Cooking with the Great Cooks

Cooking with the Great Cooks

ARLENE FELTMAN SAILHAC
Founder of De Gustibus

Published by Tess Press, an imprint of
Black Dog & Leventhal Publishers, Inc.
151 West 19th St.
New York, NY 10011

Printed in Hong Kong
ISBN 1-57912-505-0

b d f h g e c a

ACKNOWLEDGMENTS

During the sixteen-year existence of
De Gustibus at Macy's, many people have given their
support and encouragment.

First, my profound thanks to all the wonderful chefs
and cooks who have taught at
De Gustibus at Macy's.

Thanks to my priceless assistants who are always there
for me in a million ways: Jane Asche, Barbara Bjorn,
Pam Carey, Corrine Gherardi, Yonina Jacobs, Nancy
Robbins,
and Betti Zucker.

Thanks to Barbara Teplitz for all her help and support
throughout the years, and to Gertrud Yampierre for
holding the office together.

Thanks to Ruth Schwartz for believing in
the concept of De Gustibus and helping to orchestrate
its initiation at Macy's.

Thanks to J. P. Leventhal and Pamela Horn of Black
Dog & Leventhal Publishers for providing the vehicle
to put our cooking classes into book form and for
being so encouraging.

Thanks to Marty Lubin for his wonderful design.

Thanks to my agent Judith Weber for her help and
advice.

Special thanks to Judith Choate, who shaped all my
words into meaningful prose and never ceased to
amaze me with her knowledge of food and her
patience and calm, and to Steve Pool for getting these
words into the computer with smiles and enthusiasm.

Finally, thanks to all the faithful De Gustibus cus-
tomers who have made all our classes spring to life.

Contents

French Cooking

New American Cooking

Southwest Cooking

Introduction

Cooking with Great Cooks compiles five books in the De Gustibus series into one—*Southwest Cooking, French Cooking for the Home, The Art of New American Cooking, Rustic Italian Cooking, and Mediterranean Cooking.* We have created this book to be a complete kitchen compendium. Organized by menu, it provides hundreds of suggestions for what to serve on every occasion—from robust dinners and colorful buffets, to late-night suppers, spring lunches, and celebrations year-round.

Cooking with Great Cooks gives the home cook a vast repertoire from which to create the most basic stocks and breads, to choosing an interesting vinaigrette to toss on a salad, or a bold side dish for your tried-and-true roast chicken.

When we started De Gustibus in 1980, we had no inkling of the variety of cuisines that would become an integral part of American cooking. As American and international cuisines have changed and our tastes have broadened, De Gustibus has stayed on the cutting edge of the culinary experience. We have invited teachers, cooks, and chefs to De Gustibus both because of their recognition in the American cooking scene, and because of their challenging, unique, current, and above all, noteworthy cooking styles.

The goal of the cooking demonstrations at De Gustibus is to make the art of the grand master chefs and cooks accessible and practical for the home kitchen. In these recipes, each chef leads the way and holds out a helping hand to the home cook. New and unfamiliar ingredients, untried techniques, and even a little dazzle all find a place in the amateur's kitchen.

ARLENE FELTMAN SAILHAC
1997

Strategies for Cooking from Our Great Chefs and Cooks

Before beginning to prepare any meal, regardless of how simple or how complicated, take the following steps to heart:

1 Read through the entire menu and its recipe in advance.

2 Complete as many recipes, or steps, as possible ahead of time, taking care to allow time for defrosting, reheating, bringing to room temperature, or whatever the recipe requires before serving.

For each menu, we provide a feature entitled "What You Can Prepare Ahead of Time." This offers timesaving hints for the cook who is preparing the entire menu, or elements of it, and wants to do much of the preparation before the actual day of the meal. While many foods taste better fresh rather than reheated, we include these lists for your convenience, as suggestions only—not as required do-ahead instructions.

3 Place all the ingredients for a particular recipe on, or in, individual trays, plates, or bowls according to the specific steps in the recipe. Each item should be washed, chopped, measured, separated—or whatever

is called for—before you begin to cook. This organizational technique, known as the mise en place (from the French, it literally means "putting in place"), is the most valuable lesson we at De Gustibus have learned from the pros. We strongly urge you to cook this way.

Note that when a recipe calls for a particular ingredient to be cut in a certain size or shape, it matters. The final result is often dependent upon the textures and colors, as well as the flavor, of the ingredients.

4 Use only the best ingredients available. All good chefs and cooks stress this. Try to find the exact ingredient called for, but if you cannot, substitute in the recipe or glossary, or use your common sense.

5 Rely on your taste buds. They will not lie!

6 Clean up as you work.

Use the following menu suggestions in full, or plan meals around one or two elements from a menu. Educate yourself, and have fun with new ingredients and flavors.

Cooks and Chefs

COLMAN ANDREWS Food writer; Executive Editor, *Saveur Magazine,* New York, New York. Author: *Everything on the Table*

FRANCESCO ANTONUCCI Chef/Owner, Remi, New York, New York; Santa Monica, California; Mexico City, Mexico; and Tel Aviv, Israel. Author: *Venetian Taste*

LIDIA BASTIANICH Chef/Owner, Felidia *and* Becco, New York, New York. Author: *La Cucina di Lidia*

JAMES BEARD Late dean of New American Cooking, cookbook author, New York, New York

DAVID BOULEY Chef/Owner, Bouley, New York, New York

DANIEL BOULUD Chef/Owner, Restaurant Daniel, New York, New York. Author: *Cooking with Daniel Boulud*

ANTOINE BOUTERIN Chef/Owner, Bouterin, New York, New York. Author: *Cooking Provence*

CHARLES BOWMAN Chef, Peryali, New York, New York. Author: *The Periyali Cookbook*

TERRANCE BRENNAN Chef/Owner, Picholine, New York, New York

GIULIANO BUGIALLI Noted cookbook author, New York, New York

BIBA CAGGIANO Chef/Owner, Biba, Sacramento, California. Author: *Biba's Italian Kitchen, Trattoria Cooking*

DOMINICK CERRONE Chef/Owner, Solera, New York, New York

JULIA CHILD Grande Dame of French Cooking, cookbook author, and television personality, Cambridge, Massachusetts

CRAIG CLAIBORNE Cookbook author and former *New York Times* food writer, New York, New York

ANDREW D'AMICO Executive Chef/Owner, The Sign of the Dove, New York, New York

ROBERT DEL GRANDE Chef/Owner, Cafe Annie, Cafe Express, and Rio Ranch, Houston, Texas

JEAN-MICHEL DIOT Chef/Owner, Park Bistro *and* Park Avenue Gourmandise, New York, New York

ROBERTO DONNA Chef/Owner, Galileo *and* I Matti, Washington, D.C.

DEAN FEARING Executive Chef, The Mansion on Turtle Creek Restaurant, Dallas, Texas

BOBBY FLAY Executive Chef/Owner, Mesa Grill, Bolo, *and* Mesa City, New York, New York. Author: *Bold American Food*

PIERRE FRANEY Chef, cookbook author, and television personality, New York, New York

MARILYN FROBUCCINO Formerly Executive Chef, Arizona 206 *and* Cafe Mimosa, New York, New York

JOYCE GOLDSTEIN Chef/Owner, Square One, San Francisco, California. Author: *Mediterranean the Beautiful, Back to Square One, The Mediterranean Kitchen*

VINCENT GUERITHAULT Chef/Owner, Vincent Guerithault on Camelback, Phoenix, Arizona. Author: *Vincent's*

MATTHEW KENNEY Chef/Owner, Matthew's Restaurant *and* Mezze, New York, New York

JOHANNE KILLEEN AND GEORGE GERMON Chefs/Owners, Al Forno, Providence, Rhode Island. Authors: *Cucina Simpatica*

GRAY KUNZ Executive Chef, Lespinasse Restaurant, The St. Regis Hotel, New York, New York

MICHAEL LOMONACO Former Executive Chef, '21' Club, New York, New York. Author: *The '21' Cookbook: Recipes and Lore From New York's Fabled Restaurant*

CARLO MIDDIONE Chef/Owner, Vivande, San Francisco, California. Author: *The Food of Southern Italy*

WAYNE NISH Chef/Owner, March, New York, New York

BRADLEY OGDEN Chef/Owner, Lark Creek Inn, Larkspur, California. Author: *Bradley Ogden's Breakfast, Lunch & Dinner*

JAQUES PÉPIN Cookbook author, television personality, Dean of Special Programs at The French Culinary Institute, New York, New York

DEBRA PONZEK Formerly Executive Chef, Montrachet, New York, New York; Chef/Owner gourmet food store, Connecticut

ALFRED PORTALE Chef/Owner, Gotham Bar & Grill, New York, New York

WOLFGANG PUCK Chef/Owner, Spago, Chinois on Main, Granita, Los Angeles; Postrio, San Francisco, California. Author: *The Wolfgang Puck Cookbook*

MARTA PULINI Executive Chef, mad.61, New York, New York

STEPHAN PYLES Chef/Owner, Star Canyon, Dallas, Texas. Author: *New Texas Cuisine*

ANNE ROSENZWEIG Chef/Owner, Arcadia *and* Lobster Club, New York, New York

ALAIN SAILHAC Dean of Culinary Arts at The French Culinary Institute; Former Executive Chef, Le Cirque, New York, New York

CLAUDIO SCADUTTO Executive Chef, Trattoria dell'Arte, New York, New York

JIMMY SCHMIDT Chef/Owner, The Rattlesnake Club, Detroit, Michigan

ANDRÉ SOLTNER Formerly Executive Chef/Owner, Lutèce, New York, New York. Author: *The Lutèce Cookbook*

TOM VALENTI Former Executive Chef/Owner, Cascabel, New York, New York

JEAN-GEORGES VONGERICHTREN Chef/Owner, JoJo, Vong, and Jean Georges, New York, New York

BRENDAN WALSH Chef/Owner, North Street Grill, Great Neck, New York

DAVID WALZOG Chef, Tapika, New York, New York

ALICE WATERS Chef/Owner, Chez Panise, Berkeley, California. Author: *Chez Panise Cooking, Chez Panise Menu Cookbook, Chez Panise Pizza, Pasta & Calzone*

PAULA WOLFERT Noted food writer and cookbook author, San Francisco, California. Author: *The Cooking of the Eastern Mediterranean, Paula Wolfert's World of Food, The Cooking of Southwest France, Couscous and Other Good Foods from Morocco*

Techniques

CUTTING VEGETABLES

Into julienne: Using a small, very sharp knife, a mandoline, or an inexpensive vegetable slicer, cut vegetables into thin, uniform sticks, usually about ¼-inch thick and 1 to 2 inches long. This process is easiest when each vegetable is first cut into uniform pieces. For instance, trim a bell pepper into two or three evenly shaped pieces and then proceed to cut into a julienne.

Into dice: Trim vegetables into uniform rectangles. Using a very sharp knife, cut into strips ranging in width from ⅛ to ¼ inch, depending upon the size dice you require. Lay the strips together and cut into an even dice by cross cutting into squares ⅛ to ¼ inch across. When dicing bell peppers, it is particularly important to trim all the membranes and ridges so that you have an absolutely smooth rectangle.

Tourner: This French term literally means "to turn." When used to describe the preparation of vegetables, it means to trim them into small, uniform shapes (generally oval or olive-shaped) using a very sharp knife or parer. The vegetable to be turned is usually cut into quarters and then each piece is made uniform by trimming the flesh as you turn it in your fingers. The vegetable should have seven sides. This preparation facilitates the uniform cooking of the vegetables.

BLANCHING VEGETABLES

Place trimmed vegetables (or fruit) into rapidly boiling water for a brief period, often no more than 30 seconds, then immediately drain and plunge into ice cold water to stop the cooking process. Blanching serves to set color and flavor, firm up the flesh, and/or loosen the skin.

ROASTING VEGETABLES

Preheat the oven to 350 degrees F.

For root vegetables, trim and peel if desired. If small, cut in half lengthwise; if large, cut into quarters. Toss with a small amount of olive oil and salt and pepper to taste. For tomatoes, cut in half, and seed if desired. For onions, peel if desired. If large, cut in half. Rub with olive oil, salt, and pepper.

Place the vegetables on a heavy-duty baking sheet and bake until tender when pierced with a fork.

NOTE: To slow-roast tomatoes, cut as above, and bake at 200 degrees F for about 3 hours, or until they are almost dried. Alternatively, if you have a gas oven with a pilot light, lay cut-side down on a baking sheet and place in the oven with the pilot light on for at least 12 hours, or until almost dry.

PREPARING CHILES

The intense heat of the chile is mainly found in the seeds, the placenta (the fleshy part near the stem end), and the white veins that run down the inside of the chile. When removing these parts, some cooks prefer to use rubber gloves. Whether you choose to wear gloves or not, be sure to wash your hands well after working with chiles. Also, keep your hands away from your eyes and mouth until your hands are clean and the chile oil has completely dissipated. Both fresh and dried chiles can be stemmed, seeded, and deveined before use. Dried chiles are frequently reconstituted by soaking them in hot water or broth for about 30 minutes, or until softened.

THREE METHODS FOR ROASTING CHILES AND BELL PEPPERS

Using a fork with a heatproof handle, hold the chile or pepper close to the flame of a gas burner, without actually placing it in the flame, until the skin puffs and is charred black on all sides. Turn to ensure that the entire chile or pepper is charred. Immediately place the charred chile or pepper in a plastic bag and seal. Allow to steam for about 10 minutes.

Remove the chile or pepper from the bag and pull off the charred skin. Stem and seed. Dice, chop, or puree as required.

If using an electric stove, place the entire chile or pepper in a large, dry cast-iron skillet over medium heat. Cook slowly, turning frequently, until completely charred. Proceed as above.

To roast several chiles or peppers at a time, place on a baking sheet under a preheated broiler as close to the heat as possible without touching the flame. Roast until the skin puffs and is charred black, turning as necessary to char the entire chile or pepper. Then proceed as above.

When roasting chiles, remember that their oils are very potent. As the skin blackens, you may feel burning in your throat and eyes, which may cause some momentary discomfort. When roasting a large number of chiles, it is best to do so under a broiler to contain the potency.

TOASTING CHILES

Dried red chiles are often toasted before using. This is done to heighten their aroma, flavor, and, according to some experts, digestibility.

Remove the stem and, using a sharp knife, slit the chile open lengthwise. Remove the seeds and veins and flatten the chile out. Heat a griddle over medium heat until hot. Add the flattened chile, skin-side up, and toast for 4 seconds. Turn over and toast for 3 seconds more, being careful not to burn the chile. The chile should just darken slightly and begin to release its aroma; if it burns, it will turn bitter.

MAKING CHILE POWDER

Using the method described above in "Toasting Chiles," toast the chiles over very low heat for about 1 minute per side, or until completely moisture-free and crisp. Do not burn!

Tear the toasted chiles into small pieces and process in an electric coffee grinder, spice grinder or mini food processor to a very fine powder. Cover tightly and store in the freezer.

MAKING CHILE PUREE

For fresh chiles: Stem, seed, and remove the membranes. Place in a food processor fitted with the metal blade and process until smooth. You may need to add a drop or two of water to create a puree. Use immediately.

For dried chiles: Toast as directed above. Tear into pieces and place in hot water to cover for 15 to 30 minutes (depending upon the age and the chile as well as the toughness of the skin), or until the chile is completely reconstituted. Drain well and place in a blender. Process until smooth. Strain through a fine sieve to remove any bits of tough skin. Cover and refrigerate for up to 3 days or freeze for up to 6 months.

TOASTING SPICES AND SEEDS

Toast spices and seeds in a heavy cast-iron skillet over medium heat, stirring or shaking the pan frequently. Toast for 2 to 5 minutes, depending on the ingredient, or until it turns a shade darker and is fragrant.

Toasting and Skinning Nuts

Preheat oven to 400 degrees F. Lay the nuts in a single layer on a baking sheet or pie tin. Using a spray bottle such as those used to mist plants, lightly spray the nuts with cool water. Roast for 5 to 10 minutes, depending on the nut's size and oil content, or until golden. Remember, since nuts have a high oil content, they can burn very quickly. Immediately remove from oven and transfer to a cool plate or tray to cool. If you leave them on the baking sheet, they will continue to cook. If the nuts have skins, immediately spread them on a clean kitchen towel. Let them cool slightly and then wrap them in the towel and rub the nuts back and forth to remove the skins.

If you do not need to toast nuts but want to skin them, put them in boiling water for 1 minute. Drain well. Place in a clean kitchen towel and rub the nuts to remove the skins.

Pitting Olives

Place olives between two kitchen towels and pound gently with a mallet or the broad side of a cleaver. Unwrap and remove the pits from the flesh.

Cooking Pasta

Pasta, whether fresh or dried, should be cooked in ample boiling, salted water just until it is *al dente,* or still firm to the bite. Usually 2 gallons of water is enough to cook
1 pound of pasta.

To ensure the best possible taste and texture, the chefs always add salt just at the point when the water comes to a boil before adding pasta.

Making Bread Crumbs

One slice of fresh bread yields approximately ½ cup fresh bread crumbs.

One slice dried (or toasted) bread yields approximately ⅓ cup dried bread crumbs.

Trim crusts from slices of firm, good-quality fresh or dried white bread. Cut the bread into cubes and place in a food processor fitted with the metal blade. Pulse until crumbs are formed.

Store fresh bread crumbs in a tightly covered container in the refrigerator for up to 3 days.

Store dried bread crumbs in a tightly covered container at room temperature for up to 1 month.

Grating Cheese

Italian hard cheeses, such as Parmigiano-Reggiano, should be purchased in chunks and grated as needed. You can purchase a grater made especially for Parmesan cheese in Italian markets or kitchen equipment shops. Alternatively, you can use the traditional 4-sided kitchen grater or even a small Mouli grater. Do not use a food processor—the speed of the blade creates heat, which will change the taste and texture of the cheese.

Rendering Duck Fat

Place pieces of duck fat in a non-stick sauté pan and cook over very low heat, stirring occasionally, until the fat has melted and all the skin and connective tissue has turned brown and crisp. Remove the "cracklings" from the fat. (Reserve for a salad garnish, if desired.) Strain the fat through a paper coffee filter or a triple layer of cheesecloth to remove any remaining cooked particles. Store, tightly covered and refrigerated, for up to 1 month. Use as you would any animal fat to pan fry potatoes or other foods.

Zesting Citrus Fruits

For strips of zest or chopped zest, using a vegetable peeler, a sharp paring knife, or a zester, remove *only* the thin layer of oily colored outer skin of any citrus fruit (the white pith beneath the colored skin tastes bitter). Then cut into thinner strips or chop as required. For grated zest, carefully remove the colored outer skin using the smallest holes of a metal grater.

MAKING CHOCOLATE CURLS

For ease of handling, you will need at least a 4-ounce solid block of cool, room-temperature chocolate. Using a paper towel, grasp one end of the chocolate block, holding it so that the paper protects it from the heat of your hand. Using a very sharp potato peeler, gradually peel off a thin sheet of chocolate from the top to the bottom, moving the peeler toward you. The chocolate will curl as it peels off the block. The lighter the pressure, the tighter the curls will be. If the chocolate is too warm, it will not curl; if it is too cold, it will break into slivers.

GRATING CHOCOLATE

Small amounts of solid, room temperature chocolate may be grated on a nutmeg grater. Larger amounts can be processed in a food processor fitted with the metal blade. Grate only as much as you need, since if stored, grated chocolate tends to melt back together.

USING AN ICE WATER BATH

Place the container of hot cooked food in a larger container (or a plugged sink) filled with enough ice and cold water to come at least halfway up the sides of the hot container. Stir the food from time to time to speed cooling. An ice water bath is used to cool foods quickly in order to halt cooking and prevent bacteria formation. Foods cooled in this fashion are often further chilled with refrigeration or freezing.

USING A MORTAR AND PESTLE

The ingredients to be ground or pulverized are placed in the mortar, a bowl-shaped container. The pestle, an easily gripped hand-sized club with a rounded or pointed end, is rotated, pressing the ingredient against the bottom and sides of the mortar, until the desired consistency is reached. A mortar and pestle, one of the world's most ancient kitchen devices, may be made of hardwood, marble, or glazed stone.

Pantry Recipes

CHICKEN, DUCK, OR TURKEY STOCK

MAKES ABOUT 4 CUPS
PREPARATION TIME: ABOUT 40 MINUTES
COOKING TIME: ABOUT 2 HOURS AND 30 MINUTES

2 quarts (8 cups) water

2 chicken carcasses or duck carcasses or 5 pounds turkey bones, cut in small pieces

3 onions, chopped

1 carrot, chopped

2 ribs celery, chopped

3 sprigs fresh thyme

3 sprigs fresh parsley

1 bay leaf

1 tablespoon white peppercorns

We supply standard stock recipes for chicken, duck or turkey, and beef, lamb or veal stock used in the recipes. Homemade stock adds a depth of flavor to a dish not possible with canned broth. However, if time is a factor, use canned chicken (or beef) broth, buying those brands that are labeled "low-sodium." Do not use diluted bouillon cubes; they are excessively salty.

1 In a large saucepan or stockpot, combine the water and chopped carcasses. Bring to a simmer over medium heat and skim the surface of any foam.

2 Add the onions, carrots, celery, thyme, parsley, bay leaf, and peppercorns. Bring to a boil, reduce the heat, and simmer for 1½ to 2 hours, skimming fat and foam from the surface as necessary, until reduced to 4 cups.

4 Pour the stock into a fine sieve and strain, extracting as much liquid as possible. Discard the solids. Cool to tepid (this can be done by plunging the stockpot into a sinkful of ice), cover, and refrigerate for 6 hours or until all fat particles have risen to the top. Spoon off solidified fat and discard. Heat the stock over medium-high heat for about 30 minutes. Adjust the seasonings and use as directed in recipe.

5 To store, cool to tepid (this can be done by plunging the stockpot into a sinkful of ice), cover, and refrigerate for 2 to 3 days or freeze in 1-cup quantities (for ease of use) for up to 3 months.

Beef, Lamb, or Veal Stock

Makes about 3 quarts
Preparation time: about 40 minutes
Cooking time: about 7 hours

¼ cup plus 2 tablespoons vegetable oil

4 pounds beef, lamb, or veal marrow bones, cut into 2-inch pieces

3 onions, peeled and quartered

1 carrot, peeled and chopped

1 rib celery, chopped

1 tomato, quartered

1 bay leaf

1 tablespoon black peppercorns

2 sprigs fresh thyme

3 cloves garlic, crushed

Approximately 1 gallon (16 cups) water

1 Preheat the oven to 450 degrees F.

2 Using ¼ cup of oil, lightly oil the bones. Spread the bones in a single layer in a large roasting pan. Roast the bones, turning occasionally, for 20 minutes, or until bones are dark golden-brown on all sides.

3 Transfer the bones to a large saucepan or stockpot. Add the remaining oil to roasting pan and stir in the onions, carrot, celery, and tomato. Cook on top of the stove for about 15 minutes over medium-high heat until brown, stirring frequently.

4 With a slotted spoon, transfer the vegetables to the stockpot. Add the bay leaf, peppercorns, thyme, and garlic.

5 Pour off the fat from the roasting pan and discard. Return the pan to moderate heat and deglaze it with 2 cups of water, scraping up any particles sticking to the bottom. Remove from the heat and add this liquid to the stockpot. Pour enough of the remaining water into the stockpot to cover the bones by 2 inches. Bring to a boil, reduce the heat, and let the stock barely simmer, uncovered, for 6 hours, skimming fat and foam from the surface as necessary. Remove from the heat. Cool slightly and chill in the refrigerator for 12 hours or overnight.

6 Pour the stock into a fine sieve into a clean pan. Discard the solids. Spoon off any trace of fat. Place stockpot over high heat and bring stock to a rolling boil. Lower heat and simmer for 30 minutes or until flavor is full-bodied and liquid has slightly reduced. Use as directed in the recipe.

7 To store, cool to tepid (this can be done by plunging the stockpot into a sinkful of ice), cover, and refrigerate for 2 to 3 days or freeze in 1-cup quantities (for ease of use) for up to 3 months.

FISH STOCK

MAKES ABOUT 3 CUPS

PREPARATION TIME: ABOUT 20 MINUTES

COOKING TIME: ABOUT 25 MINUTES

---

2 sprigs fresh parsley

2 sprigs fresh thyme

1 small bay leaf

2 pounds fish bones (saltwater fish such as sole, John Dory, turbot, halibut, or other very fresh, non-oily fish), cut into pieces

2 tablespoons canola or other flavorless oil

1 small onion, chopped

1 small rib celery, chopped

1 cup dry white wine

Making fish stock is easier and faster than making chicken or beef stock. Substituting a canned broth is tricky in recipes calling for fish stock, but if you have no time to make stock, substitute low-sodium canned chicken broth for fish stock.

---

1 Make a bouquet garni by tying together with kitchen twine the parsley, thyme, and bay leaf. Set aside.

2 Clean the fish bones under cold running water.

3 Heat the oil in a large saucepan or stockpot over medium heat. Add the fish bones and vegetables. Lower the heat and lay a piece of wax paper directly on bones and vegetables in the pan. Cook for 10 minutes, stirring once or twice to prevent browning. Be careful not to push the paper into the pan.

4 Remove the wax paper. Add the wine and enough water to cover the bones and vegetables by 2 inches. Add the bouquet garni. Increase the heat to high and bring to a boil. Skim the surface of all foam. Lower the heat and simmer for 20 to 25 minutes.

5 Strain the stock through an extra-fine sieve. Discard the solids. Use as directed in recipe or cool to tepid (this can be done by plunging the stockpot into a sinkful of ice), cover tightly, and refrigerate for 2 to 3 days or freeze in 1-cup quantities (for ease of use) for up to 3 weeks.

VEGETABLE STOCK

MAKES ABOUT 3 CUPS
PREPARATION TIME: ABOUT 20 MINUTES
COOKING TIME: ABOUT 2 HOURS

---

3 quarts cold water

1 carrot, peeled and chopped

1 potato, peeled and chopped

1 large onion, chopped

3 ribs celery, chopped

½ leek, white part only, chopped

1 small tomato, chopped

1 tablespoon salt or to taste

2 cloves garlic, peeled

1 teaspoon chopped fresh parsley

½ teaspoon black peppercorns

Making vegetable stock is easy and fast. Substituting a canned broth is difficult, as finding a good one can be a problem. Low-sodium vegetable bouillon cubes, sold in health food stores, are a good substitute. Low-sodium canned chicken broth can also be used in recipes calling for vegetable stock.

---

1 In a 5-quart saucepan, bring 1 cup of the water to a boil over medium-high heat. Add the carrot, potato, onions, celery, leeks, tomato, and salt. Cook for 5 minutes, stirring occasionally.

2 Add the remaining 11 cups of water to the pan, along with the garlic, parsley, and peppercorns. Bring to a simmer, reduce the heat to low, and simmer gently for 2 hours.

3 Strain the liquid through a fine sieve into a bowl. Discard the vegetables. Let cool for 1 hour and then pour the stock through a fine sieve again. Use as directed in the recipe.

4 To store, cover and refrigerate for up to 3 days or freeze in 1-cup quantities (for ease of use) for up to 3 months.

COOKED BEANS

MAKES ABOUT 2½ CUPS COOKED BEANS
PREPARATION TIME: ABOUT 10 MINUTES
COOKING TIME: 1 TO 2 HOURS
SOAKING TIME: AT LEAST 4 HOURS

1 cup dried black, white, fava, or other beans

Cooking dried beans is simply a matter of reconstituting them by soaking, followed by long, slow cooking. You can double or triple the recipe. Cooked beans keep in the freezer for up to one month. Lentils and black-eyed peas do not require soaking before cooking.

1 Check the beans for pebbles and other debris. Rinse them in a colander. Put the beans in a large pot and add about 10 cups of water (or 10 times the amount of the beans). Cover and let soak at room temperature for at least 4 hours. Change the water 3 or 4 times during soaking. If the beans are particularly old, let them soak for 8 hours or overnight.

2 Drain the beans, rinse with cold water, and return to the pot. Add fresh cold water to cover the beans by about 2 inches. Bring to a boil over high heat, skim the foam that rises to the surface, and reduce the heat to a simmer. Cover and cook for 1 to 2 hours, until tender, adding more water to the pot as necessary. The beans are done when they are fork-tender. Drain and proceed with the specific recipe.

NOTE: To prepare the beans by the "quick-soak method," put the beans in a large pot and add enough water to cover by 3 inches. Bring to a boil and boil for 5 minutes. Remove from the heat, cover, and soak for no less than 1 hour and no longer than 2 hours. Drain and discard the soaking water. Rinse well. Proceed with the cooking instructions above.

ROASTED GARLIC

1 or more whole garlic heads (bulbs) or 1 or more cloves garlic

You may roast whole heads of garlic (bulbs) or you may cut each head in half, crosswise, or separate each one into individual cloves.

1 Preheat the oven to 200 degress F.

2 Lightly wrap the garlic in aluminum foil. Place on a pie plate or small baking sheet. Bake for 1 hour for a whole head, 15 minutes for individual cloves, or until the pulp is very soft. Remove from the oven. Unwrap and allow to cool.

For whole heads: Cut in half crosswise, and working from the closed end, gently push the soft roasted garlic from the skin. Discard the skin.

For individual cloves: Slit the skin using a sharp knife point. Gently push the soft roasted garlic from the skin. Discard the skin.

CLARIFIED BUTTER

MAKES ABOUT 3 CUPS

2 pounds unsalted butter, cut into pieces

Clarified butter burns less easily than other butter because during the clarifying process, the milk particles are removed. For the same reason it stores longer.

1 Melt the butter in a medium-sized saucepan over very low heat. Skim off the foam that rises to the top using a ladle, taking care to remove as little of the clear, yellow fat as possible.

2 Let the butter cool slightly and settle. Carefully strain the butter through a fine sieve into a clean, glass container, leaving the milky residue on the bottom of the saucepan. Discard the residue.

3 Cover and refrigerate for up to 2 weeks or freeze for up to 1 month.

Flour Tortillas

Makes 10 to 12 tortillas
Preparation time: about 10 minutes
Cooking time: 30 to 40 minutes
Resting time: about 30 minutes

2 cups sifted all-purpose flour, plus additional for dusting

1 teaspoon baking powder

½ teaspoon salt

½ teaspoon granulated sugar

1 tablespoon solid vegetable shortening

Approximately ½ cup warm water

This simple tortilla recipe from Dean Fearing does not require any unusual ingredients or even a tortilla press.

1 Assemble the *mise en place* trays for this recipe.

2 Sift the dry ingredients together into a bowl. Cut in the shortening with a fork or pastry blender until the mixture resembles coarse meal. Add just enough warm water to make a soft dough.

3 Turn the dough out onto a well-floured surface and knead for 3 to 5 minutes. Cover the dough and let it rest for 30 minutes in a warm, draft-free area.

4 Form the dough into 2-inch balls between the palms of your hands. On a lightly floured surface, roll out each ball into a circle about 7 inches in diameter and ¼ inch thick.

5 Heat a cast-iron griddle or skillet over medium-high heat. Place a tortilla on the ungreased griddle and cook for about 2 minutes, or until lightly browned around the edges. Turn over and cook for about 1 minute longer, or until the edges are brown.

6 Wrap tightly in foil to keep warm, and repeat with the remaining tortillas. If cooking in advance, wrap in foil and store at cool room temperature for an hour or so, or in the refrigerator for longer, until needed. Reheat, still wrapped in foil, in a 300 degree F. oven for 10 to 15 minutes, or until heated through.

❧ If these are for chips, undercook the tortillas slightly.

CORN TORTILLAS

MAKES 8 TORTILLAS
PREPARATION TIME: ABOUT 10 MINUTES
COOKING TIME: ABOUT 35 MINUTES

¾ cup stone-ground yellow or blue cornmeal or masa harina

1 tablespoon plus 1 teaspoon corn oil

⅛ teaspoon salt

About 2 tablespoons hot water

■ Special Equipment: tortilla press, optional

1 Preheat the oven to 175 degrees F. or 200 degrees F. if that is the lowest setting. Assemble the *mise en place* trays for this dish.

2 In a small bowl, combine the cornmeal, 1 tablespoon of the oil, and the salt until just blended. Add just enough water to form the dough into a ball.

3 Divide the dough into 8 even, small balls. Place each ball between 2 sheets of wax paper and flatten in a tortilla press. Alternatively, using a rolling pin, roll out each ball into a circle ⅙-inch thick.

4 Heat a cast-iron griddle or skillet over medium-high heat. Lightly brush with the remaining 1 teaspoon of the oil. Peel off one sheet of wax paper from a tortilla and place it, dough side down, on the griddle. Cook for 2 minutes. Remove the other sheet of wax paper, turn the tortilla over, and cook for 2 minutes more, or until slightly browned and firm.

5 Wrap in a kitchen towel and keep warm in the oven, and repeat with the remaining tortillas.

❧ If the dough crumbles or cracks around edges while rolling, add a bit more water and reform.

❧ If these are for chips, undercook the tortillas slightly.

❧ Tortillas may be made early in the day. Store, covered and refrigerated in the towel or in aluminum foil.

Tortilla Chips

PREPARATION TIME: ABOUT 5 MINUTES
COOKING TIME: ABOUT 3 MINUTES PER CHIP

Corn or Flour Tortillas (page 26)
Oil for deep frying

■ Special Equipment: deep-fry
thermometer

1 Cut the tortillas into quarters or sixths, depending upon the size you want.

2 Heat the oil in a deep fat fryer or deep skillet to 325 degrees F. Add the tortilla pieces, a few at a time, and fry, stirring continuously, for 3 minutes, or until crisp. Using a slotted spoon, remove the chips from the oil and drain on paper towels.

❧ If you don't have a deep-fry thermometer, you can check for proper oil temperature by dropping a ½-inch bread cube into the oil. When small bubbles begin to surround the cube and it starts to turn golden, the oil is the correct temperature. Remove the bread cube with tongs or chopsticks.

Tostadas

PREPARATION TIME: ABOUT 5 MINUTES
COOKING TIME: ABOUT 3 MINUTES PER TOSTADA

Corn Tortillas (recipe page 26)
Oil for shallow-frying

Heat ¼ inch of oil in a large, heavy skillet over high heat to 325 degrees F. Cook the tortillas, one at a time, for about 3 minutes, or until crisp and golden. Do not deep-fry. Tostadas are best eaten as they are fried. If this is not possible, drain well and place on a baking sheet lined with paper towels. Reheat in in a preheated 350 degree F. oven for 2 to 3 minutes, or until hot.

ACHIOTE PASTE

MAKES ABOUT ½ CUP
PREPARATION TIME: ABOUT 15 MINUTES
STANDING TIME: AT LEAST SEVERAL HOURS

---

1 tablespoon achiote seeds

1 teaspoon black peppercorns

1 teaspoon dried oregano

4 whole cloves

½ teaspoon cumin seeds

1 one-inch piece of cinnamon stick

1 teaspoon coriander seeds

1 teaspoon salt

5 cloves garlic, minced

2 tablespoons cider vinegar

1½ teaspoons all-purpose flour

1 Assemble the *mise en place* trays for this recipe.

2 Put the achiote, peppercorns, oregano, cloves, cumin, cinnamon, and coriander into an electric coffee grinder, spice grinder, or mini food processor and process until fine. Transfer to a small bowl and stir in the salt.

3 Place the garlic in another small bowl and sprinkle with 2 teaspoons of the ground spices. Using the back of a spoon, mash the garlic and spice mixture into a smooth paste. Blend in the remaining spice mixture, the vinegar, and flour. Scrape into a glass or ceramic container with a lid. Let stand at room temperature for several hours, or overnight, before using. Store tightly covered in the refrigerator for up to 3 months.

CHILE-FLAVORED VINEGAR

MAKES ABOUT 2 CUPS
PREPARATION TIME: ABOUT 5 MINUTES
STANDING TIME: ABOUT 1 WEEK

---

2 cups good-quality white wine vinegar

2 green chiles, halved lengthwise

1 small dried red chile

1 clove garlic

To make this vinegar, select a dried red chile with the amount of "heat" you prefer. There is no need to remove the seeds from the chiles unless you want to. Likewise, there is no need to remove the chiles from the vinegar after they have soaked in it.

Combine all the ingredients in a glass jar with a tight-fitting lid. Let sit in a cool dark place for 1 week before using. Store in the refrigerator for up to 6 months.

Cooking with Great Cooks

FRENCH COOKING

DAVID BOULEY:
Autumn Elegance—
A Dinner with a Hint of France

DANIEL BOULUD:
A Lovely Lunch or Sunday Supper

ANTOINE BOUTERIN:
A Tribute to the End of Summer

JULIA CHILD:
Classic French for Friends

AUTUMN ELEGANCE—
A DINNER WITH A HINT OF FRANCE

Acorn and Butternut Squash Soup with Roasted Chestnuts
SOUPE DE COURGES AUX MARRONS RÔTIS

Guinea Hen with Quince Purée and Chanterelles
PINTADE À LA PURÉE DE QUOINGS ET AUX CHANTERELLES

Deep Chocolate Marquise
MARQUISE PROFONDE DE CHOCOLAT

WINE SUGGESTIONS:

Light-bodied Champagne (*first course*)

White Burgundy or Viognier (*second course*)

Late Bottled Vintage Port (*dessert*)

WHAT YOU CAN PREPARE AHEAD OF TIME

Up to 1 week ahead: Prepare the Chicken Stock (if making your own).

The day before: Make the quince purée and the mushroom liquid for the Guinea Hen. Cover separately and refrigerate. Make the Chocolate Marquise. Cover and refrigerate.

Early in the day: Make the chestnut purée for the Acorn and Butternut Squash Soup. Fry the celery leaves for the soup garnish.

David Bouley came to De Gustibus very early in his cooking career to assist Alain Sailhac, then chef at Le Cirque in New York City. Soon after, American-born David left Le Cirque to become head chef of a restaurant in San Francisco opened by Roger Vergé, the esteemed French chef. When Chef Vergé taught one of our classes, David returned to New York to cook with him, and we once again had the pleasure of his talents at the school.

Shortly thereafter, David returned to New York City. Within a couple of years, he had opened Bouley, a restaurant that reflects his love of France and has the feeling of a French country inn. Anyone who follows the New York restaurant scene knows how quickly David garnered four-star accolades for his innovative food. Over the years, Bouley has remained at the top of New York's favorite restaurant list. David Bouley has returned to demonstrate many classes at De Gustibus. His enthusiasm, his knowledge of culinary techniques, and his imaginative way of combining the classic with the revolutionary continue to delight audiences.

◁ Deep Chocolate Marquise

Acorn and Butternut Squash Soup with Roasted Chestnuts

SERVES 6
PREPARATION TIME: ABOUT 30 MINUTES
COOKING TIME: ABOUT 1 HOUR AND 45 MINUTES

Soupe de Courges aux Marrons Rôtis

This is an aromatic soup combining the rich, sweet taste of our American fall squashes with the intense flavor of the roasted French chestnut, all accented by the innovative use of celery water and crisp celery leaves.

1 pound fresh chestnuts
3 one-pound acorn squash, halved and seeded
3 one-and-one-half-pound butternut squash, halved and seeded
¼ teaspoon freshly grated nutmeg
¼ teaspoon ground cinnamon
1 teaspoon ground mace
2 tablespoons light brown sugar
¼ cup honey
8 tablespoons unsalted butter, melted
2 quarts water
1 rib celery, chopped
Salt and freshly ground white pepper to taste
½ cup celery leaves (optional)
1 cup vegetable oil (if using celery leaves)
¼ cup heavy cream, softly whipped
2 tablespoons minced fresh lemon thyme

■ Special Equipment: chinois; deep-fry thermometer

1 Preheat the oven to 350 degrees F. Assemble the *mise en place* trays for this recipe.

2 With a sharp knife cut an "X" on one end of each chestnut and place on a baking sheet. Bake for about 20 minutes, until the chestnuts open and the flesh is tender. Transfer to a plate and allow to cool slightly.

3 When the chestnuts are cool enough to handle, peel with a small sharp knife or your fingers. Put the peeled chestnuts in a small saucepan and cover with water. Bring to a simmer and cook for 5 to 6 minutes, until the flesh is soft. Drain and press the flesh through a chinois or other fine sieve into a medium bowl. Set aside.

4 Meanwhile, place the squash halves, cut side up, in a large shallow baking dish. Dust with the nutmeg, cinnamon, mace, and brown sugar. Drizzle with the honey and

DAVID BOULEY: Acorn and Butternut Squash Soup with Roasted Chestnuts

melted butter. Cover the dish tightly with aluminum foil. Bake for 40 minutes, or until tender.

5 In a medium-sized saucepan, combine the chopped celery and the water, and bring to a boil over medium-high heat. Reduce the heat and simmer for 45 minutes. Strain, discarding the solids. Set the celery water aside.

6 Remove the squash from the oven and scrape the flesh from the skin. Process the squash in a food processor just until almost smooth; there will be some lumps. Press the flesh through a chinois or other fine sieve into a medium-sized saucepan. Slowly stir in the reserved celery water. Season to taste with salt and white pepper.

7 Place the soup over medium heat and simmer for about 4 minutes, or until just heated through.

8 Meanwhile, if using, rinse the celery leaves and pat dry with paper towels. In a small saucepan, heat the oil to 325 degrees F. on a deep-fry thermometer. Fry the leaves for 15 seconds, or until crisp. Lift from the oil with a slotted metal spoon or tongs and drain on paper towels.

9 Fold the whipped cream into the reserved chestnut purée. Stir in the lemon thyme.

10 Ladle the soup into 6 warm soup bowls. Using 2 table-spoons, shape the chestnut mixture into 6 small ovals, placing one in the center of each serving. Garnish with the fried celery leaves, if using, and serve.

▶ You may use 8 ounces canned unsweetened chestnut purée, but you will not get the same roasted flavor you will get when you roast the chestnuts yourself.

▶ If you are using the fried celery leaves as a garnish, choose pale, tender leaves. Fry them until crisp, but not brown. Store, uncovered, at room temperature, for up to 6 hours. However, if weather is damp, do not fry any earlier than 1 hour before use, or they will wilt.

▶ A chinois is a fine-meshed cone-shaped French sieve. While other fine-meshed sieves can be used when a chinois is called for, the result may not be as fine in texture. The shape enables the cook to press as much flavor from the solid ingredients as possible because the solids adhere to the sides of the sieve, making it easy to press against them with the back of a spoon.

Guinea Hen with Quince Purée and Chanterelles

SERVES 6
PREPARATION TIME: ABOUT 30 MINUTES
COOKING TIME: ABOUT 2 HOURS

Pintade à la Purée de Quoings et aux Chanterelles

Quinces are fall fruits, related to apples and pears, but they cannot be eaten raw. When cooked, they provide the perfect accent to many dishes. Look for firm, yellow-skinned fruit and store in a cool, dry place—but not the refrigerator. To capture the true essence of Chef Bouley's dish, buy chanterelles from Nova Scotia, if possible.

2 pounds button mushrooms, wiped clean, trimmed, and chopped
2 quarts water
6 large quinces, peeled, quartered, and seeded
6 cups Chicken Stock
⅓ cup chopped celery
⅓ cup chopped carrot
⅓ cup chopped onion
1 sprig fresh thyme
1 bay leaf
⅛ teaspoon dried marjoram

Salt and freshly ground black pepper to taste
3 two-and-one-half-pound guinea hens
1 teaspoon walnut oil
2 pounds chanterelles, wiped clean, trimmed, and sliced
8 shallots, minced
¼ cup fresh tarragon leaves
1 roasted clove garlic

■ Special Equipment: chinois

1 Assemble the *mise en place* trays for this recipe.

2 In a medium-sized saucepan, combine the button mushrooms and water over medium-high heat. Bring to a boil. Reduce the heat and simmer for about 45 minutes, or until the liquid has reduced to ½ cup. Strain into a bowl, pressing on the mushrooms. Discard the solids and reserve the liquid.

3 Meanwhile, in a medium-sized saucepan combine the quinces, chicken stock, celery, carrot, onion, thyme, bay leaf, and marjoram. Bring to a boil over medium-high heat. Reduce the heat and simmer for 25 to 30 minutes, until the quinces are very soft. Drain the liquid and reserve for another use. Discard the thyme and bay leaf. Pass the remaining solids through a chinois or other fine sieve into a small saucepan. Taste and adjust the seasoning with salt and pepper. Set aside.

4 Preheat the oven to 375 degrees F.

5 Generously season the guinea hens with salt and pepper. Put in a shallow pan and roast for about 45 minutes, or until cooked through and the juices run clear when the flesh is pricked with the tip of a sharp knife. Remove from the oven and let rest for 10 minutes before carving.

6 While the hens are roasting, heat the walnut oil in a large sauté pan over medium heat. Add the chanterelles, shallots, and tarragon. Sauté for about 10 minutes, or until the vegetables are very soft. Push the roasted garlic pulp from the skin and add to the chanterelles. Add the reserved mushroom liquid and stir to combine. Remove from the heat and keep warm.

7 Place the quince purée over low heat just to warm through.

8 Using a boning knife, remove the breast halves from the hens. Slice each half, diagonally, into thin slices. Remove the legs with the thighs attached.

9 Spoon the warm quince purée into the centers of 6 warm dinner plates. Arrange a sliced breast half around one side of each serving of purée. Lay the legs on the other side. Arrange the chanterelle mixture on top of the breast meat, and drizzle some of the liquid from the chanterelles over all. Serve immediately.

DAVID BOULEY: Guinea Hen with Quince Purée and Chanterelles

▶ When buying walnut oil, purchase the smallest quantity possible, as it is expensive and it turns rancid very rapidly. A small amount of this flavorful oil adds a distinctive, nutty fragrance to vinaigrettes, baked goods containing walnuts, sautés, or sauces. Store tightly covered in the refrigerator. It usually does not keep for longer than 2 months.

▶ You can substitute small chickens, pheasants, or Rock Cornish game hens for guinea hens.

Deep Chocolate Marquise

Marquise Profonde de Chocolat

This rich, dark, luxurious chocolate dessert is a true indulgence. Use the best bittersweet chocolate you can find for the most intense flavor.

LADYFINGERS:

8 large eggs, separated
1½ cups plus 2 tablespoons granulated sugar
⅞ cup all-purpose flour
⅞ cup cornstarch
2 teaspoons pure coffee extract
2 teaspoons pure vanilla extract

MARQUISE:

6 large egg yolks
1¼ cups plus 2 tablespoons confectioners' sugar
8 ounces bittersweet chocolate, coarsely chopped
1 cup unsalted butter
2 tablespoons orange-flavored liqueur, such as Cointreau or Grand Marnier
Grated zest of 2 oranges (about 2 tablespoons)
½ cup Dutch-processed cocoa powder
1¼ cups heavy cream, softly whipped
Whipped cream, for garnish
6 fresh mint sprigs, for garnish

1 Assemble the *mise en place* trays for this recipe. Preheat the oven to 325 degrees F. Lightly butter and flour 2 baking sheets. Lightly butter an 8-inch spring-form pan.

2 To make the ladyfingers, using an electric mixer set on medium-high speed, beat the egg yolks with 1 cup plus 2 tablespoons of sugar for 3 to 4 minutes until pale yellow and thick.

3 In another bowl, using an electric mixer set on medium-high speed, beat the egg whites and the remaining ½ cup of sugar until stiff and shiny.

4 Whisk together the flour and cornstarch. Fold the dry ingredients into the egg yolk mixture, alternating with the meringue. When well combined, divide the mixture in half. Stir coffee extract into one half of the batter and vanilla extract into the other half.

5 Spoon the coffee-flavored batter into a pastry bag fitted with a plain tip. Pipe batter onto the baking sheets, making 4-inch strips about ½ inch apart. When all the coffee batter is gone, fill the pastry bag with the vanilla batter and make more ladyfingers.

6 Bake for about 15 minutes until light golden. Cool the ladyfingers completely on wire racks.

7 To make the marquise, put the egg yolks and confectioners' sugar in a medium-sized bowl set over a larger bowl filled with very warm water. Using a hand-held electric mixer set on medium speed, beat until well mixed. Increase the speed to medium-high and beat for 4 to 5 minutes until the mixture is pale yellow and thick. Remove from the water and set aside.

8 In the top half of a double boiler, melt the chocolate over barely simmering water. Transfer to a large bowl and set aside.

9 In a small saucepan, melt the butter over medium-low heat. Stir in the liqueur and orange zest.

10 Whisk the butter mixture into the chocolate, alternating with the cocoa. When well blended, fold in the beaten egg yolk mixture. Fold in the whipped cream.

11 Line the sides of the springform pan with alternating flavors of ladyfingers, positioning them so that they stand up straight around the pan. Spoon the chocolate marquise mixture into the pan and smooth the top with a spatula. Cover with plastic wrap and refrigerate for at least 4 hours.

12 To serve, carefully remove the sides of the springform pan. Slice the cake and serve each piece with whipped cream and a sprig of mint.

▶ **You can substitute high-quality ladyfingers sold in French bakeries for homemade ladyfingers. They also are sold packaged in specialty stores. Be sure to buy slender, French-style ladyfingers rather than plump, American style.**

A LOVELY LUNCH OR SUNDAY SUPPER

Curried Cream of Cauliflower and Apple Soup
SOUPE CRÈME DE CHOUX-FLEURS ET POMME AU CURRY

Beef Shank Terrine with Leeks and Horseradish Sauce
TERRINE DE BOEUF AUX POIREAUX AVEC SAUCE AU RAIFORT

Warm Apricot Tarts with Pistachios
TARTE TATIN AUX ABRICOTS ET À LA PISTACHE

WINE SUGGESTIONS:

Alsace or California Sparkling Wine (*first course*)

Red Burgundy or Pomerol (*second course*)

Muscat de Beaumes-de-Venise or German Auslese Riesling (*dessert*)

WHAT YOU CAN PREPARE AHEAD OF TIME

Up to 1 week ahead: Prepare the Chicken Stock (if making your own).

Up to 3 days ahead: Prepare the Beef Terrine. Wrap in plastic and refrigerate.

Up to 1 day ahead: Make the Curried Cream of Cauliflower and Apple Soup. Cool, then cover and refrigerate. Reheat over medium heat.

Early in the day: Prepare the apple garnish for the soup. Reheat in the top of a double boiler. Make the Horseradish Sauce. Make the Apricot Tarts. Do not cover them with pastry or unmold them until just before serving.

I first met Daniel Boulud when he was a sous-chef at the Polo restaurant in New York. Although very young at the time, he was already an accomplished chef, having begun his training as a fourteen-year-old apprentice in France.

Daniel taught his first demonstration class when he became the executive chef at La Régence, the French-style restaurant at New York's Hotel Plaza Athenée. We were all awed by his abilities. Now owner of his own restaurant, Daniel, on the East Side of Manhattan, Chef Boulud always puts a great deal of thought into the kitchen skills and tricks he shares with home cooks. Consequently, we are consistently thrilled by his classes. His support of the efforts of De Gustibus has been a boon to our students in understanding what great French cooking is all about.

◁ Beef Shank Terrine with Leeks and Horseradish Sauce

Curried Cream of Cauliflower and Apple Soup

Soupe Crème de Choux-Fleurs et Pomme au Curry

Smooth and creamy with a sweet, spicy taste, this soup is the perfect starter to any festive meal. The fact that it can be prepared a day in advance and reheated at the last minute makes it an even better first course for the busy host or hostess. The soup is also tasty served cold.

4 cups Chicken Stock
1½ tablespoons unsalted butter
1 cup chopped onions
2 teaspoons curry powder
¾ teaspoon saffron threads (or saffron powder)
1 cup sliced tart apples, such as Granny Smith
4 cups cauliflower florets
1 cup heavy cream
Salt and freshly ground white pepper to taste

GARNISH:

1 cup diced tart apples, such as Granny Smith
1 tablespoon water
1 teaspoon curry powder
¼ teaspoon saffron threads (or saffron powder)
Salt and freshly ground white pepper to taste
1 tablespoon chopped fresh chives

1 Assemble the *mise en place* trays for this recipe.

2 In a medium-sized saucepan, warm the stock over low heat.

3 In a large saucepan, melt the butter over medium heat. Add the onions, curry powder, and saffron and cook, stirring frequently, for about 2 minutes, until the onions begin to soften. Add the sliced apples and cook, stirring frequently, for 5 minutes. Stir in the cauliflower and warm chicken stock, increase the heat, and bring to a boil. Reduce the heat and simmer for 20 to 30 minutes, until the cauliflower is very tender.

4 Transfer the soup, in batches if necessary, to a blender or a food processor fitted with the metal blade and process until very smooth. Pour into a medium-sized saucepan and stir in the cream. Season to taste with salt and white pepper and keep warm over very low heat.

5 To make the garnish, combine the diced apples and water in a small saucepan over medium heat and bring to a simmer. Stir in the curry powder and saffron, and season to taste with salt and white pepper. Cover and cook for about 3 minutes. Strain through a fine sieve, reserving the solids. Return the apples to the pan to keep warm.

6 Ladle the soup into warm soup bowls. Sprinkle the diced apple and chopped chives over the top.

DANIEL BOULUD: **Curried Cream of Cauliflower and Apple Soup**

Beef Shank Terrine with Leeks and Horseradish Sauce

Terrine de Boeuf aux Poireaux avec Sauce au Raifort

This terrine is great on its own as a light summer lunch, served with a salad, a crisp baguette, a bowl of fresh fruit—and, of course, a light French wine!

10 pounds well trimmed beef shank, cut into large pieces, or 1 whole beef shank, well trimmed
2 carrots, peeled and chopped
2 ribs celery, chopped
1 sprig fresh thyme
2 whole cloves
1 bay leaf
1 tablespoon salt, or to taste
5 peppercorns
10 large leeks, washed, trimmed, and green part removed
1½ tablespoons unflavored gelatin
2 tablespoons cold water
2 tablespoons fresh tarragon leaves
Freshly ground black pepper
Horseradish Sauce (recipe follows)
½ cup peeled, seeded, and diced tomatoes
1 tablespoon minced fresh chives

■ Special Equipment: 12 x 4 x 4-inch terrine mold or loaf pan

1 Assemble the *mise en place* trays for this recipe.

2 Put the beef in a large heavy saucepan and add enough cold water to cover. Bring to a boil, reduce the heat to low, and simmer for 30 minutes, skimming the surface frequently.

3 Add the carrots, celery, thyme, cloves, bay leaf, salt, and peppercorns, and simmer for 1½ hours.

4 Meanwhile, tie a piece of kitchen twine around each leek to hold it together. Distribute the leeks around the beef. Cover and cook for 30 to 45 minutes longer, or until meat is fork-tender. Remove from the heat and let the meat cool slightly in the liquid.

5 Using a slotted spoon, carefully remove the leeks from the pan. Untie them, place in a shallow dish, and set aside.

DANIEL BOULUD: Beef Shank Terrine with Leeks and Horseradish Sauce

6 Carefully transfer the beef shank to a shallow dish, and set aside.

7 Strain the stock through a coarse sieve, and discard the solids. Strain again through an extra-fine sieve. Skim the fat from the surface of the stock. (Or refrigerate it for several hours and then lift the hardened fat from the surface.)

8 Measure 2 cups of the stock into a small saucepan and heat over very low heat. Reserve the remaining stock for another purpose.

A TRIBUTE TO THE END OF SUMMER

Tomato Tart with Lime Butter
TARTE AUX TOMATES ET BEURRE DE CITRONS VERTS

Red Snapper with Tomatoes and Caramelized Garlic
ROUGET À LA TOMATE ET AIL CARAMELISÉ

Chicken in Parchment with Thyme
POULET EN PAPILLOTE AU THYM

Sweet Green Tomato Pie
TARTE DOUCE DE TOMATES VERTES

WINE SUGGESTION:

Sauvignon Blanc

WHAT YOU CAN PREPARE AHEAD OF TIME

Up to 1 week ahead: Prepare the Chicken Stock (if making your own).

Early in the day: Prepare the filling for the Tomato Tart. Cover and refrigerate. Bake the pastry shell and make the filling for the Sweet Tomato Pie. Prepare garlic, tomatoes, and onions for the Red Snapper. Cover separately and refrigerate. Assemble the chicken and thyme packets. Refrigerate.

In the afternoon: Line the tart pan for the Tomato Tart. Refrigerate.

Just before serving: Make the Lime Butter for the Tomato Tart. Keep warm in a double boiler.

I was first introduced to Antoine Bouterin by the late Gregory Usher, then of the famous French cooking school La Varenne. Antoine had just moved to New York and Gregory felt that we at De Gustibus should experience this great French chef's talents and food. Great he was in the kitchen—but he was not so great with the English language. However, with a translator at his side, Antoine performed miracles and the class was, as Gregory had promised, a rousing success. As Chef Bouterin's reputation grew in America, so did his command of English, and he has returned to teach many times, without a translator. We like nothing better than to lure him from his kitchen at Le Périgord, a New York City restaurant, to share his food and skills with our students. The food is redolent with the flavors of his native Provence, and equally warming is his sunny Provençal disposition. This menu is especially interesting in that the chef showcases tomatoes, at their very best at the end of the summer, in every recipe.

◁ Chicken in Parchment with Thyme

Tomato Tart with Lime Butter

Tarte aux Tomates et Beurre de Citrons Verts

This tart is not only a sensational first course, but would also be a wonderful brunch or light lunch entrée.

TART:

½ pound frozen puff pastry, thawed
2 pounds ripe tomatoes, cored, peeled, seeded, and finely chopped
Juice of 1 large lemon
2 shallots, minced
2 cloves garlic, minced
½ teaspoon minced fresh parsley
¼ teaspoon minced fresh basil
¼ teaspoon minced fresh thyme
Salt and freshly ground black pepper to taste
2 tablespoons olive oil

LIME BUTTER:

Juice of 1 large lime
8 tablespoons unsalted butter, cut into tablespoon-size pieces
2 tablespoons heavy cream
Salt and freshly ground black pepper to taste
½ cup peeled, seeded, and diced ripe tomatoes, for garnish

■ Special Equipment: six 4-inch tartlet pans (not with removable bottoms); pastry weights, dried beans, or rice

1 Preheat the oven to 400 degrees F. Assemble the *mise en place* trays for this recipe.

2 On a floured surface, roll out the pastry to approximately a 15-inch square. Using a sharp knife, cut the pastry into six 5¼-inch squares. Gently fit each square into a 4-inch tartlet pan. Trim the excess dough from the edges. Prick

ANTOINE BOUTERIN:
Tomato Tart with
Lime Butter

46

the bottom of the pastry shelves all over with a fork. Line the pastry shells with aluminum foil cut about 2 inches larger than the pan so that there is no overhang. Spread pastry weights, dried beans, or rice over the foil. Set the tartlet pan on a baking sheet and bake for about 15 minutes, until the pastry is lightly browned. Lift out the foil and weights. Gently lift the baked shells from the tartlet pans and set the pastry shells on a wire rack to cool. Do not turn off the oven.

3 Meanwhile, put the tomatoes in a colander and let drain for about 15 minutes. Pat dry with paper towels.

4 In a glass or ceramic bowl, combine the tomatoes, lemon juice, shallots, garlic, parsley, basil, thyme, and salt and pepper to taste. Stir in the olive oil.

5 Put the baking sheet back in the oven for about 5 minutes. Lift the hot sheet from the oven and position the tartlet shells on it. Spoon approximately 2 tablespoons of the tomato mixture into each shell. Do not overfill. Bake for about 15 minutes, or until centers are firm. As the tartlets

bake, pat the filling with paper towel 2 or 3 times to absorb excess liquid. Grind a light coating of pepper over the top of each tartlet. Let cool for 5 minutes before serving.

6 Meanwhile, make the lime butter: In a small nonreactive saucepan, combine the lime juice with an equal amount of water (about ⅓ cup). Bring to a boil over high heat, and boil for about 3 minutes, or until reduced by half. Whisk in the butter, a tablespoon at a time, until well incorporated. Stir in the cream and season to taste with salt and pepper. Pour into the top half of a double boiler and place over hot water to keep warm.

7 Spoon the lime butter onto plates. Set the tartlets on top, and garnish with the diced tomatoes. Serve immediately.

▶**It's important to let the tomatoes drain to remove excess moisture and then to blot them during baking. Have the paper towels ready—folded two or three thick—before opening the oven door. Work quickly so as not to let too much heat escape.**

Red Snapper with Tomatoes and Caramelized Garlic

Rouget à la Tomate et Ail Caramelisé

SERVES 6
PREPARATION TIME: ABOUT 15 MINUTES
COOKING TIME: ABOUT 1 HOUR

This dish epitomizes the sunny flavors of Provence. Without doubt, it is a dish for garlic-lovers.

3 pounds red snapper fillets, skinned
6 tablespoons peanut oil
22 cloves garlic, peeled (2 to 3 heads)
2 tablespoons sugar
6 large ripe tomatoes, cored, peeled, seeded, and chopped
1 large onion, thinly sliced
1 cup Chicken Stock
½ teaspoon minced fresh thyme
3 large, fresh basil leaves, minced
2 large, fresh sage leaves, minced
1 bay leaf
Pinch of ground cumin
Salt and freshly ground black pepper to taste
6 sprigs fresh parsley

1 Assemble the *mise en place* trays for this recipe.

2 Remove any bones from the fish, rinse it, and pat dry with paper towels. Cut into 2-inch chunks. Cover and refrigerate until ready to cook.

3 In a small sauté pan, heat 2 tablespoons of the oil over medium heat. Add the garlic cloves and sauté for 6 to 7 minutes, until lightly browned. Stir in the sugar. Cook, stirring continuously, for about 3 minutes, until the garlic is caramelized.

4 Using a slotted spoon, transfer the garlic cloves to a paper towel to drain. Mash 4 of the cloves and set aside. Keep the remaining 18 cloves warm.

5 In a large sauté pan, heat 2 tablespoons of the oil over medium heat. Add the chopped tomatoes and cook, stir-

ring frequently, for 20 to 30 minutes, until all the liquid has evaporated. The tomatoes will be smooth and thick. Remove from the heat.

6 In a medium-sized sauté pan, heat the remaining 2 tablespoons of oil over medium heat. Add the onion and sauté for about 5 minutes, until softened and lightly browned. Stir in the mashed garlic, the tomatoes, stock,

thyme, basil, sage, bay leaf, cumin, and salt and pepper to taste. Add the fish and cook, stirring occasionally, for about 10 minutes, until cooked through. Remove the bay leaf.

7 Place equal portions of the fish and vegetable sauce in the center of 6 warm dinner plates. Garnish each plate with 3 garlic cloves and a sprig of parsley.

Chicken in Parchment with Thyme

SERVES 6
PREPARATION TIME: ABOUT 15 MINUTES
COOKING TIME: ABOUT 25 MINUTES

Poulet en Papillote au Thym

This recipe calls for cooking the chicken in parchment, but heavy-duty aluminum foil is an easy and accessible option for the home cook. The foil packets can also be placed on the grill for perfect summertime entertaining.

6 skinless, boneless chicken breast halves, trimmed
1 cup chopped leeks, white parts only
½ cup diced celery
1 cup cored, peeled, seeded, and diced tomatoes
Grated zest of 1 lemon
3 cloves garlic, sliced
3 tablespoons chopped scallions
1 tablespoon minced fresh thyme
Salt and freshly ground black pepper to taste
24 to 30 fresh spinach leaves, washed, dried, stems removed
6 tablespoons dry white wine

1 Preheat oven to 400 degrees F. Assemble the *mise en place* trays for this recipe.

2 Cut 6 pieces of heavy-duty aluminum foil into rectangles approximately 18 x 20 inches.

3 Rinse the chicken and pat dry with paper towels. Using a cleaver or heavy knife, slightly flatten each breast half.

4 Combine the leeks and celery. Put about ¼ cup of the vegetables toward the bottom edge of each piece of foil. Lay a chicken breast on top, and put 4 to 5 spinach leaves on top of the chicken.

5 Combine the tomatoes, lemon zest, garlic, scallions, thyme, and salt and pepper to taste. Divide this mixture evenly among the packets, spooning it on top of the chicken. Sprinkle 1 tablespoon of the wine over each one.

6 Fold the top half of each sheet of foil over the chicken so that the edges meet like a book. Fold the bottom edges up to make a 1-inch fold. Fold the 1-inch closure in half, making a ½-inch fold, and fold over once more with a ½-inch fold. Fold the sides in the same way. You should have formed a packet, closed tightly around the ingredients. Place on a large baking sheet and bake for 20 to 25 minutes, or until the foil packages swell up. Serve in the packets, letting your guests slit open the foil at the table, and enjoy the fragrant aroma that steams out.

ANTOINE BOUTERIN: **Chicken in Parchment with Thyme**

◁ ANTOINE BOUTERIN: Red Snapper with Tomatoes and Caramelized Garlic

Sweet Green Tomato Pie

Tarte Douce de Tomates Vertes

This unusual French dessert calls for unripe tomatoes. In rural America, green tomato pie is often served as dessert. In both countries, the recipes were created to utilize bumper crops that gardeners feared would not reach ripeness before the autumn frost. This pie has a wonderful fresh taste, as citrus again heightens the flavor of the tomatoes.

2 lemons
5 tablespoons water
½ cup granulated sugar
½ pound puff pastry, thawed
1 large egg
1 tablespoon arrowroot
4½ tablespoons unsalted butter
3 pounds green tomatoes, cored, peeled, seeded, and sliced into ¼-inch slices
3 large egg whites
1 tablespoon confectioners' sugar

■ Special Equipment: 9-inch tart pan with removable bottom; pastry weights, beans, or rice

1 Preheat the oven to 400 degrees F. Assemble the *mise en place* trays for this recipe.

2 Using a sharp knife, carefully remove the yellow-colored peel from 1 of the lemons, avoiding the bitter white pith. Cut the peel into a fine julienne. Grate the zest from the remaining lemon and set aside.

3 In a small saucepan, combine the julienned peel, the water, and 3 tablespoons of the sugar. Bring to a boil over high heat, and cook for 4 to 5 minutes, until all the water has evaporated. Drain the lemon peel on paper towels and set aside.

4 On a lightly floured surface, roll out the pastry to a circle about ⅛ inch thick and approximately 12 inches round. Transfer the pastry to a 9-inch tart pan with a removable bottom. Gently fit the pastry into the pan, and trim off any excess. Prick the bottom of the pastry all over with a fork. Line the pastry shell with aluminum foil and spread pastry weights, dried beans, or rice over the foil. Bake for about 15 minutes, until the pastry is lightly browned. Lift out the foil and weights, and set on a wire rack to cool. Do not turn off the oven.

5 In a small bowl, beat the egg with the arrowroot.

6 In a large sauté pan, melt the butter over medium heat. Cook the tomato slices for about 5 minutes, or until softened, stirring gently every so often and taking care not to tear the slices. Sprinkle 3 tablespoons of the sugar over them and stir gently. Spoon some liquid from the pan into the egg mixture and stir to temper it. Add the egg mixture to the pan, and stir gently. Remove from the heat, and stir in the julienned lemon peel. Pour this mixture into the partially baked pastry shell, and let the filling cool slightly.

7 In a large bowl, using an electric mixer, beat the egg whites until soft peaks form. Add the remaining 2 tablespoons of sugar and beat until stiff peaks form. Fold the lemon zest into the meringue. Using a spatula, spread the meringue evenly over the tomato filling, swirling and lifting the meringue to make an attractive design.

8 Bake for about 5 minutes, until the meringue is golden. Sprinkle with the confectioners' sugar and serve immediately.

▶ When making a tart with a filling as moist as this one, do not expect the pastry to stay firm and crisp. It will soften a little beneath the filling.

▷ ANTOINE BOUTERIN: Sweet Green Tomato Pie

CLASSIC FRENCH FOR FRIENDS

Artichoke Bottoms Filled with Poached Oysters
COEURS D'ARTICHAUTS FARCIES AUX HUÎTRES POCHÉES

Apple Soufflé on a Platter with Apricot Sauce
SOUFFLÉ DE POMMES À L'ASSIETTE AVEC SAUCE AUX ABRICOTS

WINE SUGGESTIONS:

Premier Cru Chablis or California Chardonnay (*first course*)

Late Harvest Muscat or Riesling (*dessert*)

WHAT YOU CAN PREPARE AHEAD OF TIME

Up to 3 days ahead: Prepare and cook the artichokes for the Artichoke Bottoms. Cover and refrigerate.

Up to 2 days ahead: Prepare and cook the diced apples for the Apple Soufflé. Cover and refrigerate. Prepare the Apricot Sauce for the Apple Soufflé. Cover and refrigerate.

The day before: Prepare the croutons for the Apple Soufflé. Cover and refrigerate.

Early in the day: Make the artichoke sauce, leaving out the oysters. Top with a film of heavy cream to prevent drying out. Cover and refrigerate. Prepare the oysters and refrigerate separately. Gently fold into the sauce as it reheats.

Julia Child was one of the very first superstars we invited to teach at De Gustibus. This was during the time when we were still housed in an off-off Broadway theater and our kitchen was composed of two electric burners. Julia arrived with one of her favorite kitchen tools, a blowtorch. During her demonstration, she flamboyantly showed the class how to peel the skins from tomatoes and caramelize a tart using her handy flamethrower!

From the beginning, Julia has been very supportive of our efforts to bring demonstrations by notable chefs to "regular people." She had not visited us for some years until recently, when she came as an honored guest at a special program at De Gustibus. In her own words, "What fun it is to be back at De Gustibus. It has been a number of years and how nice it is to see the advances from that funny little attic theater to this very chic Macy's environment."

Julia Child is truly a remarkable person. This is a very simple menu—only two dishes!—but the flavors are perfectly balanced and the food sublime.

◁ Artichoke Bottoms Filled with Poached Oysters

APRICOT SAUCE
Sauce á l'Abricot

MAKES ABOUT 3 CUPS

8 ounces dried apricots, rinsed and drained
½ cup water
½ cup dry vermouth
1 cinnamon stick or ¼ teaspoon ground cinnamon
½ lemon, quartered and seeded
½ cup granulated sugar, or more to taste
16 ounces canned apricot halves packed in water
⅛ teaspoon salt
1 to 2 teaspoons unsalted butter, softened (optional)

1 In a medium-sized saucepan, combine the dried apricots, water, and vermouth. Let soak for at least 1 hour, or overnight if the fruit is especially dry. (You may need to add another ¼ cup of water for longer soaking.)

2 Add the cinnamon stick and lemon to the pan of apricots, and bring to a simmer over medium heat. Cook for 20 minutes.

3 Stir in the sugar and the canned apricots, with their juices. Reduce the heat to low and cook, stirring frequently to prevent the sauce from scorching and sticking, for 20 to 30 minutes, or until thick and almost caramelized. Taste frequently, and add additional sugar, a tablespoonful at a time, if the sauce is too tart.

4 Transfer the apricot mixture to a blender or a food processor fitted with the metal blade. Blend until smooth. Blend in the butter, if using. Serve hot or cold.

▶ **This sauce can be made up to 1 week in advance, covered, and refrigerated. It can also be frozen for up to 3 months.**

▷ JULIA CHILD: Apple Soufflé on a Platter with Apricot Sauce

A TASTE OF PROVENCE

Mediterranean Seafood Soup
L'AÏGO

Braised Lamb Shanks with Dried Mediterranean Fruits
JARRET D'AGNEAU AUX FRUITS DE BRANCONNIER

Chocolate Tarte with Orange Salad
TARTE SABLÉE AU CHOCOLAT AVEC SALADE D'ORANGE

WINE SUGGESTIONS:

Rosé de Provence, Gavi, or Pinot Grigio (*first course*)

Full-Bodied Pinot Noir or lighter Zinfandel (*second course*)

Vintage Character Port (*dessert*)

WHAT YOU CAN PREPARE AHEAD OF TIME

Up to 1 week ahead: Make the pastry for the Chocolate Tart. Fit it into the pan, wrap tightly in aluminum foil, and freeze. Thaw at room temperature before baking. (Thawing will take between 30 minutes and 1 hour, depending on the heat of the day.)

Up to 3 days ahead: Marinate the lamb shanks and reduce and strain the braising liquid for the Braised Lamb. Combine the meat and liquid, cover, and refrigerate. Reheat in the oven with the fennel mixture.

Up to 2 days ahead: Dice the dried fruits for the Braised Lamb. Cover tightly and refrigerate.

The day before: Prepare the orange juice and zest for the Braised Lamb. Cover and refrigerate.

The night before: Prepare all the vegetables for the Mediterranean Seafood Soup. Cover and refrigerate.

Early in the day: Prepare the lobster for the Mediterranean Seafood Soup. Cover and refrigerate. Cut the fennel and apples for the Braised Lamb into julienne. Toss separately with fresh lemon juice, cover, and refrigerate. Prepare the Orange Salad for the Chocolate Tart.

Jean-Michel Diot was one of our best surprises. I had expected Jacques Chibois, executive chef of the Royal Grey in Cannes and consultant at New York's Peninsula Hotel, to be part of one of our French series. At the last moment, he had an emergency in France and couldn't come. "Don't worry," said Chef Chibois, "I'll send my chef from the Peninsula. He trained with me and is terrific!" What he didn't tell me was that his terrific chef had only been in New York for six weeks, did not speak a word of English, and had never taught a cooking class.

After some anxiety, the class took place and this terrific chef, Jean-Michel Diot, received a standing ovation from the students. His food reflected all of the flavors and colors of the South of France, he smiled a lot, and his sous-chef was a great translator. It was one of our most exciting classes.

Jean-Michel subsequently learned English, opened three restaurants in New York City, and is now considered one of the city's leading chefs.

◁ Braised Lamb Shanks with Dried Mediterranean Fruits

JEAN-MICHEL DIOT   A TASTE OF PROVENCE

marinade, reserving the liquid. Reserve the vegetables and bouquet garni separately.

5 In the Dutch oven, heat 2 tablespoons of the olive oil over medium-high heat. Add the lamb shanks and sear, turning frequently, for 10 to 15 minutes, or until well browned. Transfer to paper towels to drain.

6 Add the marinated vegetables to the pot and cook for 5 to 6 minutes, until they have just begun to release their liquid. Transfer to a bowl with a slotted spoon, and set aside.

7 Using a wooden spoon, stir the flour into the juices remaining in the pot. Cook, stirring constantly, for about 3 minutes, or until the flour is golden brown.

8 Return the lamb shanks and vegetables to the pot. Add the tomatoes, the reserved marinade, and the bouquet garni. Increase the heat to high and bring to a boil. Reduce the heat and simmer for about 20 minutes, or until the liquid is reduced by half.

9 Stir in 2 cups of the water. Cover and transfer to the oven. Cook for about 2 hours or until the meat is very tender.

10 Meanwhile, dice the figs, apricots, dates, and raisins.

Cut the mint leaves into fine julienne and combine with the diced fruit. Set aside.

11 About 45 minutes before the meat is ready, peel and core the apples and cut into ⅛-inch-thick slices.

12 In a large ovenproof sauté pan, heat the remaining 2 tablespoons of oil over medium heat. Add the fennel and sauté for about 5 minutes, just until it begins to brown. Stir in the apples and orange zest and juice. Stir in the remaining 1 cup of water, cover, and cook in the oven for 30 minutes.

13 Arrange the fennel mixture in the center of a large platter. Place the lamb shanks on top. Cover with a piece of aluminum foil to keep warm.

14 Place the Dutch oven over high heat, bring the liquid to a boil for about 5 minutes, until reduced and slightly thickened. Skim off any fat that rises to the surface. Strain into a saucepan and stir in the dried fruit mixture. Simmer for 4 to 5 minutes, until fruit softens. Season to taste with salt and pepper.

15 Ladle some of the sauce over the top of the lamb. Serve with the remaining sauce on the side.

SERVES 6
PREPARATION TIME: ABOUT 30 MINUTES
COOKING TIME: ABOUT 1 HOUR AND 15 MINUTES
CHILLING AND COOLING TIME: ABOUT 3 HOURS AND 25 MINUTES

Chocolate Tart with Orange Salad

Tarte Sablée au Chocolat avec Salade d'Orange

A chocolate dessert as seductive as this one tastes even better when served with an orange salad for a slightly acidic accent and refreshing note.

1¾ cups unsalted butter, at room temperature
2 cups granulated sugar
5 large eggs
¼ teaspoon salt
1½ cups all-purpose flour
12 ounces bittersweet chocolate
¼ cup cornstarch
2 large egg yolks
1 tablespoon confectioners' sugar
Orange Salad (recipe follows)

■ Special Equipment: 10-inch tart pan with removable bottom. Pastry weights, dried beans, or rice.

1 Assemble the *mise en place* trays for this recipe.

2 In a large bowl, using an electric mixer set on medium-high speed, beat 12 tablespoons of the butter, ½ cup of the granulated sugar, 1 of the eggs, and the salt for 3 to 4 minutes, until light colored and thick. Reduce the speed to medium-low and slowly add the flour, about ½ cup at a time, being careful not to overmix the dough. Form the dough into a flattened ball, wrap in plastic, and refrigerate for at least 2 hours.

3 Preheat the oven to 350 degrees F.

4 Lay a large piece of waxed paper on a lightly floured surface and dust the paper with flour. Put the chilled dough on the paper and sprinkle lightly with flour. Lay a second

62

JEAN-MICHEL DIOT: **Chocolate Tart with Orange Salad**

sheet of waxed paper over the dough, and roll it out to a 13-inch circle. Carefully transfer the paper-wrapped pastry to the refrigerator and chill for about 15 minutes.

5 Peel off the top piece of waxed paper and carefully transfer the chilled dough, paper side up, to a 10-inch tart pan with a removable bottom. Gently lift off the remaining piece of waxed paper, fit the pastry into the pan, and trim off any excess. Prick the bottom of the pastry all over with a fork. Line the pastry shell with aluminum foil, and spread pastry weights, dried beans, or rice over the foil. Bake for 10 to 15 minutes, until lightly browned. Lift out the weights and foil and and set on a wire rack to cool. Do not turn off the oven.

6 In the top half of a double boiler, melt the chocolate over barely simmering water. Beat in the remaining 1 cup of butter, a little at a time, until well incorporated. Remove from the heat.

7 In a large bowl, using an electric mixer set on medium-high speed, beat the egg yolks, the remaining 4 eggs, and 1½ cups of sugar for 3 to 4 minutes, until light and creamy. Whisk in the cornstarch until well blended. Slowly whisk in the chocolate mixture.

8 Scrape the mixture into the partially baked pastry shell. Bake for about 1 hour, or until the center is set. Transfer to a wire rack to cool for at least 1 hour before serving.

9 Just before serving, dust the tart with confectioners' sugar. Cut into wedges and serve with the Orange Salad on the side.

ORANGE SALAD
Salade d'Orange

MAKES ABOUT 4 CUPS

8 oranges
2 tablespoons bitter orange marmalade
3 tablespoons granulated sugar

1 With a small, sharp knife remove the colored peel from 4 of the oranges, being careful to avoid any bitter white pith. Cut the peel into fine julienne.

2 Blanch the julienne in boiling water for 15 seconds. Drain and refresh under cold running water. Pat dry and set aside.

3 Working over a bowl, cut all the peel and pith from all 8 oranges, letting any juices drip into the bowl. Slice between the membranes to free each segment, dropping the segments into the bowl. Squeeze the juice from the membranes and discard them.

4 Add the marmalade, reserved zest, and the sugar to the orange segments. Stir to combine. Cover and refrigerate until ready to serve.

A TYPICAL FRENCH MEAL

Creamy Carrot Soup
SOUPE DE CAROTTES À L'ANETH

Fillet of Beef with Horseradish Sauce
FILET DE BOEUF À LA FICELLE AVEC SAUCE AU RAIFORT

Thin Apple Tart
TARTE AUX POMMES À LA MINUTE

WINE SUGGESTIONS:

Chardonnay (*first course*)

Red Bordeaux, St. Estèphe or Pauillac (*second course*)

Calvados (*dessert*)

WHAT YOU CAN PREPARE AHEAD OF TIME

Up to 1 week ahead: Prepare the Chicken Stock (if making your own). Prepare the Beef Stock (if making your own).

Up to 2 days ahead: Make the Carrot Soup. Cover and refrigerate.

The day before: Make the Horseradish Sauce. Cover and refrigerate.

Early in the day: Prepare all the vegetables for the Fillet of Beef. Place in a sealed plastic bag and refrigerate. Tie the beef with the kitchen twine. Cover and refrigerate. Bake the Thin Apple Tart. Before serving, heat in a preheated 300 degree F. oven for 5 minutes.

It was a thrill and an honor to have Pierre Franey teach in the De Gustibus kitchen. For many of us, Pierre is the essence of the charming French chef. He enchanted us with his stories of his early cooking days and amazed us with tales of his experiences at *The New York Times.*

Pierre's first visits to De Gustibus were in our "formative years," and he was one of the first "real" French chefs to teach a class. None of us had ever seen such order around the stove. I don't know what was more impressive—his organizational skills or his fastidious presentation. We had never witnessed what was to Chef Franey perfectly normal, well-learned culinary practice. More than any other chef, he taught us how important the basic cooking habits are in accomplishing great meals. Furthermore, Pierre made good cooking really accessible. Not only is he a great French chef, he is a warm human being who enjoys cooking for family and friends.

◁ Creamy Carrot Soup

Creamy Carrot Soup

Soupe de Carottes à l'Aneth

This simple soup has great taste, it can be made in advance, and it can be served hot or cold. What more could a home cook ask?

2 tablespoons unsalted butter
1 cup minced onions
5 cups sliced carrots
Salt and freshly ground black pepper to taste
4 cups Chicken Stock
½ cup ricotta cheese
2 tablespoons port wine
2 tablespoons chopped fresh dill

1 Assemble the *mise en place* trays for this recipe.

2 In a medium-sized saucepan, melt the butter over medium heat. Add the onions and cook, stirring occasionally, for 4 to 5 minutes, until softened.

3 Stir in the carrots and season to taste with salt and pepper. Add the chicken stock and bring to a boil. Reduce the heat and simmer, partially covered, for 30 minutes. Strain, reserving the liquid.

4 Transfer the carrot mixture to a blender or a food processor fitted with the metal blade. Add the ricotta and 1 cup of the reserved liquid. Process until smooth. Scrape back into the saucepan and add the remaining liquid.

5 Return the soup to the heat and bring to a boil. Remove from the heat and stir in the port and dill. Serve hot. Alternately, allow to cool just to warm room temperature, cover, and refrigerate for at least 4 hours until well chilled. Stir in the port and dill just before serving cold.

Fillet of Beef with Horseradish Sauce

Filet de Boeuf à la Ficelle avec Sauce au Raifort

Although, for this menu, the meat should be cooked just before serving, all the other components of the recipe can easily be prepared in advance. However, the beef is also terrific cold, so the dish could be cooked early in the day, especially during warm weather, when cold meals are always welcome.

1¼ pounds center-cut fillet of beef
4 cups Beef Stock
1 bay leaf
2 sprigs fresh parsley
3 sprigs fresh thyme, chopped, or ½ teaspoon dried thyme
Salt and freshly ground black pepper to taste
1 large leek, white part only, washed and cut into julienne (about 2 cups)
1 large parsnip, peeled and cut into julienne (about 2 cups)
2 carrots, peeled and cut into julienne (about 2 cups)
1 small onion, halved and finely sliced (about ½ cup)
Horseradish Sauce (recipe follows)

1 Assemble the *mise en place* trays for this recipe.

2 Carefully tie the meat lengthwise and crosswise with kitchen twine, leaving a long end of string as a handle to facilitate removing the meat from the cooking liquid.

3 In a large, heavy saucepan or flame-proof casserole with lid, combine the stock, bay leaf, parsley, thyme, and salt and pepper to taste. Add the beef, leaving the length of string outside the pan.

4 Cover the pan, bring the stock to a simmer over medium-high heat, and cook for exactly 5 minutes. Immediately add the leeks, parsnips, carrots, and onion and stir to distribute them. Cover and simmer for exactly 7 minutes. Remove from the heat and let stand, covered, for 5 minutes.

▷ PIERRE FRANEY: Fillet of Beef with Horseradish Sauce

5 Remove the beef from the pan and cut into thin slices (no more than ½-inch thick). Arrange on a warm platter. Spoon the vegetables around the meat and spoon a little of the liquid over all. Serve with the Horseradish Sauce passed on the side.

▶ If you cannot buy a center-cut fillet but instead buy an end of the fillet, trim the tapering ends before cooking.

▶ You can, of course, lift the meat from the pan with tongs rather than using the string as a handle, but do not pierce it with a fork.

▶ Substitute drained white bottled horseradish for grated horseradish in the horseradish sauce, if necessary.

HORSERADISH SAUCE
Sauce au Raifort

MAKES ABOUT ½ CUP

½ cup sour cream
2 tablespoons freshly grated horseradish, or to taste
1 teaspoon white wine vinegar
⅛ teaspoon Tabasco
Salt and freshly ground black pepper to taste

In a bowl, combine the sour cream, 2 tablespoons of horseradish, the vinegar, and Tabasco. Stir to blend. Season to taste with salt and pepper, and add more horseradish, if desired.

Thin Apple Tart

SERVES 6
PREPARATION TIME: ABOUT 20 MINUTES
COOKING TIME: ABOUT 20 MINUTES

Tarte aux Pommes à la Minute

This is one of my favorite French desserts. It is so simple and the apple flavor just shines!

1½ cups all-purpose flour, chilled
6 tablespoons unsalted butter, chilled and cut into pieces
3 tablespoons plus 2 teaspoons granulated sugar
¼ cup cold water
3 large, tart apples, such as Granny Smith, peeled, cored, and thinly sliced
1 tablespoon unsalted butter, melted

■ Special Equipment: dark-colored, 12-inch pie pan or pizza pan

1 Preheat the oven to 450 degrees F. Assemble the *mise en place* trays for this recipe.

2 Put the flour, butter, and 2 teaspoons of the sugar in a food processor fitted with the metal blade. With the motor running, slowly add the water through the feed tube and process for about 1 minute, until the dough forms a ball.

3 Transfer the dough to a lightly floured surface and roll out into a circle about 13 inches in diameter. Press into a 12-inch shallow black steel or aluminum pie pan or pizza

pan about ½ inch deep. Trim any dough that rises up the side of the pan to make a flat round.

4 Sprinkle the dough with 1 tablespoon of the sugar. Arrange the apple slices neatly in an overlapping circular pattern on the dough, starting from the center and forming concentric rings. The center will rise to a slight peak, but it will flatten during baking. If there is space in the middle, fill it with some chopped apple. Sprinkle the apples with the remaining 2 tablespoons of sugar.

5 Bake for about 20 minutes, until the apples are lightly browned and soft and the sugar has begun to brown.

6 Remove the tart from the oven, and turn the oven setting to broil.

7 When the broiler is hot, place the tart under it for 1 minute to caramelize the sugar on top. The rims of the apple slices should be well browned, but watch carefully so that the pastry does not get too brown. Remove from the broiler and brush the top with the melted butter. Cut into wedges and serve hot.

▶ **Cut the apples as thin as possible. They should be as uniformly shaped as possible for even cooking. You can cut them into either circles or half-moon shapes.**

◁ PIERRE FRANEY: Thin Apple Tart

COLONIAL FRANCE—
FRENCH FOOD WITH A TOUCH OF ASIA

*Sautéed Shrimp with Marinated Spaghetti Squash
and Curry-Cilantro Vinaigrette*
POÊLE DE CREVETTES ET SPAGHETTI DE COURGES AU CURRY

Spicy Broth of Bass and Halibut Flavored with Lovage
CONSOMMÉ ÉPICÉ DE FLÉTANS ET BAR DE L'ATLANTIQUE
AVEC LIVÈCHES ("CÉLERI BÂTARD")

Chilled Soup of Santa Rosa Plums Flavored with Vanilla
SOUPE GLACÉE AUX PRUNES PARFUMÉE DE VANILLE

WINE SUGGESTIONS:

Dry Riesling (German or Washington State)

Premier Cru Chablis

WHAT YOU CAN PREPARE AHEAD OF TIME

Up to 1 week ahead: Prepare the Fish Stock (if making your own). Prepare the Vegetable Stock (if making your own).

The day before: Make the Chilled Soup of Santa Rosa Plums. Cover and refrigerate.

Early in the day: Prepare all the components for the Sautéed Shrimp except the shrimp. Store separately, covered, in the refrigerator. Prepare the Curry-Cilantro Vinaigrette, but do not add the cilantro until just before serving. Cover and store at room temperature. Make the pistachio-coated ice cream balls for the Chilled Soup of Santa Rosa Plums. Set on a baking sheet in a single layer and freeze until ready to use.

Gray Kunz is a dazzling chef. He grew up in Switzerland, where he trained with Freddy Girardet, one of the world's great cooking gurus, before spending a number of years cooking in Asia. Recently, he brought his genius to New York. Now chef at the acclaimed restaurant Lespinasse at the Hotel St. Regis, Gray Kunz continues to receive accolades for his refined flavors.

Chef Kunz has an eye for detail both in the kitchen and on the plate. His marriage of zesty Asian ingredients with classic French techniques has opened new horizons for the De Gustibus students. Totally interested in our classroom enthusiasms, Gray has been a great supporter of our students and a great friend to all of us.

◁ Chilled Soup of Santa Rosa Plums Flavored with Vanilla

Sautéed Shrimp with Marinated Spaghetti Squash and Curry-Cilantro Vinaigrette

SERVES 6
PREPARATION TIME: ABOUT 25 MINUTES
COOKING TIME: ABOUT 1 HOUR

Poêle de Crevettes et Spaghetti de Courges au Curry

A perfectly light but flavor-packed first course. The Asian flavors add a refreshing zing to the otherwise sweetly bland spaghetti squash. The squash mixture is so delicious that you will want to serve it alone as a tasty salad or side dish.

1 two-to-two-and-one-half-pound spaghetti squash
1 small candy cane beet or regular beet, cooked, peeled, and thinly sliced
⅓ cup thinly sliced firm but ripe papaya
¼ cup thinly sliced hothouse cucumber
Grated zest of 1 lime
1 tablespoon minced fresh ginger
1½ teaspoons minced fresh parsley
3 tablespoons rice wine vinegar
2½ tablespoons corn oil
1 teaspoon granulated sugar
¼ teaspoon salt
¼ teaspoon freshly ground white pepper
6 jumbo shrimp, peeled and deveined
1 ounce mesclun greens or other delicate leaf salad mix
Curry-Cilantro Vinaigrette (recipe follows)

1 Preheat the oven to 375 degrees F. Assemble the *mise en place* trays for this recipe.

2 Prick the squash with a fork in a few places to prevent it from bursting. Put it in a shallow baking dish and bake for 1 hour, or until it depresses easily when gently pressed. Remove from the oven and immediately cut lengthwise in half. Allow to cool for about 10 minutes.

3 Remove and discard the seeds from the squash. Using a kitchen fork, lift the strands of "spaghetti" from each half. Measure out 2 cups of squash and place in a large bowl. Let squash cool. Reserve any remaining squash for another use.

4 Add the beet, papaya, cucumber, lime zest, ginger, and parsley to the squash, and toss well.

5 In a small bowl, whisk together the vinegar, 1½ tablespoons of the oil, the sugar, salt, and white pepper. Pour over the squash mixture and toss. Taste and adjust the seasoning. Set aside.

6 In a small sauté pan, heat the remaining 1 tablespoon of oil over medium-high heat. Add the shrimp and sauté for 2 minutes, or until the shrimp turns pink and opaque. Remove from the heat.

7 Mound the squash mixture in the center of 6 plates. Surround with the mesclun. Put the shrimp on top of the squash mixture, drizzle the Curry-Cilantro Vinaigrette over all, and serve immediately.

▶ Select a papaya that is just ripe. It should be firm but slightly yielding. If it is too green, the flesh will be unpleasantly hard; if too ripe, it will not hold up well in the salad.

▶ If papayas are unavailable, you could use a firm but ripe mango.

CURRY-CILANTRO VINAIGRETTE
MAKES ABOUT ⅓ CUP

3 tablespoons vegetable oil
1½ tablespoons white wine vinegar
¾ teaspoon curry powder
1½ tablespoons Vegetable Stock or water
½ teaspoon fresh lemon juice, or to taste
Salt and freshly ground black pepper to taste
Granulated sugar to taste
2 tablespoons chopped fresh cilantro

1 In a small bowl, whisk together the oil, vinegar, and curry powder. Add the stock. Season to taste with lemon juice, salt, pepper, and a pinch of sugar. Add more sugar, if desired.

2 Just before serving, stir in the cilantro.

▷ GRAY KUNZ: Sautéed Shrimp with Marinated Spaghetti Squash and Curry-Cilantro Vinaigrette

Spicy Broth of Bass and Halibut Flavored with Lovage

SERVES 6
PREPARATION TIME: ABOUT 25 MINUTES
COOKING TIME: ABOUT 35 MINUTES

Consommé Épicé de Flétans et Bar de l'Atlantique avec Livèches ("céleri bâtard")

This is a perfectly simple fish course that can easily become a main course for a light lunch.

½ **pound fresh black sea bass fillet, skinned, trimmed, and cut into ½-inch cubes**

½ **pound fresh halibut fillet, skinned, trimmed, and cut into ½-inch cubes**

Salt and freshly ground black pepper to taste

3 **leaves lovage, chopped, or ¼ cup chopped celery leaves**

1 **teaspoon vegetable oil, or more if necessary**

4 **cups Fish Stock**

4 **tablespoons unsalted butter, cut into pieces**

2½ **tablespoons minced shallots**

½ **teaspoon minced garlic**

Cayenne pepper to taste

½ **cup cored, peeled, seeded, and diced tomatoes**

¼ **cup diced green bell pepper**

⅓ **cup thinly sliced leeks**

■ **Special Equipment: mortar and pestle**

1 Assemble the *mise en place* trays for this recipe.

2 Put the lovage in a mortar and add the vegetable oil. Using a pestle, grind into a paste, adding additional oil if necessary for a pesto-like consistency. Alternatively, mince the chopped lovage leaves and mix them with the oil in a small bowl, pressing down and grinding with the edge of a wooden spoon until the mixture forms a paste-like consistency.

3 In a medium-sized saucepan, bring the stock to a boil over medium-high heat. Reduce the heat to low. Using a whisk, beat the butter into the stock, a piece at a time, until emulsified. Do not add the next piece until the one before is incorporated. Stir in the shallots and garlic. Season to taste with salt and black pepper and cayenne. Bring the mixture to a gentle boil.

GRAY KUNZ: Spicy Broth of Bass and Halibut Flavored with Lovage

4 Season the fish with salt and pepper to taste.

5 Add the tomato, pepper, and leeks to the pan and return to a gentle boil. Add the fish. As soon as the liquid returns to a gentle boil, remove the pan from the heat and stir in the lovage mixture. Taste and adjust the seasoning, if necessary.

6 Ladle the fish and broth into 6 warm, shallow soup bowls. Serve immediately.

▶Lovage, called céleri bâtard, or "false celery," in France because its flavor and aroma are similar to celery, is extremely potent. Use it sparingly. Lovage is easy to grow in a vegetable garden. It is sold at greengrocers and farm markets. As indicated in the recipe, you can substitute celery leaves for lovage if necessary.

▶If you like the flavor of lovage, make small amounts of lovage "pesto" as described in Step 2, cover and refrigerate. Use it to flavor stews, soups, salads, or sauces or to season roasted or grilled meats.

▶If you cannot find black sea bass, substitute any firm-fleshed white fish or use all halibut. Recommended substitutes include grouper, striped sea bass, and snapper.

Chilled Soup of Santa Rosa Plums Flavored with Vanilla

SERVES 6
PREPARATION TIME: ABOUT 20 MINUTES
COOKING TIME: ABOUT 1 HOUR
CHILLING TIME: AT LEAST 4 HOURS

Soupe Glacée aux Prunes Parfumée de Vanille

This dessert is best made in the summer, when plums are at their most succulent. For fewer calories and no fat, eliminate the ice cream. The idea of serving "soup" for dessert is a delicious one you may not have tried.

2½ pounds overripe red plums, preferably Santa Rosa, washed
½ cup plus 1 tablespoon granulated sugar, or to taste
1 vanilla bean, split in half lengthwise
Juice of 1 lemon, or more to taste
10 cups water
Dash of Mirabelle eau-de-vie or other plum-flavored liqueur
1 cup chopped, toasted pistachio nuts
1 pint high-quality vanilla ice cream

1 Assemble the *mise en place* trays for this recipe.

2 Cut 6 silver dollar-sized slices from the sides of 2 or 3 plums. Chop the remaining plum flesh, discarding the pits.

3 In a medium-sized saucepan, combine the sliced and chopped plums, ½ cup of the sugar, the vanilla bean, lemon juice, and water. Bring to a simmer over medium heat. Reduce the heat to low and simmer, uncovered, for 20 minutes.

4 Using a slotted spoon, carefully transfer 6 plum slices to a plate and sprinkle with the remaining 1 tablespoon of sugar. Set aside. Continue simmering the chopped plum mixture, uncovered, for about 40 minutes more.

5 Strain the chopped plum mixture through a fine sieve into a glass or ceramic bowl, pushing against the solids to extract all the juice. Discard the solids. Taste, and add a little more sugar, if necessary. Cover and refrigerate for about 4 hours, or until well chilled.

6 Just before serving, stir the eau-de-vie or plum liqueur into the soup. Taste, and add lemon juice, if necessary. Ladle the soup into 6 well-chilled, shallow soup bowls.

7 Place the pistachios in a shallow bowl. Scoop out 6 small balls of ice cream and roll each one in the pistachios. Place an ice cream ball in the center of each bowl of soup, lay a sugared plum slice on top, and serve immediately. If not using ice cream, simply garnish the soup with the plum slices.

▶When a recipe calls for overripe plums, select those that feel heavy and juicy and are very "giving" when pressed. Avoid any that are still firm—or that show signs of spoilage.

TALKING TURKEY IN THE FRENCH MANNER

Lettuce Soup
SOUPE DE LAITUES

Scallopine of Turkey Breast with Morel and Cognac Sauce
ESCALOPE DE JEUNE DINDE AUX MORILLES AVEC SAUCE AU COGNAC

Fricassee of Turkey and Brown Rice
FRICASÉE DE DINDE AU RIZ BRUN

Baked Apples
POMMES BONNE FEMME

WINE SUGGESTIONS:

Champagne (*first course*)

California Pinot Noir or Red Burgundy (*second course*)

Syrah or Merlot (*third course*)

Calvados (*dessert*)

WHAT YOU CAN PREPARE AHEAD OF TIME

Up to 1 week ahead: Prepare the Turkey or Chicken Stock (if making your own).

Up to 1 day ahead: Make the Lettuce Soup, but if serving hot, do not add the lettuce. Cool, cover, and refrigerate, and reheat just before serving, adding the shredded lettuce. If serving cold, add the lettuce, cool, cover, and refrigerate. Prepare the Fricassee of Turkey, but do not add the peas and parsley. Cool, cover, and refrigerate. Reheat in a preheated 300 degree F. oven for 30 minutes, adding additional liquid if necessary, and stir in the peas and parsley just before serving.

Early in the day: Prepare the components of the Scallopine of Turkey Breast. Cover separately and refrigerate.

J acques Pépin is the Rachmaninoff of chefs. When he first came to De Gustibus, we had never seen a chef so adroit, skillful, and speedy with a knife. Jacques's technical skills were amazing.

Over the years, he has done many demonstration classes for us, so we have come to understand his philosophy of cooking. He has taught us how to cook efficiently, that we must never waste anything, and that the expensive product is not always the best. When Jacques demonstrated the following menu, it was not as easy to get "turkey parts" as it is now. His menu utilizes his practical and economic approach to ingredients by providing separate recipes for different parts of the turkey. Early in our history, Jacques set the standard for excellence that we strive to maintain at De Gustibus.

◁ Baked Apples

Lettuce Soup

Soupe de Laitues

Not only is this soup easy to make—it is delicately beautiful to look at. A French favorite not often seen in the American kitchen, lettuce soup, which has a potato base, can be served hot or cold.

5 tablespoons unsalted butter
1 cup chopped onions
1 cup chopped leeks, washed and drained
8 cups Turkey or Chicken Stock
4 cups diced, peeled baking potatoes
1 teaspoon salt
2 small heads Boston lettuce, leaves separated, washed, and dried

1 Assemble the *mise en place* trays for this recipe.

2 In a large saucepan, heat 3 tablespoons of the butter over medium heat. Add the onions and leeks and sauté for about 2 minutes. Add the stock, potatoes, and salt and bring to a boil. Reduce the heat to low and simmer, partially covered, for about 40 minutes, until the potatoes are very tender.

3 Transfer the mixture to a blender or a food processor fitted with the metal blade, and blend until smooth. You may have to do this in batches to avoid overflow. Return the soup to the pan and set over low heat.

4 Stack the lettuce leaves a few at a time, roll them up cigar fashion, and slice into chiffonade (thin strips).

5 In a medium-sized saucepan, heat the remaining 2 tablespoons of butter. Add the chiffonade and sauté for about 3 minutes, until wilted. Stir into the soup. Adjust seasoning to taste.

6 Ladle the soup into 6 warm soup bowls and serve immediately.

JACQUES PÉPIN: Lettuce Soup

Scallopine of Turkey Breast with Morel and Cognac Sauce

SERVES 6
PREPARATION TIME: ABOUT 35 MINUTES
COOKING TIME: ABOUT 50 MINUTES
SOAKING TIME (MUSHROOMS ONLY): ABOUT 30 MINUTES

Escalope de Jeune Dinde aux Morilles avec Sauce au Cognac

Scallopine of turkey breast is much less expensive than veal but just as elegant with the morels and Cognac—a typically practical French solution!

3 ounces dried morels
4 cups lukewarm water
6 slices turkey breast, each about 6 ounces and about ⅜-inch thick
1½ teaspoons salt, or more to taste
1 teaspoon freshly ground black pepper, or more to taste
2 to 3 tablespoons unsalted butter
½ cup chopped shallots
1 tablespoon finely chopped garlic
2 tablespoons Cognac
1½ cups heavy cream
1 teaspoon potato starch or cornstarch (optional)
Few drops of fresh lemon juice

1 Assemble the *mise en place* trays for this recipe.

2 In a bowl, combine the morels and water. Let the mushrooms soak for about 30 minutes, until reconstituted and softened.

3 Drain the morels, reserving the soaking liquid. Remove any dirty or sandy stems. Cut in half lengthwise, or quarter if very large.

4 Strain the reserved soaking liquid through a fine sieve lined with paper towels into a small saucepan. Bring to a boil over medium-high heat. Reduce the heat to low and simmer for about 30 minutes, until reduced to 1 cup.

5 Preheat the oven to 175 degrees F.

6 Season the turkey slices on both sides with the salt and pepper.

7 In a large skillet, melt 1 tablespoon of the butter over medium-high heat. When hot, add 2 of the turkey slices. Cook for about 2 minutes, turning once. Arrange in a single layer in a large shallow ovenproof dish, and keep warm in the oven. Cook the remaining turkey slices in the same way, adding more butter as needed.

8 When all the turkey is cooked, add the shallots and garlic to the skillet. Reduce the heat to medium and cook for about 30 seconds. Add the Cognac to the skillet. Carefully ignite the Cognac and flambé; it will extinguish almost immediately.

9 Add the reduced mushroom liquid and the cream. Bring to a boil, stirring to scrape up any browned bits. Stir in the juices that have accumulated around the turkey slices. Strain the sauce into a clean saucepan. Stir in the morels, place over medium heat, and bring to a boil. Reduce the heat and simmer for about 3 minutes. Season to taste with

JACQUES PÉPIN: Scallopine of Turkey Breast with Morel and Cognac Sauce

salt and pepper. If the sauce seems thin, dissolve the potato starch or cornstarch in 1 tablespoon of cold water and whisk it into the simmering sauce so that it thickens enough to thinly coat the back of a spoon. Stir in the lemon juice.

10 Arrange the turkey slices on a warm serving platter and spoon the sauce and mushrooms over them. Serve immediately.

▶ You can slice the turkey from a whole turkey breast half, or you can buy packaged turkey cutlets, which are usually cut about ⅜ inch thick.

▶ Whenever you work with raw poultry, be sure to wash the work surfaces and utensils, as well as your hands, with warm, soapy water before proceeding with another task. This prevents the spread of salmonella bacteria.

▶ Even cooked turkey should not be left at room temperature for longer than necessary. Refrigerate any leftovers as soon as the main course is over.

Fricassee of Turkey and Brown Rice

SERVES 6
PREPARATION TIME: ABOUT 30 MINUTES
COOKING TIME: 1 HOUR AND 45 MINUTES TO 2 HOURS

Fricassée de Dinde au Riz Brun

This is a great dish with which you can feed a crowd. It is inexpensive, nutritious, and easy to make ahead of time. And, if there are any leftovers, it's even better when reheated. Either this or the Scallopine of Turkey Breast can be served as a main course. Or you can serve both.

2 turkey legs and 2 turkey wings (about 5 pounds)
3 tablespoons unsalted butter
1½ pounds yellow onions, chopped
4 ounces loose-packed sun-dried tomatoes, chopped
3 tablespoons chopped garlic
1 teaspoon ground cumin
½ teaspoon red pepper flakes
3 bay leaves
2 teaspoons salt
1 teaspoon freshly ground black pepper
1½ cups brown rice
5 cups water
1 cup tiny peas, blanched in boiling water for 1 minute
¼ cup chopped fresh parsley

1 Assemble the *mise en place* trays for this recipe.

2 Using a cleaver, cut each turkey leg into 5 pieces and each wing into 2 pieces. Remove any tough tendons.

JACQUES PÉPIN: Fricassee of Turkey and Brown Rice

80

3 In a large skillet or Dutch oven, melt the butter over medium heat. Add the turkey pieces and sear, turning frequently, for about 15 minutes, or until well browned on all sides.

4 Add the onions and cook for about 10 minutes until the onions soften. Add the sun-dried tomatoes, garlic, cumin, hot pepper flakes, bay leaves, and salt and pepper. Stir in the rice and water, increase the heat, and bring to a boil. Cover, reduce the heat, and simmer for about 1 hour and

10 minutes, or until all the liquid has been absorbed and the turkey meat and rice are very tender.

5 Remove from the heat, and remove the bay leaves. Stir in the peas and parsley, and serve immediately.

▶ **Fresh peas are best for this recipe, but you may use high-quality frozen or canned tiny peas.**

▶ **You can have the butcher chop the turkey into pieces. Ask him to remove the tendons at the same time.**

Baked Apples

SERVES 6
PREPARATION TIME: ABOUT 15 MINUTES
COOKING TIME: ABOUT 1 HOUR

Pommes Bonne Femme

A simple dessert straight from the kitchen of "la grand'mère."

6 large, tart apples, such as Russet, Granny Smith, or Pippin, cored
⅓ cup apricot jam
⅓ cup pure maple syrup
3 tablespoons unsalted butter, cut into 6 pieces

1 Preheat the oven to 375 degrees F. Assemble the *mise en place* trays for this recipe.

2 With the point of a knife, cut an incision about ⅛ inch to ½ inch wide through the skin all around each apple, about a third of the way down from the stem end. As the apples cook, the flesh expands and the tops of the apples will lift up like a lid above this cut. Without this scoring, the apples will burst.

3 Stand the apples upright in a gratin dish or other attractive ovenproof dish. Coat the apples with the apricot jam and maple syrup and dot them with the butter. Bake for 30 minutes.

4 Baste the apples with the cooking juices and bake for 30 to 40 minutes longer, or until the apples are plump, brown, and soft to the touch. Serve warm.

▶ **If you prepare the apples early in the day, bake them while you are dining so that they are served hot from the oven.**

▶ **Delicious served with a slice of pound cake or with sour cream or ice cream.**

A PERFECT MARRIAGE

Roasted Eggplant Roulade with Oregano and Marinated Goat Cheese

PAUPIETTE D'AUBERGINES AU FROMAGE DE CHÈVRE MARINÉ A L'ORIGAN

Lamb Stew with Fall Fruits and Vegetables

LE SAUTÉ D'AGNEAU AUX ARTICHAUTS, POMMES, ET HARICOTS NOIRS

Crème Brûlée Le Cirque

WINE SUGGESTIONS:

Sauvignon Blanc or Pinot Blanc (*first course*)

Châteauneuf-du-Pape (*second course*)

Aged Tawny Port (*dessert*)

WHAT YOU CAN PREPARE AHEAD OF TIME

Up to 1 week ahead: Prepare the Lamb Stock (if making your own).

Up to 3 days ahead: Prepare the brown sugar for the Crème Brûlée.

Up to 1 day ahead: Prepare the Roasted Eggplant Roulade. Prepare the lamb cubes for the Lamb Stew. Cover and refrigerate. Soak the black beans for the Lamb Stew.

Early in the day: Prepare and cook the artichokes, potatoes, and black beans for the Lamb Stew. Cover and refrigerate. Prepare the diced tomatoes and minced herbs for the Lamb Stew. Cover separately and refrigerate. Bake the Crème Brûlée. Cool, cover, and refrigerate without the sugar. Caramelize the sugar on the top just before serving.

It is very hard to view your husband objectively. It is even harder when you run cooking classes and he is a well-known French chef whose meals, whether at home or at work, are always delicious! I have learned more about French food from Alain than from anyone else, simply because I see him cook it every day.

Although known for his knowledge of French culinary techniques and his intimacy with the classic French repertoire, Alain is a very modern chef. When he teaches, he makes himself totally accessible. He seems to know what diners demand in a contemporary menu and he has a flexibility about cooking that can accommodate their needs. He also has a quiet patience with his students and me! Needless to add, in my eyes, he is a great chef —and an even greater husband!

◁ Roasted Eggplant Roulade with Oregano and Marinated Goat Cheese

83

10 Put the potatoes in a medium-sized saucepan, with enough cold water to cover. Add salt to taste and a few drops of lemon juice. Cover and bring to a boil over medium-high heat. Reduce the heat and simmer for 8 to 10 minutes, or until just tender. Drain and set aside.

11 In a very large, deep sauté pan or Dutch oven, heat 1 tablespoon of the olive oil over medium-high heat. Sauté the meat, in 2 or 3 batches, for about 10 minutes, until browned. Do not crowd the pan. Spoon off liquid as it accumulates in the pan. When all the meat is browned, set the lamb aside.

12 Pour off the fat in the pan. Add 1 cup of water and deglaze over medium heat, stirring to scrape up any brown bits sticking to the bottom. Cook for 8 to 10 minutes, stirring, until most of the liquid has evaporated. Return the lamb to the pan.

13 Heat 1 tablespoon of the olive oil in a medium-sized sauté pan over medium-high heat. Add the carrots, celery, and onions and sauté for 10 to 12 minutes, until browned. Add the chopped garlic and sauté for 1 minute longer.

14 Add the stock and 2 more cups of water to the meat, increase the heat, and bring to a boil. Add the sautéed vegetables, reduce the heat to low, cover, and simmer for 1½ hours, or until the lamb is very tender.

15 Skim the fat from the top of the stew. Using a slotted spoon, transfer the meat to a platter and set aside.

16 Strain the cooking liquid and vegetables through a fine sieve into a large saucepan, pushing against the solids to extract all the liquid. Discard the solids. Stir in the bean and apple purée. Add the lamb and keep warm over very low heat.

17 Meanwhile, in a medium-sized saucepan, heat the remaining 2 tablespoons of olive oil over medium heat. Add the mushrooms and sauté for 8 minutes, or until tender. Stir in the artichokes and potatoes to just heat through. Check the seasonings.

18 Spoon the lamb with the sauce into the center of a serving platter. Arrange the vegetable mixture around it. Sprinkle the tomatoes over the vegetables. Sprinkle with the minced parsley, thyme, and oregano, and serve immediately.

ALAIN SAILHAC:
Lamb Stew with Fall
Fruits and Vegetables

Crème Brûlée Le Cirque

SERVES 6
PREPARATION TIME: ABOUT 15 MINUTES
COOKING TIME: ABOUT 35 MINUTES
DRYING TIME (BROWN SUGAR ONLY): 24 HOURS
COOLING TIME: AT LEAST 30 MINUTES

This is the ultimate crème brûlée, the most classic of all French desserts. There are now many Americanized versions, but, in my opinion, this is the one and only, rich and delicious "burnt cream."

½ cup packed light brown sugar
4 cups heavy cream
1 vanilla bean, split
½ cup plus 2 tablespoons granulated sugar
6 large egg yolks

■ Special Equipment: Shallow 8-ounce oval ramekins

1 Spread the brown sugar on a small baking sheet. Place, uncovered, in a dry spot for at least 24 hours, or until the sugar is quite dry. Push through a fine sieve. Set aside.

2 Assemble the *mise en place* trays for this recipe.

3 Preheat the oven to 350 degrees F.

4 In a medium-sized saucepan, heat the cream and vanilla bean over medium heat for 3 minutes, or until just warm.

5 In a bowl, whisk together the granulated sugar and egg yolks. When well blended, whisk in the cream. Strain through a fine sieve into a bowl.

6 Divide the mixture among 6 eight-ounce shallow oval ramekins. Place in a shallow roasting pan and add enough hot water to come halfway up the side of the ramekins. Bake for about 30 minutes, or until set and a knife inserted in the center comes out clean. The custards will still be soft; do not overbake.

7 Transfer the custards to wire racks to cool for at least 30 minutes.

8 Preheat the broiler.

9 Spoon the brown sugar into a fine sieve and sprinkle evenly over the tops of the custards. Broil for about 15 seconds to melt and burn the sugar topping. Watch carefully to prevent charring. Serve immediately.

ALAIN SAILHAC: Crème Brûlée *Le Cirque*

▶ Many chefs use a blow torch or a crème brûlée iron to make the brittle burnt sugar topping. Here, the broiler is equally effective because the sugar is already so dry.

A TRADITIONAL ALSATIAN DINNER

Onion Tart
TARTE AUX OIGNONS

Stuffed Breast of Veal
POITRINE DE VEAU

Potato Pancakes
GALETTES AUX POMMES DE TERRE

Chocolate Mousse
MOUSSE AU CHOCOLAT

WINE SUGGESTIONS:

Alsatian Riesling or Sparkling Wine (*first course*)

Red Villages-level Burgundy or Chianti Classico (*second course*)

Ruby Port (*dessert*)

WHAT YOU CAN PREPARE AHEAD OF TIME

Up to 1 week ahead: Make the pastry for the Onion Tart. Line tart pan with the pastry, wrap tightly, and freeze. Thaw before filling.

Up to 2 days ahead: Stuff and cook the Breast of Veal. Skim the pan juices. Cool quickly, and refrigerate the veal and juices in the roasting pan. Reheat for 30 minutes in a preheated 300 degree F. oven before serving.

Early in the day: Chop the onions for the Onion Tart. Cover and refrigerate. Make the stuffing for the Breast of Veal, if not already stuffed and baked. Cover and refrigerate. As a safety precaution, do not stuff the veal until ready to cook. Make the batter for the Potato Pancakes. Cook just before serving. Make the Chocolate Mousse.

André Soltner of Lutèce is an inspiration to all home cooks. He is the only chef ever to orchestrate an entire De Gustibus class by himself, showing us firsthand that it is quite possible to cook a grand meal without a fully staffed kitchen. He never ceases to amaze me.

Chef Soltner always plays to a full house at De Gustibus. And what a maestro! Every audience has been mesmerized both by his cooking and by his stories of the road he took to become one of the world's superstar chefs. An afternoon with André is always one of the highlights of the season's classes. He leaves us all eagerly anticipating his next visit.

◁ Stuffed Breast of Veal and Potato Pancakes

A Vegetable Tasting

Napoléon of Roquefort and Boursin
MILLEFEUILLE DE ROQUEFORT ET BOURSIN

Wild Mushroom Crêpes
GÂTEAU DE CRÊPES AUX CHAMPIGNONS SAUVAGES

Beet Tartare
TARTARE DE BETTERAVES ROUGES

Passion Fruit Club with Strawberries
"CLUB" DE FRUITS DE LA PASSION AUX FRAISES

WINE SUGGESTIONS:

Champagne

WHAT YOU CAN PREPARE AHEAD OF TIME

Up to 3 days ahead: Prepare the Beet Tartare. Cover and refrigerate. Bring to room temperature before serving. Bake the cookies for the Passion Fruit Club.

Up to 2 days ahead: Prepare the duxelles for the Wild Mushroom Crêpes. Cover and refrigerate. Prepare the crêpes for the Wild Mushroom Crêpes. Cover and refrigerate.

Up to 4 hours ahead: Assemble the Napoléon.

Jean-Georges Vongerichten is probably the most versatile French chef we have ever hosted at De Gustibus. Each of his classes have been unique and unpredictable. He is so filled with creative concepts and stimulating recipes that we await each visit with enormous anticipation, truly wondering, "What's cooking?"

Chef Vongerichten has presented us with classic French cuisine, bistro meals, a taste of Thailand, and, our biggest surprise, a meal made entirely of vegetables.

All of us remember Jean-Georges's first De Gustibus demonstration not for the Thai food, but for the ties. He had brought five cooks to assist him, including two of his brothers. None of them had ever done a cooking class and all were absolutely delighted with an audience and a photographer. Although ready to face home cooks, however, they did not feel appropriately dressed for a formal portrait. So, since we were at Macy's, they all went downstairs to the shops. These chic French chefs returned wearing new, fashionably narrow ties, ready to pose for the camera.

◁ Wild Mushroom Crêpes

Napoléon of Roquefort and Boursin

Millefeuille de Roquefort et Boursin

This delicious cheese dish can be served either as an appetizer or as a cheese course after the meal. Best of all, it can be cooked in advance and reheated just before serving.

3 sheets phyllo dough, thawed
4 tablespoons unsalted butter, melted
4 ounces Roquefort cheese
4 ounces Boursin cheese
½ cup heavy cream, softly whipped
1 tablespoon chopped fresh chives
½ teaspoon Cognac
Salt and freshly ground black pepper to taste

■ Special Equipment: pastry bag with a plain tip (optional)

1 Preheat the oven to 450 degrees F. Assemble the *mise en place* trays for this recipe.

2 Stack the phyllo sheets on a baking sheet, brushing each one with some of the melted butter, making sure to brush all the way to the edges of the phyllo. Trim the stack into a 12-inch square. Discard the trimmings. Bake for 3 to 4 minutes, until golden brown. Allow to cool for at least 20 minutes.

3 In a blender or a food processor fitted with the metal blade, blend the Roquefort and Boursin cheese until smooth. Scrape into a bowl and gently but thoroughly fold in the whipped cream. Fold in the chives and Cognac, and season to taste with salt and pepper.

4 Using a very sharp knife, cut off a 3 x 12-inch strip from the cooled phyllo stack. Set aside.

5 Spoon the cheese mixture into a pastry bag fitted with a plain tip, and pipe evenly over the baked rectangle, making sure the piped lines touch each other. Or, gently spread the cheese over the phyllo with a spatula. Cover with plastic wrap and refrigerate for 1 hour, or until the cheese is firm.

6 Preheat the oven to 200 degrees F.

7 Lift the plastic wrap off the cheese-covered phyllo rec-tangle. Using a sharp knife, cut it into three 3 x 12-inch strips. Stack the strips, one on top of the other. Place the reserved plain strip on the top. Gently lifting each one with a spatula, transfer the napoléon to a baking sheet and warm in the oven for 1 minute.

8 Remove from the oven and cut crosswise into six 2 x 3-inch rectangles. Serve immediately.

▶ Do not put the napoléon together more than four hours before serving or the pastry will get soggy.

JEAN-GEORGES VONGERICHTEN: Napoléon of Roquefort and Boursin

Wild Mushroom Crêpes

Gâteau de Crêpes aux Champignons Sauvages

This is a basic crêpe recipe made special with mushrooms and a soy vinaigrette. Any type of wild mushrooms may be used.

6 tablespoons unsalted butter
1 shallot, chopped
1 clove garlic, chopped
4 ounces fresh porcini mushrooms, wiped clean, trimmed, and roughly chopped
4 ounces fresh shiitake mushrooms, wiped clean, trimmed, and roughly chopped
4 ounces fresh button mushrooms, wiped clean, trimmed, and roughly chopped
Salt and freshly ground black pepper to taste
1 tablespoon minced fresh chervil
1 tablespoon minced fresh chives
1 cup all-purpose flour
3 large eggs
1 cup milk
¼ cup soy sauce
¼ cup fresh lemon juice
1 cup olive oil

1 Assemble the *mise en place* trays for this recipe.

2 In a medium-sized sauté pan, melt 2 tablespoons of the butter over medium-high heat. Add the shallot and garlic and sauté for about 3 minutes, until translucent.

3 Stir in the mushrooms and season to taste with salt and pepper. Reduce the heat and sauté for about 5 minutes, or until all the liquid from the mushrooms has evaporated.

4 Transfer the mushrooms to a blender or a food processor fitted with the metal blade. Process, using on/off turns, until finely chopped. Scrape the mushrooms into a bowl and stir in the chervil and chives. Set aside.

5 In a small saucepan, melt the remaining 4 tablespoons of butter over medium heat. Heat for about 3 minutes, or until golden brown. Take care the butter does not burn. Remove from the heat.

JEAN-GEORGES VONGERICHTEN: Wild Mushroom Crêpes

6 In a bowl, whisk together the flour, eggs, milk, and salt to taste until smooth. Whisk in browned butter. Cover and refrigerate for 20 minutes.

7 Preheat the oven to 400 degrees F.

8 To make the crêpes, heat a 6- or 7-inch nonstick crêpe pan over medium heat. Pour in just enough batter (about 2 tablespoons) to cover the bottom of the pan. Cook for 1 minute, or until light brown on the bottom and set. Care-

97

Passion Fruit Club with Strawberries

"Club" de Fruits de la Passion aux Fraises

These represent an innovative French chef's exploration of a favorite American sandwich. The exotic flavor of the passion fruit gives an arresting taste to the pastry cream.

COOKIE TRIANGLES:
4 cups all-purpose flour
¾ cup granulated sugar
1 cup unsalted butter
1 teaspoon pure vanilla extract
2 large eggs
2 tablespoons water

PASSION FRUIT FILLING:
¾ cup milk
⅔ cup passion fruit purée (see note)
1 vanilla bean, split
⅓ cup granulated sugar
2 tablespoons all-purpose flour
1 large egg
2 tablespoons heavy cream, softly whipped
18 strawberries, washed, hulled, and halved lengthwise
3 tablespoons confectioners' sugar

1 Assemble the *mise en place* trays for this recipe.

2 To make the cookies, in a bowl, combine the flour and sugar. Using two kitchen knives, cut in the butter until the mixture resembles coarse meal.

3 In a small bowl, whisk together the vanilla, eggs, and water. Add to the flour mixture and stir to make a stiff dough. Form into a ball, wrap in plastic, and allow to rest for 1 hour at room temperature.

4 Preheat the oven to 350 degrees F. Make a cardboard triangle pattern that is 1½ inches long from apex to base.

5 On a lightly floured surface, roll out the dough to a large circle about ⅛ inch thick.

6 Lay the cardboard pattern on the dough and, using a small sharp knife, cut out 20 or more triangles. (You will

◁ JEAN-GEORGES VONGERICHTEN: Passion Fruit Club with Strawberries

need only 18 but make extra to allow for breakage.) Transfer the triangles to an ungreased baking sheet. Bake for about 10 minutes, until very lightly browned. Remove from the oven, lift from the pan, and cool on a wire rack.

7 To make the passion fruit filling, in a medium-sized, heavy-based saucepan, combine the milk, passion fruit purée, and vanilla bean. Bring to a boil over medium heat. Remove from heat.

8 In a medium-sized bowl, whisk together the sugar, flour, and egg. Slowly whisk in the hot milk mixture and then return the mixture to the saucepan. Place over medium heat and bring to a boil, whisking continously. Reduce the heat and cook, whisking continuously, for about 5 minutes until thick. Remove from the heat and allow to cool.

9 Remove the vanilla bean from the cooled pastry cream. Fold in the whipped cream.

10 On a work surface, lay out 6 of the cookie triangles. Place a strawberry half in each corner. Spoon a little passion fruit pastry cream into the center. Top each one with another cookie and repeat the layer with strawberries and pastry cream. Top with the remaining cookies and serve immediately.

Note: Passion fruit purée can be difficult to find. Try ordering it from a specialty store or buy some from a local restaurant. (It is easily available to restaurants through wholesalers.) If you cannot find passion fruit purée, substitute peach purée.

▶ If the strawberries are large, you may have to quarter them. In that case, you will need only 9 berries.

▶ To make passion fruit purée yourself, purée the flesh of 12 passion fruits in a food processor fitted with the metal blade. Strain the purée into a nonreactive saucepan and add ½ cup of sugar. Cook, stirring, over medium heat until the sugar dissolves. Increase the heat and bring to a boil. Immediately take the purée from the heat and strain again. Let it cool to room temperature and use it as instructed, or refrigerate it until needed.

NEW AMERICAN COOKING

JAMES BEARD:
A Thanksgiving Alternative

CRAIG CLAIBORNE:
A Totally '50s Lunch

MICHAEL LOMONACO:
A Late-Night Supper

WAYNE NISH:
A Dinner Filled with Remembrances
of the Flavors of the South of France

BRADLEY OGDEN:
A Leisurely Sunday Lunch

DEBRA PONZEK:
A Winter Dinner

ALFRED PORTALE:
A Modern Dinner

WOLFGANG PUCK:
The Flavors of Spring

ANNE ROSENZWEIG:
A Menu for All Seasons

ALICE WATERS:
A Pasta Party

A THANKSGIVING ALTERNATIVE

Cornish Game Hens with
Crumb and Sausage Stuffing

Beet and Carrot Puree

Quince Tart

WINE SUGGESTIONS:

Pinot Noir *(main course)*
Late Harvest Riesling *(dessert)*

WHAT YOU CAN PREPARE AHEAD OF TIME

Up to 3 days ahead: Make the Beet and Carrot Puree. Cover and refrigerate. Reheat as directed.

The day before: Make the Quince Tart. Cover loosely and store in a cool area of the kitchen.

Early in the day: Make the Crumb and Sausage Stuffing for the hens. Cover and refrigerate. Do not stuff the hens until ready to roast.

Having James Beard teach at De Gustibus was a complete culinary experience. It was like having the father of all fathers cooking in our presence, talking about our favorite subject, and his: food. Mr. Beard made his love and understanding of American ingredients come alive at our stove. He reminisced about the quince trees growing in the yard of his boyhood home and told of his excitement at discovering the old-fashioned quince tart that we include here, on the menu of the award-winning Coach House restaurant in New York City.

James Beard prepared this menu for a small gathering at Thanksgiving, but he felt it would also make a warming fall dinner. Although this class came late in the career of this giant of American cuisine, it was an afternoon we will never forget. James Beard truly paved the way for New American cooking.

◁ JAMES BEARD: **Quince Tart**

Cornish Game Hens with Crumb and Sausage Stuffing

SERVES 6
PREPARATION TIME: ABOUT 15 MINUTES
COOKING TIME: ABOUT 1 HOUR AND 30 MINUTES

Individual game hens are a great alternative to the mammoth holiday turkey. They require a shorter cooking time and particularly appeal to those who want both white and dark meat.

6 Rock Cornish game hens (about 1 pound each), rinsed and patted dry
1/2 cup unsalted butter
1/4 cup sliced scallions
8 ounces bulk sausage meat
1 tablespoon chopped fresh tarragon
2 teaspoons salt, or to taste
1 teaspoon freshly ground black pepper, or to taste
4 cups fresh bread crumbs
1/4 cup chopped fresh parsley

1 Preheat the oven to 400 degrees F. Assemble the *mise en place* trays for this recipe.

2 In a large sauté pan, melt the butter over medium-high heat. Add the scallions and sauté for 4 minutes, or until just limp. Stir in the sausage meat, tarragon, salt, and pepper. Cook for 8 to 10 minutes, or until the sausage begins to lose its pinkness. Add the bread crumbs and parsley and stir until well combined. Remove from the heat and let cool completely.

3 Place an equal portion of the stuffing into each of the hens. Truss the cavities closed (see page 93) by sewing with kitchen twine, or secure them with skewers.

4 Place the stuffed hens on a rack in a large roasting pan, breast side up. Roast for 15 minutes. Turn hens over and baste for another 15 minutes with the accumulated juices.

5 Reduce the oven temperature to 350 degrees F. Turn the birds breast side up, baste again, and roast for about 45 minutes longer, or until just tender; do not overcook.

6 Remove the pan from oven and allow the hens to rest for 5 minutes before serving. Spoon the pan juices over the hens and serve on warm dinner plates.

▶ To test the hens for doneness, wiggle the legs and pierce the joint between the body and thigh with a sharp knife. If legs move freely and the juices run clear, the birds are ready.

▶ Do not stuff the birds until just before cooking. Harmful bacteria may develop in the stuffing as it sits in the uncooked bird.

▷ JAMES BEARD: Cornish Game Hens with Crumb and Sausage Stuffing; Beet and Carrot Puree

A Totally '50s Lunch

*Janice Okun's Buffalo Chicken Wings
with Blue Cheese Dressing*

Mrs. Reardy's Shrimp and Artichoke Casserole

Hazelnut Cheesecake

Wine Suggestions:

Beer or Chardonnay

What You Can Prepare Ahead of Time

Up to 2 days ahead: Make the Blue Cheese Dressing for the Buffalo Chicken Wings.

Early in the day: Prepare the chicken wings for frying. Wrap tightly and refrigerate. Deep-fry just before serving. Prepare the components of the Shrimp and Artichoke Casserole. Cover and refrigerate the shrimp, mushroom-cream sauce, and the artichokes separately. Assemble the casserole just before baking. Bake the Cheesecake.

Craig Claiborne's lunch will take you back in time to roller skates, hula hoops, saddle shoes, and Junior League cookbooks. This menu could be the centerpiece of a nostalgia party, as you transport your guests to another time and place.

Having Craig Claiborne teach at De Gustibus was truly a memorable experience. We had all read his *New York Times* column, his newspaper and magazine articles, and used his cookbooks with great frequency. In some ways, it seemed as though we were old friends. To have such a culinary personage in our kitchen was thrilling.

Mr. Claiborne is a cook who believes in exactitude. In preparation for his class, we had carefully measured all the ingredients, but he insisted on remeasuring and reweighing everything. Having written thousands of recipes for the home cook, he sent us a clear message: "You can never be too careful when you are writing for the public."

◁ Craig Claiborne: Mrs. Reardy's Shrimp and Artichoke Casserole

Janice Okun's Buffalo Chicken Wings with Blue Cheese Dressing

Here's a great recipe for one of America's all-time favorite bar foods. Craig Claiborne brings chicken wings into the dining room as an appetizer, but you could easily increase the amount for a big bowl of tasty party fare.

BLUE CHEESE DRESSING:

1 cup mayonnaise
1/2 cup sour cream
1/4 cup crumbled blue cheese
2 tablespoons minced onion
1 teaspoon minced parsley
1 tablespoon fresh lemon juice
1 tablespoon white vinegar
Salt and freshly ground black pepper to taste
Cayenne pepper to taste

CHICKEN WINGS:

4 pounds chicken wings
Salt and freshly ground black pepper to taste
About 4 cups peanut, vegetable, or corn oil, for deep-frying
4 tablespoons salted butter
2 tablespoons hot red pepper sauce
1 tablespoon white vinegar
24 to 30 four-inch celery sticks

1 Preheat the oven to 250 degrees F. Assemble the *mise en place* trays for this recipe.

2 To make the dressing, combine the mayonnaise, sour cream, blue cheese, onion, parsley, lemon juice, and vinegar in a bowl. Add salt, pepper, and cayenne to taste. Cover and refrigerate for at least 1 hour.

3 To prepare the chicken, wash the wings and dry well. Cut off and discard the small tip of each wing. Cut apart the wings at the joint. Sprinkle with salt and pepper to taste.

4 In a deep-fat fryer or a large, deep saucepan, heat the oil over medium-high heat until almost smoking. Add half of the wings and cook for about 10 minutes, stirring occasionally or turning with tongs, until golden brown and crisp. Drain well on paper towels or a brown paper bag. Put the drained wings on a baking sheet and keep warm in the oven while you cook the remaining wings. Drain well and place on the baking sheet in the oven.

CRAIG CLAIBORNE: Janice Okun's Buffalo Chicken Wings with Blue Cheese Dressing

5 In a small saucepan, melt the butter over low heat. Stir in the hot sauce and vinegar.

6 Put the chicken wings on a warm serving platter and pour the butter mixture over them. Serve with the Blue Cheese Dressing and celery sticks.

▶ If you wish to avoid some of the fat in this dish, prepare the recipe through step 3, then in a non-stick baking dish, bake the wings in the oven at 400 degrees F. for about 25 to 30 minutes, or until the wings are brown and crisp. Continue as directed preparing the sauce and serving.

Mrs. Reardy's Shrimp and Artichoke Casserole

SERVES 6
PREPARATION TIME: ABOUT 20 MINUTES
COOKING TIME: ABOUT 45 MINUTES

Ah, for the days of cholesterol, fat, and calorie ignorance! I suspect that you could replace the butter with canola oil, the milk and cream with skim milk. But I also suspect the result would be less than rich and delicious. Save this recipe for a day when calories don't count and enjoy yourself!

7 tablespoons unsalted butter
1 pound medium shrimp (unshelled)
4 1/2 tablespoons all-purpose flour
3/4 cup milk
3/4 cup heavy cream
Salt and freshly ground black pepper to taste
4 ounces fresh mushrooms, sliced (about 1 1/4 cups)
1 nine-ounce package frozen artichoke hearts, thawed and well drained
2 tablespoons sherry
1 tablespoon Worcestershire sauce
1/4 cup freshly grated Parmesan cheese
Paprika

1 Preheat the oven to 375 degrees F. Assemble the *mise en place* trays for this recipe. Grease a 2-quart casserole or baking dish with 1 tablespoon of the butter.

2 In a pan of rapidly boiling salted water, cook the shrimp for 3 minutes or until just opaque. Drain and refresh under cold running water. Peel and devein. Set aside.

3 In a medium-sized saucepan, melt 4 1/2 tablespoons of the butter over medium-high heat. Whisk in the flour until blended. Gradually whisk in the milk and cream, and cook, whisking constantly, for 3 to 4 minutes, until the sauce is thick and smooth. Season to taste with salt and pepper. Remove from the heat and set aside.

4 In a small sauté pan, melt the remaining 1 1/2 tablespoons butter over medium heat. Add the mushrooms and sauté for about 5 minutes, or until softened. Remove from the heat.

5 Arrange the artichokes in the bottom of the prepared casserole. Scatter the shrimp over the artichokes. Spoon the mushrooms over the shrimp and artichokes.

6 Add the sherry and Worcestershire sauce to the cream sauce. Pour over the shrimp and artichokes. Sprinkle with the Parmesan cheese and dust with paprika.

7 Bake for 30 minutes, or until golden and bubbling. Serve hot.

▶ You can substitute canned artichoke hearts. Be sure to use those packed in water—not marinated artichoke hearts.

Hazelnut Cheesecake

There is nothing as overwhelmingly wonderful as a cheesecake—smooth, rich, and oh-so-delicious. A real indulgence.

2 tablespoons unsalted butter, softened
Approximately 1/3 cup graham cracker crumbs
1 1/2 cups toasted, blanched hazelnuts or toasted, blanched almonds
2 pounds cream cheese, at room temperature
1/2 cup heavy cream
4 large eggs
1 3/4 cups granulated sugar
1 teaspoon pure vanilla extract

1 Preheat the oven to 300 degrees F. Assemble the *mise en place* trays for this recipe. Generously grease a 9-by-3-inch-deep springform pan. Sprinkle the graham cracker crumbs over the pan, tilting it so that they cover the bottom and sides. Shake out the excess crumbs. Using 2 large sheets of aluminum foil, double-wrap the outside of the springform pan.

2 Place the nuts in a blender or food processor fitted with the metal blade. If you want the cheesecake to have a crunchy texture, process the nuts for about 20 seconds, until they are coarse-fine. If you want a smooth texture, process for about 1 minute, until they are almost paste-like.

3 Using an electric mixer set at low speed, beat the cream cheese, cream, eggs, sugar, and vanilla in a large bowl. As the ingredients blend, increase the speed to medium-high and continue beating until smooth. Add the nuts and beat until thoroughly incorporated.

4 Scrape the batter into the prepared pan and shake the pan gently to level the mixture. Set the pan inside a slightly wider pan and pour boiling water into the larger pan to a depth of about 1/2 inch, or until the water comes about halfway up the sides of the springform pan.

5 Bake for 2 hours. Turn off the oven and let the cake cool in the oven for 1 hour.

6 Remove the pans from the oven and lift the cake out of the water bath. Place on a wire rack and allow to sit for at least 2 hours.

7 Carefully remove the sides of the springform pan and set the cheesecake on a serving dish. Serve lukewarm or at room temperature, or refrigerate until about an hour before serving. Let the cake come to room temperature before serving.

▶ You can make this cheesecake in a 9-by-3-inch-deep cake pan. When the cheesecake is completely cool, invert it onto a serving plate by placing the plate over the top of the cake and turning both upside down.

▷ CRAIG CLAIBORNE: Hazelnut Cheesecake

A LATE-NIGHT SUPPER

Smoked Trout Mousse on Pumpernickel

Shrimp Ravioli with Tomatoes and Olives

*Chocolate Strudel and Poached Pears
with Cinnamon Sauce*

WINE SUGGESTIONS:

Cocktails or Champagne *(first course)*
Gavi or Frascati *(second course)*
Late Bottled Vintage Port *(dessert)*

WHAT YOU CAN PREPARE AHEAD OF TIME

Up to 1 week ahead: Make the Shrimp Ravioli and freeze on a baking sheet until solid. Transfer to a rigid container, cover, and freeze. Just before serving, cook, without thawing, for 3 to 4 minutes.

Up to 3 days ahead: Poach the pears for the dessert. Cover and refrigerate in the poaching liquid. Bring to room temperature before serving.

The day before: Make the Smoked Trout Mousse. Cover and refrigerate. Let the mousse come to room temperature before piping. Make the Cinnamon Sauce. Cover and refrigerate.

Early in the day: Dice and drain the tomato garnish for the Smoked Trout Mousse. Make the sauce for the Shrimp Ravioli. Cover and refrigerate. Reheat before serving. Prepare the Shrimp Ravioli if not already made. Cover and refrigerate. Bake the Chocolate Strudel.

Michael Lomonaco's menu is a perfect after-theater meal, as it can be prepared in advance. Since Chef Lomonaco's first passion was to be in the theater, after the theater is a particularly appropriate time to taste his food. He once thought he would have a career as an actor, but it is lucky for us that his equal fervor for fine food became the appetite that had to be fed.

Perhaps it is his love of traditional music that has allowed Michael to combine his taste for thoroughly modern cooking with the demands of convention at the world-famous '21' Club. I particularly like this menu because it allows you to offer hors d'oeuvres to your hungry guests as they arrive.

◁ MICHAEL LOMONACO: **Smoked Trout Mousse on Pumpernickel**

Smoked Trout Mousse on Pumpernickel

SERVES 6
PREPARATION TIME: ABOUT 20 MINUTES

You can use any fine smoked fish for this mousse. Since it multiplies easily, you could also serve it in an attractive bowl, with crackers, pita crisps, or toast points for an easy hors d'oeuvre for a large party.

1 tomato, cored, peeled, seeded, and diced
6 ounces boned, skinned, smoked trout fillets
3 tablespoons heavy cream
6 tablespoons unsalted butter, softened
6 slices pumpernickel bread
24 small, fresh dill sprigs

1 Assemble the *mise en place* trays for this recipe.

2 Put the tomato in a strainer set over a plate to catch the juices. Set aside.

3 In a blender or a food processor fitted with the metal blade, combine the fish fillets and cream and process to a thick paste. Add the butter and pulse to combine. Scrape the mixture into a small bowl. Cover and refrigerate for 15 minutes.

4 Trim the crusts from the bread, and cut each slice into 4 triangles. Spoon the trout mousse into a pastry bag fitted with a star tip. Pipe an equal portion of mousse onto each bread triangle. Garnish each one with a sprig of dill and a few cubes of drained tomato.

Shrimp Ravioli with Tomatoes and Olives

SERVES 6
PREPARATION TIME: ABOUT 1 HOUR AND 15 MINUTES
COOKING TIME: ABOUT 25 MINUTES

This type of Italian tomato sauce is known as *puttanesca*, a word that, in polite company, translates to "streetwalker." It's a naughty name for a zesty and quite addictive sauce. Try it simply spooned over linguine or spaghetti.

SAUCE:

1/4 cup plus 2 tablespoons olive oil
2 ounces canned anchovies, drained
1/2 to 1 teaspoon red pepper flakes, to taste
3 pounds very ripe plum tomatoes, cored, peeled, seeded, and chopped
2 tablespoons chopped shallots
2 tablespoons plus 1 1/2 teaspoons chopped garlic
4 ounces Niçoise olives, pitted and chopped
1/4 cup small capers, well drained
3 tablespoons chopped fresh flat-leaf parsley
1 1/2 tablespoons chopped fresh basil
Freshly ground black pepper to taste

RAVIOLI:

1 pound large shrimp, peeled and deveined
1 tablespoon plus 1 1/2 teaspoons olive oil
3 tablespoons chopped shallots
1 1/2 teaspoons chopped garlic
3 tablespoons chopped fresh flat-leaf parsley
3 tablespoons chopped fresh cilantro
1 1/2 tablespoons chopped fresh thyme
Salt and freshly ground black pepper to taste
1 egg white, lightly beaten
1 package wonton wrappers (about 50 wrappers)

1 Assemble the *mise en place* trays for this recipe.

2 To make the sauce, heat the oil in a large sauté pan over medium heat. Add the anchovies and red pepper flakes and cook for about 4 minutes or until the anchovies "melt."

3 Add the tomatoes and cook, stirring occasionally, for 5 to 10 minutes, until very soft. Stir in the shallots, garlic,

▷ MICHAEL LOMONACO: Shrimp Ravioli with Tomatoes and Olives

118

olives, capers, parsley, and basil. Season to taste with pepper. Remove the pan from the heat and set aside.

4 To make the ravioli filling, use a sharp knife to cut the shrimp into nuggets the size of peas.

5 In a medium-sized sauté pan, heat the oil over medium heat. Add the shrimp and sauté for 2 minutes, or until just cooked. Stir in the shallots, garlic, parsley, cilantro, and thyme. Season to taste with salt and pepper. Remove from the heat and allow to cool (about 20 minutes).

6 When the shrimp mixture is cool, stir in the egg white.

7 Separate the wonton wrappers. Using a small pastry brush dipped in cold water, moisten the edges of 1 wonton wrapper. Place 1 teaspoon of the cooled shrimp mixture in the center. Fold over diagonally into a triangle and pinch the edges together to seal. Put the ravioli on a parchment-lined baking sheet and continue making ravioli until all the wrappers are used.

8 Meanwhile, in a large pot, bring 2 quarts of water to a boil over high heat. When boiling, lightly salt the water.

9 Drop the ravioli into the boiling water one by one. Stir gently to prevent sticking and return the water to a slow boil. Cook for 1 to 2 minutes, until the ravioli bob to the surface of the pot. Lift the ravioli out of the water with a slotted spoon and carefully put into a colander to drain.

10 While the ravioli are cooking, warm the sauce over low heat.

11 Place the ravioli on a warm serving platter, and spoon the warm sauce over the top. Serve immediately.

▶ **The ravioli could also be made with traditional pasta dough, but the wonton wrappers make an especially easy preparation.**

Chocolate Strudel and Poached Pears with Cinnamon Sauce

SERVES 6
PREPARATION TIME: ABOUT 45 MINUTES
COOKING AND BAKING TIME: ABOUT 50 MINUTES

Each component of this dessert can be prepared in advance. The pears can be poached and the strudel rolled so that the dessert can be assembled just before serving.

3 ripe Bosc pears, peeled, cored, and halved lengthwise
1½ cups water
¾ cup semisweet white wine, such as Muscat de Beaumes-de-Venise or Muscat from Northern Italy
3 tablespoons granulated sugar
1 teaspoon ground cinnamon
6 sheets frozen filo pastry, thawed according to package directions
½ cup unsalted butter, melted
¼ cup chopped walnuts
6 ounces bittersweet chocolate, finely chopped
1 tablespoon unsweetened cocoa powder
Cinnamon Sauce (recipe follows)
6 fresh mint sprigs

1 Assemble the *mise en place* trays for this recipe.

2 In a medium-sized, nonreactive saucepan, combine the pears, water, wine, sugar, and cinnamon, and bring to a boil over high heat. Reduce the heat to low and simmer for 10 to 12 minutes, or until the pears are tender but not soft. Remove from heat and let the pears cool in the liquid.

3 Preheat the oven to 375 degrees F.

4 Lay 1 filo sheet on a work surface. Lightly brush it with melted butter, and sprinkle with 1 tablespoon of the walnuts. Lay another filo sheet on top, brush with butter and sprinkle with walnuts. Repeat the layering process with the remaining sheets, leaving the top sheet plain.

5 Sprinkle the chopped chocolate evenly over the top sheet of filo and then sprinkle with the cocoa powder. Starting from a long side, roll up jelly-roll fashion into a log. Brush with the remaining melted butter.

6 Transfer the strudel to a baking sheet. Bake for about 20 minutes, or until golden. Cool on the baking sheet for about 10 minutes.

7 Using a serrated knife, cut the strudel into slices no more than 1/2 inch thick.

8 Drain the pears well. Cut each half lengthwise from the stem end into thin slices, keeping it intact at the stem end.

9 Spoon the Cinnamon Sauce onto 6 dessert plates. Fan a pear half out on each plate. Place a strudel slice beside each pear. Garnish each plate with a mint sprig and serve.

▶ **When working with filo pastry, it is important to keep the sheets you are not using covered with a damp dish towel or cloth. Wrap unused filo well in plastic and foil and freeze.**

CINNAMON SAUCE
MAKES ABOUT 3/4 CUP

1 large egg yolk, at room temperature
2 tablespoons granulated sugar
1/2 cup milk
1/4 teaspoon ground cinnamon

1 In a medium-sized bowl, whisk together the egg yolk, sugar, and cinnamon until smooth.

2 Heat the milk in the top half of a double boiler until scalded (just below a boil). Gradually add the milk to the egg mixture, whisking constantly. Return the mixture to the double boiler and cook over hot water, whisking constantly, for 2 to 3 minutes until thick enough to coat the back of a spoon. Remove the pan from the heat and allow to cool. Use as soon as it's cool, or cover and refrigerate until ready to serve.

MICHAEL LOMONACO: **Chocolate Strudel and Poached Pears with Cinnamon Sauce**

A Dinner Filled with Remembrances of The Flavors of the South of France

Provençal Vegetable Tart with Seared Tuna

Striped Bass with Artichokes and Aïoli

Vanilla Custard with Maple-Roasted Peanuts

Wine Suggestions:

White Côtes du Rhône or Rosé *(first course)*

Sauvignon Blanc *(second course)*

Tawny Port *(dessert)*

Up to 2 days ahead: Make the Aïoli for the Striped Bass with Artichokes and Aïoli. Cover and refrigerate.

Early in the day: Cook the artichokes for both the Provençal Vegetable Tart and the Striped Bass. Cover and store at cool room temperature. Prepare the remaining components for the Provençal Vegetable Tart, except the tuna. Cover the vegetables and refrigerate. Wrap the salad and herbs in damp paper towels and refrigerate. Wrap the pastry in wax paper and refrigerate. Bake the Vanilla Custards. Cover and refrigerate. Chop the peanuts.

Up to 1 hour before the party: Cook the tuna for the Provençal Vegetable Tart.

Wayne Nish prepared this menu some years ago, when he was the executive chef at La Colombe d'Or Restaurant in New York City. After the wonderful class, we all went home inspired to recapture his wonderful flavors and to bring a taste of France into our American kitchens.

Chef Nish subsequently went on to become chef and co-owner of the critically acclaimed March Restaurant, where he added other more exotic flavors to his menu. Recently he returned to the flavors of France when he became co-owner of La Colombe d'Or, while retaining his interest at March. This early menu reflects some of Wayne's long-held food enthusiasms. I think that you will find that the flavors and colors—which echo each other from appetizer to entrée—make this challenging meal a memorable one.

◁ WAYNE NISH: Provençal Vegetable Tart with Seared Tuna

Provençal Vegetable Tart with Seared Tuna

SERVES 6
PREPARATION TIME: ABOUT 1 HOUR AND 30 MINUTES
COOKING TIME: ABOUT 30 MINUTES
CHILLING TIME (PASTRY ONLY): 1 HOUR AND 30 MINUTES

The simple tastes of Provence combine in an unusual fashion to make this a very contemporary dish. Since all of the components can be prepared in advance, it is an especially appealing appetizer for the busy cook.

TART PASTRY:

3/4 cup unsalted butter
1/2 cup solid vegetable shortening
1 1/2 cups sifted all-purpose flour
1/2 teaspoon kosher salt
1/2 cup ice water

TOPPING:

3 baby artichokes, trimmed, or artichoke hearts (not marinated)
1 large ripe tomato, cored, peeled, seeded, and cut into strips 1 to 1 1/2 inches long
2 teaspoons chopped fresh thyme
Salt and freshly ground black pepper to taste
1 clove garlic, sliced
1/2 lemon, quartered
1 cup plus 3 tablespoons extra-virgin olive oil
1 large zucchini, trimmed, cored, and cut into 2-inch long *bâtonnets*
1/2 cup fresh peas or fava beans
1/2 cup tomato juice
12 ounces sashimi-quality tuna, about 1 inch thick, cut into slices, 2-inches by 2-inches

SALAD:

2 cups mesclun or other baby salad greens, rinsed and dried
1 tablespoon chopped fresh basil leaves
1 tablespoon chopped fresh tarragon leaves
1 tablespoon chopped fresh parsley leaves
1 tablespoon chopped fresh chives
1 tablespoon chopped fresh chervil sprigs

■ Special Equipment: 3-inch round cookie cutter

1 Assemble the *mise en place* trays for this recipe.

2 To make the tart pastry, cut the butter and shortening into tablespoon-sized pieces. Wrap the butter and shortening separately in plastic wrap and freeze for 30 minutes.

3 Combine the flour and salt in the bowl of a food processor fitted with the metal blade. Add the chilled butter and pulse until the mixture is the consistency of coarse meal. Add the shortening and pulse for 3 to 4 seconds longer.

4 With the motor running, slowly add the ice water and process until the dough comes together in a smooth, sticky ball. Wrap in plastic wrap and refrigerate for 1 hour.

5 Roll out the dough between 2 sheets of plastic wrap to a rectangle about 1/4 inch thick. Place on a baking sheet and freeze for about 30 minutes.

6 Preheat the oven to 350 degrees F.

7 Using a 3-inch round cookie cutter, cut the dough into 6 circles. Place on an ungreased baking sheet. Cover the circles with parchment paper, waxed paper, or foil, and set another baking sheet on top of pastry circles. Bake for 7 minutes. Remove the top baking sheet and the paper and bake for 3 or 4 minutes longer. Turn the pastries over and bake for another 3 to 4 minutes or until the pastry is golden. Remove to a wire rack to cool. Reduce the oven temperature to 300 degrees F.

8 To prepare the topping, cook the artichokes in boiling salted water for 10 minutes, or until tender. Drain well and let cool.

9 In a small bowl, combine the tomato strips, 1 teaspoon of the thyme, and salt and pepper to taste. Set aside.

10 Cut the artichokes in half lengthwise. Place in a small, ovenproof dish and add the garlic, the remaining 1 teaspoon thyme, the lemon quarters, and salt and pepper to taste. Cover tightly with aluminum foil and bake for 10 minutes. Uncover and let cool.

11 Meanwhile, in small sauté pan, heat 1 teaspoon of the olive oil over medium heat. Add the zucchini, season to taste with salt and pepper, and sauté for 2 minutes, or until just beginning to color. Remove from the heat and set aside.

▷ WAYNE NISH: Provençal Vegetable Tart with Seared Tuna

12 Blanch the peas or fava beans in boiling salted water for 30 seconds. Drain and refresh under cold running water. Set aside. (If using fava beans, peel them after blanching.)

13 Place the tomato juice in a blender with the motor running, and add 1 cup of olive oil in a slow, steady stream until fully emulsified. Season to taste with salt and pepper. Set aside.

14 In a large, heavy sauté pan, heat 1 tablespoon of the oil over medium heat. Sear the tuna for 15 to 20 seconds on all sides; it should be rare in the middle. Transfer to a cutting board and allow to cool.

15 Cut the tuna into long, thin slices about ¼ to ⅛ inch thick. Season the slices lightly with the remaining 1 tablespoon plus 2 teaspoons olive oil and salt.

16 To make the salad, toss the salad greens with the fresh herbs.

17 Place a pastry disk in the center of each appetizer plate. Arrange the tomato, artichokes, peas or beans, and zucchini on the disks and top each one with a small mound of the herb salad. Drape the sliced tuna over the salad, and drizzle with the tomato and oil dressing. Serve at once.

▶ **Freshness is always important when purchasing fish. Sashimi-quality tuna refers to the freshest, highest-quality tuna available, because it is the tuna used for Japanese sashimi, fish served raw. For this recipe, buy the very best tuna you can find.**

Striped Bass with Artichokes and Aïoli

SERVES 6
PREPARATION TIME: ABOUT 45 MINUTES
COOKING TIME: ABOUT 55 MINUTES
RESTING TIME (AIOLI ONLY): 8 HOURS

Aïoli is the richly flavored garlic mayonnaise favored throughout Provence as an accompaniment to lightly steamed or grilled poultry, fish, or fresh vegetables. Here, it highlights a simply cooked bass.

6 small artichokes, trimmed, or large artichoke hearts (not marinated)
1 whole head garlic, halved crosswise
1 lemon, quartered
1 tablespoon chopped fresh thyme
Salt and freshly ground black pepper to taste
6 six-ounce striped bass fillets with skin
Kosher salt to taste
¼ cup extra-virgin olive oil
Aïoli (recipe follows)

1 Preheat the oven to 300 degrees F. Assemble the *mise en place* trays for this recipe.

2 Cook the artichokes in boiling, salted water for 12 to 15 minutes, or until tender. Drain and let cool slightly.

3 Cut the artichokes in half lengthwise. Place the artichokes, garlic, lemon, thyme, and salt and pepper to taste in a small ovenproof dish. Cover tightly with aluminum foil and bake for 20 minutes. Uncover and set aside to cool.

4 Heat 2 ten-inch, medium-weight skillets over medium-high heat for 4 to 5 minutes.

5 Lightly season both sides of the fish with kosher salt.

6 Pour half the olive oil into each pan. Place 3 of the fish fillets in each pan, skin-side down. Cover the pan with a lid or another skillet laid upside down so that it resembles a dome. Cook the fish for 6 minutes, without turning. Transfer to paper towels to drain.

7 Place a fish fillet in the center of each warm dinner plate. Lay 2 artichoke halves next to each one. Spoon Aïoli over all, or place on one side of the plate, and pass the remaining Aïoli on the side.

▶ **The striped bass can be replaced with red snapper or another firm-fleshed saltwater fish.**

▷ WAYNE NISH: Striped Bass with Artichokes and Aïoli

AÏOLI

MAKES ABOUT 2⅔ CUPS

18 cloves garlic, 6 cloves minced and 12 left whole
¾ cup extra-virgin olive oil
1½ cups peanut oil
6 large egg yolks
¼ cup heavy cream
3 tablespoons fresh lemon juice
2 teaspoons kosher salt

1 In a small sauté pan, combine the whole garlic cloves and 2 tablespoons olive oil. Cover and cook over very low heat, stirring occasionally, for about 15 minutes, or until the garlic is very soft.

2 In a blender, combine the softened garlic and minced fresh garlic with 4 tablespoons peanut oil and blend until smooth. Set aside.

3 In a medium-sized glass or ceramic bowl, beat the egg yolks with a hand-held electric mixer set at high speed until well blended. While continuing to beat, gradually add ½ cup of the remaining peanut oil in a slow, steady stream until completely emulsified. Stir in the cream and lemon juice and transfer the mixture to a heavy saucepan. Cook over low heat just until bubbles form around the edges. Remove from heat and let the mixture stand for 2 to 3 minutes (this will kill any bacteria in the raw eggs). Return the mixture to the bowl and gradually whisk in the remaining ¾ cup peanut oil until incorportaed.

4 Whisk in the garlic puree and salt. Using the mixer set at medium speed, beat in the remaining 10 tablespoons olive oil a little at a time until incorporated.

5 Cover and refrigerate for at least 8 hours before using. Whisk well before serving.

Vanilla Custard with Maple-Roasted Peanuts

SERVES 6
PREPARATION TIME: ABOUT 20 MINUTES
COOKING AND BAKING TIME: 35 TO 40
MINUTES

These simple baked custards, with their pure, uncomplicated flavors, are the perfect ending to an elaborate meal.

4 cups milk
¾ cup granulated sugar
8 large egg yolks
2 tablespoons pure vanilla extract
⅛ teaspoon salt
1 cup high-quality pure maple syrup
4 ounces maple-roasted peanuts, coarsely chopped

■ Special Equipment: 6 six-ounce ramekins or custard cups

1 Assemble the *mise en place* trays for this recipe.

2 In a medium-sized, heavy saucepan, combine the milk and sugar. Cook over low heat, stirring for 5 minutes, or until the sugar is dissolved. Do not allow to boil. Transfer to a large bowl and let cool to room temperature.

3 Whisk the egg yolks, vanilla extract, and salt into the milk mixture. Strain through a fine strainer. Pour the custard into 6 six-ounce shallow ramekins or custard cups.

4 Place the cups in a large, flat roasting pan. Add enough hot water to come about ½ inch up the sides of the cups. Bake for 35 to 40 minutes, or until the custard is barely set. Remove from the oven and allow to cool in the water bath for about 5 minutes before lifting from the roasting pan and cooling completely on the counter.

5 To serve, drizzle about 2½ tablespoons of the maple syrup over each custard and sprinkle each with about 2 tablespoons of the peanuts.

▶ **The peanuts can be replaced with any glazed, roasted nuts.**

▶ **Place a tea towel or dish towel on the bottom of a roasting pan, under the custard cups, to prevent them from moving around while cooking.**

◁ WAYNE NISH: *Vanilla Custard with Maple-Roasted Peanuts*

A Leisurely Sunday Lunch

Spring Vegetable Stew with Pesto

*Creamy Polenta with Roasted Wild Mushrooms
and Fried Sage Leaves*

Apricot and Ginger Crisp

WINE SUGGESTIONS:

Sauvignon Blanc *(first course)*

Reserve Chardonnay *(second course)*

Vin Santo or Calvados *(dessert)*

WHAT YOU CAN PREPARE AHEAD OF TIME

Up to 1 week ahead: Prepare the Vegetable Stock for the Spring Vegetable Stew (if making your own). Prepare the Chicken Stock for the Creamy Polenta (if making your own).

Up to 2 days ahead: Make the Pesto for the Spring Vegetable Stew. Cover and refrigerate.

Early in the day: Prepare all the components for the Spring Vegetable Stew (including the Pesto, if not already made). Cover and refrigerate. Bake the Apricot and Ginger Crisp. Reheat in a 300-degree F. oven for 10 minutes before serving.

Up to 1 hour before the party: Fry the Sage Leaves for the Creamy Polenta. Store, uncovered, at room temperature. Combine the mushrooms with the flavorings for the Creamy Polenta.

B radley Ogden gives us a menu filled with a bounty of beautifully flavored vegetables. You will feel as though you have visited a deluxe farmer's market, as Chef Ogden has captured the down-home feeling as well as the lushness of freshly picked produce that such markets offer the city-dweller. Each course can stand on its own, but, in combination, the menu offers a wonderful contrast of flavors and textures.

Bradley Ogden first visited De Gustibus when he was executive chef at Campton Place in San Francisco, and he was quite the rising star of the contemporary American kitchen. He subsequently opened his own Lark Creek Inn in Larkspur, California, where he is able to showcase his ability to combine home-style food with contemporary taste.

◁ BRADLEY OGDEN: Creamy Polenta with Roasted Wild Mushrooms and Fried Sage Leaves

Spring Vegetable Stew with Pesto

You would have to be Peter Rabbit to make a fresher tasting stew. It's light enough to make a delightful first course, but served with homemade bread, it makes a lovely spring lunch.

1 cup fresh fava beans (1 pound unshelled)
1/2 cup fresh peas (8 ounces unshelled)
1 small head broccoli, divided into small florets (about 2 cups)
5 cups Vegetable Stock
1 pound thick asparagus spears, peeled and cut into 2-inch pieces (about 2 cups)
1 medium fennel bulb, trimmed, cored, and cut into 1-inch dice (about 1 1/2 cups)
2 tomatoes, cored, peeled, seeded, and diced
1 yellow squash, trimmed, peeled, and cut into 1/4-inch-thick slices (about 2 cups)
3/4 pound small curly spinach leaves, trimmed, rinsed, and dried
Kosher salt and freshly ground black pepper to taste
1/3 cup fresh chervil leaves
2 tablespoons fresh tarragon leaves
Pesto (recipe follows)

1 Assemble the *mise en place* trays for this recipe.

2 In a large saucepan of lightly salted, boiling water, cook the fava beans for 2 minutes, or until just tender. Using a strainer or slotted spoon, remove the beans from the boiling water. Refresh under cold running water and drain well. Remove the skins from the beans and discard. Set the beans aside.

3 Add the peas and broccoli florets to the boiling water and cook for 30 seconds. Drain, rinse under cold running water, and drain well. Set aside.

4 In a large pot, bring the stock to a boil over high heat. Add the asparagus and fennel and cook for 30 seconds.

5 Add the fava beans, peas, broccoli, and the remaining vegetables and cook for 3 minutes, or until the spinach has wilted; do not overcook. Season to taste with salt and pepper. Stir in the chervil and tarragon.

6 Ladle the stew into 6 warm, shallow soup bowls. Generously spoon the Pesto over the top, and serve immediately.

▶ Use any fresh spring vegetables in this stew—for example, black-eyed peas could replace the peas. Young bitter greens, such as mustard and kale, could be added or could replace the spinach. Fresh corn kernels could also be used later in the season, when corn is at its most succulent.

PESTO
MAKES ABOUT 1 CUP

2 tablespoons ground almonds
1/2 cup loosely packed fresh basil leaves
2 tablespoons chopped fresh flat-leaf parsley
1/2 teaspoon minced garlic
1/4 cup olive oil
2 teaspoons balsamic vinegar
1 teaspoon fresh lemon juice
2 tablespoons freshly grated Parmesan cheese
Kosher salt and freshly cracked black pepper to taste

1 Combine the almonds, basil, parsley, garlic, and olive oil in a blender or food processor fitted with the metal blade and process until smooth.

2 Transfer the puree to a glass or ceramic bowl. Stir in the vinegar, lemon juice, Parmesan cheese, and salt and pepper to taste. Cover and let rest at room temperature for several hours until ready to serve.

▶ **An easy way to peel fresh fava beans is, working down the pod, snap to release each fava bean and push it out with thumb and forefinger.**

▷ BRADLEY OGDEN: Spring Vegetable Stew with Pesto

Creamy Polenta with Roasted Wild Mushrooms and Fried Sage Leaves

SERVES 6
PREPARATION TIME: ABOUT 20 MINUTES
COOKING TIME: ABOUT 1 HOUR

The earthy mushrooms add extra body and fullness to the polenta. Without the mushrooms, the rich polenta is a terrific side dish, excellent served with a plate of grilled vegetables.

1½ cups water
1½ cups Chicken Stock
9 cloves garlic, 8 cloves sliced, 1 clove minced
¾ cup polenta
6 cups any combination of flavorful mushrooms, such as shiitakes, morels, chanterelles, Italian browns, or cèpes, trimmed
4½ tablespoons olive oil
4½ tablespoons balsamic vinegar
3 sprigs fresh thyme
3 sprigs fresh rosemary
Kosher salt and freshly cracked black pepper to taste
3 tablespoons unsalted butter
⅔ cup crème fraîche, at room temperature
¼ cup freshly grated, aged Monterey Jack cheese
¼ cup freshly grated Parmesan cheese
Fried Sage Leaves (recipe follows)

1 Preheat the oven to 350 degrees F. Assemble the *mise en place* trays for this recipe.

2 In a medium-sized, heavy-bottomed, ovenproof saucepan, bring the water, stock, and minced garlic to a full boil over high heat. Slowly whisk in the polenta. Reduce the heat and cook for 5 minutes, stirring constantly with a wooden spoon. Cover, transfer to the oven, and bake for 45 minutes, stirring 2 or 3 times to prevent sticking.

3 Meanwhile, combine the mushrooms, sliced garlic, olive oil, vinegar, thyme, rosemary, and salt and pepper to taste in a shallow roasting pan. About 20 minutes before the polenta is ready, place the pan on a rack in the lower half of the oven and roast for 20 minutes, or until lightly browned and tender.

4 Remove the polenta and mushrooms from the oven. Beat the butter, crème fraîche, and cheeses into the polenta. Taste and adjust the seasoning with salt and pepper.

5 Spoon the polenta onto 6 warm plates. Spoon the mushrooms over the polenta. Garnish with the Fried Sage Leaves and serve immediately.

▶ Crème fraîche is available in the refrigerated foods section of specialty stores and some supermarkets.

▶ Polenta is both Italian cornmeal and the dish made from it. It is served as a main course or side dish, depending on the ingredients added to it and the rest of the menu. In the first stages of cooking, it is important to stir polenta continuously. In Italy, many cooks use a stick to stir polenta, but a long-handled wooden spoon works fine.

FRIED SAGE LEAVES
MAKES ABOUT ⅔ CUP

1 cup peanut oil
⅔ cup fresh sage leaves
Salt to taste

1 In a small sauté pan, heat the oil over high heat until very hot. Add a few sage leaves and fry for about 45 seconds, until the leaves are crisp and the edges begin to curl. Using a slotted spoon or long-handled strainer, remove the crisp leaves and drain on paper towels. Continue frying until all leaves are cooked.

2 Lightly sprinkle each batch of leaves with salt as they are fried. Store at room temperature until ready to use.

▶ Wipe the sage leaves clean with a paper towel. If you must wash them, be sure they are completely dry before frying.

134

Apricot and Ginger Crisp

This is a real home-style dessert that is always a hit. You can replace the apricots with ripe peaches or nectarines, depending on what is best in the market.

1/3 cup packed light brown sugar
3/4 cup plus 3 tablespoons all-purpose flour
1/4 cup grated fresh ginger
1 1/4 teaspoons ground cinnamon
Grated zest of 1 lemon
5 cups fresh apricot halves (about 2 pounds)
2/3 cup packed dark brown sugar
1/4 teaspoon salt
1/8 teaspoon ground ginger
6 tablespoons unsalted butter, cut into 1-inch pieces and chilled
Vanilla ice cream, for serving (optional)

1 Preheat oven to 375 degrees F. Assemble the *mise en place* trays for this recipe.

2 In a large bowl, combine the light brown sugar, 3 tablespoons of the flour, the grated ginger, 1 teaspoon of the cinnamon, and the lemon zest. Add the apricots and toss gently until lightly coated. Set aside.

3 In another bowl, combine the remaining 3/4 cup flour and 1/4 teaspoon cinnamon with the dark brown sugar, salt, and ground ginger. Cut in the butter until the mixture resembles coarse meal.

4 Arrange the apricots, cut side down, in a single layer in the bottom of a 9- by 13-inch glass or ceramic baking dish. Sprinkle the topping evenly over the fruit. Bake for 20 to 30 minutes, or until the fruit is soft and the topping is crisp.

5 Serve warm, with ice cream if desired.

BRADLEY OGDEN: Apricot and Ginger Crisp

A WINTER DINNER

*Potato Crêpes with Dried Tomatoes,
Goat Cheese, and Basil*

*Salmon with Onion Confit,
Winter Vegetables, and Red Wine Sauce*

Pear Clafoutis

WINE SUGGESTIONS:

Sparkling Wine *(first course)*

Cabernet Sauvignon *(second course)*

Malvasia or German Auslese *(dessert)*

WHAT YOU CAN PREPARE AHEAD OF TIME

The day before: Prepare the tomato slices for the Potato Crêpes and allow to dry at room temperature. Cook and dice the beets and potatoes for the Salmon with Onion Confit. Dice the squash and turnip. Cover and refrigerate.

Early in the day: Make the Onion Confit for the Salmon with Onion Confit. Cover and refrigerate. Make the Red Wine Sauce for the Salmon with Onion Confit. Cover and refrigerate. Reheat just before serving.

Debra Ponzek's menu would be as appropriate at home after a day of winter sports as in an elegant dining room. Although Chef Ponzek is more than skilled at preparing sophisticated restaurant meals, she also has the rarer skill of rethinking her menus to make them accessible to the home cook. She realizes that the home menu needs to be much more practical and easy to execute with as much "do ahead" as possible. Debbie also has a special way of explaining her dishes, so that no one is ever intimidated by her suggestions. Needless to say, Debra Ponzek is one of the most popular De Gustibus chef/teachers.

◁ DEBRA PONZEK: Potato Crêpes with Dried Tomatoes, Goat Cheese, and Basil

minute, or until just crisp. Transfer the pan to the oven and roast for 4 minutes, or until medium rare.

10 In a nonstick sauté pan, melt the butter over medium-high heat. Add the diced winter vegetables and season to taste with salt and pepper. Cook for 5 minutes, or until just crisp-tender and golden. Stir in the chopped herbs.

Remove from the heat and cover with aluminum foil to keep warm.

11 Meanwhile, heat the red wine sauce over low heat.

12 Place the onion confit on one side of 6 warm serving plates. Lay the salmon partially on the confit and spoon the vegetables on the other side of the salmon. Spoon the warm sauce around the vegetables and serve immediately.

Pear Clafoutis

SERVES 6
PREPARATION TIME: ABOUT 25 MINUTES
BAKING TIME: ABOUT 40 MINUTES

Although a typically French dessert, usually made with cherries, clafoutis—here made with pears—is a welcome addition to the American table. Easy to prepare, it is delicious warm from the oven.

1 tablespoon unsalted butter, softened
1/2 cup plus 1 tablespoon granulated sugar
3 large eggs
1 vanilla bean split lengthwise or 2 teaspoons pure vanilla extract
1 1/2 cups heavy cream
1 tablespoon Poire William liqueur (pear liqueur)
6 tablespoons all-purpose flour, sifted
1 1/2 teaspoons ground cinnamon
4 ripe but firm Bartlett or Anjou pears

1 Preheat the oven to 375 degrees F. Assemble the *mise en place* trays for this recipe. Butter an 11- by 7- by 2-inch rectangular or oval baking dish with 1 tablespoon of the butter. Sprinkle with 1 tablespoon of the sugar.

2 In a large bowl, beat the eggs and the remaining 1/2 cup of sugar until light yellow and fluffy.

3 Scrape the seeds from the vanilla bean into the eggs or add the extract. Beat in the cream and liqueur. Beat in the flour and cinnamon until well blended. Set aside while you prepare the pears.

4 Peel, quarter, core, and cut the pears lengthwise into 1/4-inch thick slices. Arrange the slices in the bottom of the prepared baking dish.

◁ DEBRA PONZEK: **Salmon with Onion Confit, Winter Vegetables, and Red Wine Sauce**

5 Pour the batter over the pears. Bake for 40 minutes, or until puffed up and firm. Remove from the oven and serve immediately, as the clafoutis will quickly deflate.

DEBRA PONZEK: **Pear Clafoutis**

A MODERN DINNER

Tuna Tartare and Herb Salad

Duck wth Turnips and Medjoul Dates

Warm Chocolate Cake

WINE SUGGESTIONS:

Sauvignon Blanc *(first course)*

Merlot or Côtes du Rhône *(second course)*

Late Bottled Vintage Port *(dessert)*

WHAT YOU CAN PREPARE AHEAD OF TIME

The day before: Prepare the sauce for the Duck with Turnips and Medjoul Dates. Cover and refrigerate. Reheat just before serving.

Early in the day: Make the vinaigrette for the Tuna Tartare and Herb Salad. Cover and refrigerate. Wash and dry the mesclun salad and fresh herbs for the Tuna Tartare and Herb Salad. Wrap in damp paper towels and refrigerate. Make the croutons for the Tuna Tartare and Herb Salad.

In the afternoon: Cook the turnips and dates for the Duck with Turnips and Medjoul Dates. Bake the Warm Chocolate Cake only about 3½ hours before serving. Cover and set aside at room temperature.

Alfred Portale is another favorite De Gustibus chef. He always impresses us with his stunning combinations of flavors, spectacular presentations, and clean, clear tastes.

Chef Portale's menu truly reflects his personality—a bit sardonic, wonderfully witty, and always congenial. His combination of flavors and robust American presentations leave our audiences awed. On top of all this, Alfred is a great teacher, very clear and precise—otherwise he would leave us all overwhelmed!

◁ ALFRED PORTALE: Tuna Tartare and Herb Salad

Tuna Tartare and Herb Salad

The tuna must be absolutely pristine for this refreshing first course. Complex in presentation, it surprises by being quite easy to put together. However, it requires last-minute preparation and assembly.

GINGER VINAIGRETTE:

5 ounces fresh ginger, peeled
¾ cup grapeseed oil, or more to taste
¼ cup plus 2 tablespoons fresh lime juice, or more to taste
7 drops Tabasco
1 clove garlic, minced
1 shallot, minced

TUNA:

1 Japanese or hot-house cucumber, washed and dried
1½ pounds sashimi-grade yellowfin tuna
2 scallions, trimmed and minced
Salt and freshly ground black pepper to taste

CROUTONS:

1 long, thin baguette
3 tablespoons extra-virgin olive oil

HERB SALAD:

2 cups mesclun salad, washed and dried
¼ cup flat-leaf parsley leaves
¼ cup inch-long chive stalks
2 tablespoons fresh mint leaves
2 tablespoons fresh cilantro leaves
2 tablespoons fresh chervil leaves

1 Preheat the oven to 375 degrees F. Assemble the *mise en place* trays for this recipe.

2 To make the vinaigrette, grate the ginger. Wrap the grated ginger in a square of cheesecloth, hold it over a small bowl, and twist the cheesecloth tightly to extract the ginger juice. Stir in the grapeseed oil, lime juice, Tabasco, minced garlic, and shallot. Taste and adjust the flavors with additional oil or citrus juices, if necessary. Set aside.

3 Using the tines of a fork, make long, deep cuts down the length of the cucumber. Slice crosswise into very thin slices. Cover and refrigerate.

4 To prepare the tartare, cut the tuna into ¼-inch dice. Place in a glass or ceramic bowl and add ¾ cup of the Ginger Vinaigrette and the minced scallions and toss to mix. Season to taste with salt and pepper and set aside at room temperature.

5 To make the croutons, slice the baguette diagonally into ¼-inch slices so that you have at least 18 slices. (Cut a few extra slices in case guests want more croutons.) Lay the bread slices on a baking sheet and bake for 5 minutes or until golden, turning once. Drizzle with the olive oil and set aside.

6 To make the salad, toss the salad and herbs in a bowl. Add the remaining Ginger Vinaigrette and toss to coat.

7 Place a 3-inch round ring mold or pastry cutter in the center of a chilled serving plate. Make a circle of overlapping cucumber slices around the outside circumference of the mold. Lightly pack one portion of the tuna mixture into the mold and lift off the mold. Stand 3 or 4 croutons around the tuna, leaning them slightly outward. Arrange about ½ cup of the herb salad on top of the tuna, in between the croutons. Working quickly, assemble the remaining plates. Serve immediately with extra croutons on the side.

▶ **You can marinate the tuna in the vinaigrette for as long as 45 minutes ahead of time, but any longer will render the fish soft. Cover and refrigerate the fish during marinating, if making ahead.**

▶ **To replicate Chef Portale's presentation of this recipe exactly, put hoisin sauce in a squeeze bottle and dot each cucumber slice with a little sauce for extra garnish.**

Duck with Turnips and Medjoul Dates

Ducks and dates are made for each other: both are wonderfully sweet and juicy. Although this recipe takes time to prepare because you must make Duck Stock, the actual preparation is surprisingly easy.

2 four-and-a-half-pound Muscovy ducks

SAUCE:

Reserved bones and trimmings from ducks
1 tablespoon olive oil
1 onion, coarsely chopped
3 1/2 cups dry red wine
1 head garlic, halved crosswise
1 teaspoon black peppercorns
3 sprigs fresh thyme or 1/2 teaspoon dried thyme
2 bay leaves
1/2 teaspoon caraway seeds

DUCK:

6 tablespoons unsalted butter
4 large turnips, peeled and very thinly sliced
6 medjoul dates, pitted and thinly sliced lengthwise
4 teaspoons sweet butter
1 ounce olive oil
Salt and freshly ground black pepper

1 Preheat oven to 400 degrees F. Assemble the *mise en place* trays for the sauce portion of the recipe.

2 Cut off the duck legs and cut apart at the joint. Remove the meat from thighs, leaving it intact; remove the breast halves from the carcass, leaving them intact. Cover and refrigerate the breast and thigh meat. Chop the duck bones and trimmings into pieces.

3 To make the sauce, spread the bones and trimmings in a single layer in a large roasting pan and roast, stirring several times, for about 20 minutes, or until lightly browned.

4 Meanwhile, heat the olive oil in a large sauté pan. Cook the onions over medium-high heat for about 10 minutes, until softened and lightly browned. Remove from the heat.

5 Transfer the bones to a large stockpot and add the onions. Add the wine and enough water to cover the bones. Add the garlic, peppercorns, thyme, bay leaves, and caraway seeds. Bring to a boil over high heat, and then reduce the heat and simmer, partially covered, for 4 to 6 hours, skimming any foam that rises to the surface during cooking. Add more water if necessary.

6 Spoon the fat from the surface of the stock, or blot it with a folded paper towel. Strain the stock through a sieve into a saucepan, pressing against the solids to extract as much liquid as possible. Discard the solids. Strain the stock a second time through a fine-mesh sieve into a saucepan. Bring to a boil over medium heat and cook for 20 to 30 minutes, until reduced to about 1 1/2 cups. The sauce will be slightly syrupy. Set aside.

7 To prepare the duck, assemble the *mise en place* trays for the remaining ingredients.

8 Melt 2 tablespoons of the butter in a large sauté pan over medium-high heat. Sauté the turnips for 3 to 4 minutes, until softened and lightly browned around the edges. Add the dates during the last minute of cooking and season to taste with salt and pepper, remove from the heat, and cover to keep warm.

9 Bring the duck sauce to a boil over high heat. Reduce to a simmer and whisk in the remaining 4 tablespoons of butter, a tablespoon at a time, waiting until each one is incorporated before adding the next. Adjust the seasonings and cover to keep warm.

10 In a large sauté pan, heat olive oil over medium heat. Season the duck breasts and thighs with salt and pepper and add to the pan, skin side down. Cook for 4 to 5 minutes, until the skin is crispy. Turn and cook for 4 to 5 minutes longer, until medium-rare. Transfer to a platter or cutting board and let rest for a few minutes.

11 Slice the breasts and thighs on the diagonal into thick slices. Fan the slices in a semi-circle around the center of 6 serving plates. Gather date slivers in a bunch, wrap them with a few turnip slices and stand them lengthwise in the center of each plate. Gently fold turnip slices to form rounded cushions and place around the bundle of dates so

that it stands up. Continue adding turnip folds to the base, and intersperse with more date slivers. Spoon the sauce around the outside of the duck, and in a circle around the base of the turnip mixture.

▶ If serving six people and you don't want to plate the duck individually, fan the duck on a platter and create one turnip and date centerpiece, and serve the rest of the portions on the side.

Warm Chocolate Cake

This is about the best chocolate cake you'll ever eat. You can serve it with whipped cream or, for even more indulgence, toasted almond ice cream.

1 pound semisweet chocolate, coarsely chopped
3 ounces bittersweet chocolate, coarsely chopped
1/2 cup plus 2 tablespoons strong brewed coffee
6 large eggs
1/2 cup plus 2 tablespoons granulated sugar
1 cup heavy cream
Whipped cream or ice cream, for serving (optional)

1 Preheat the oven to 325 degrees F. Assemble the *mise en place* trays for this recipe. Butter a 10-inch round cake pan. Cut a 10-inch circle of parchment paper and fit it into the bottom of the pan. Lightly butter the parchment paper.

2 In the top half of a double boiler or in a heatproof bowl, combine the chocolates. Set over barely simmering water and allow to melt, stirring frequently. Remove from the heat, stir in the coffee, and mix until smooth. Set aside.

3 In the top half of a double boiler or in a heatproof bowl, combine the eggs and sugar. Set over boiling water and stir constantly until the sugar has dissolved and the mixture is warm. Reduce the heat to a gentle simmer.

4 Using a hand-held mixer set on medium speed, beat the egg mixture for about 5 minutes, or until it forms soft peaks. Remove the top half of the double boiler or the bowl from the heat. Gently fold a third of the beaten eggs into the melted chocolate. Fold in the rest of the egg mixture. Do not overmix; fold just until blended.

5 In a medium bowl, beat the cream until it forms stiff peaks. Gently fold into the chocolate mixture until well

blended. Scrape the batter into the prepared pan and smooth the top. Place the pan in a larger pan and add enough hot water to come 1/2 inch up the sides of the cake pan. Bake for 1 hour.

6 Turn off the oven and open the oven door for 1 minute. Close the door and allow the cake to rest in the oven for 2 hours.

7 Invert the cake onto a serving plate and lift off the pan. Peel off the parchment paper. Serve warm, with whipped cream or ice cream if desired.

ALFRED PORTALE: Warm Chocolate Cake

◁ ALFRED PORTALE: Duck with Turnips and Medjoul Dates

THE FLAVORS OF SPRING

Fresh Tuna with Maui Onions and Avocado

Grilled Salmon with Black Pepper and Ginger

Pecan Pie

WINE SUGGESTIONS:

Sparkling Wine *(first course)*

Sauvignon Blanc *(second course)*

Tawny Port *(dessert)*

WHAT YOU CAN PREPARE AHEAD OF TIME

Up to 1 week ahead: Make the pastry and line the tart pan for the Pecan Pie. Cover tightly and freeze.

Early in the day: Make the vinaigrette for the Fresh Tuna. Cover and refrigerate. Dice the onion for the Fresh Tuna. Cover and refrigerate. Make the sauce for the Grilled Salmon through step 3. Cover and refrigerate. Add the butter during reheating, just before serving. Fry the spinach leaves for the Grilled Salmon. Store, uncovered, in a dry place.

In the afternoon: Bake the pie. When cool, cover and set aside in a cool place.

Whenever Wolfgang Puck teaches at De Gustibus, we cannot keep the crowds from forming and there is always a waiting list of eager food enthusiasts. Not only is Chef Puck a magnet for our students, he also pulls remarkable flavors and tastes from the most simple ingredients.

Wolfgang is filled with good humor and his face is lit by a broad smile as he chops, minces, stirs, and mixes. He chats comfortably with his inquiring audience and makes it all seem effortless as he combines foods to bring out their maximum flavor. Never does one element overpower a dish. He and his food are absolutely joyful.

This menu is filled with the feelings of spring, much like Wolf himself. There is a slight Asian influence that adds a balance and intensity to the otherwise simple ingredients. Then he tops it off with a down-home American pie appropriate any time of year.

◁ WOLFGANG PUCK: **Grilled Salmon with Black Pepper and Ginger**

Pecan Pie

Wolfgang's classic pecan pie is a perfect dessert to end this slightly Asian meal.

PIE PASTRY:

1¾ cups all-purpose flour, sifted
1 tablespoon granulated sugar
¼ teaspoon salt
12 tablespoons unsalted butter, cut into 1-inch pieces and chilled
2 large egg yolks
2 to 3 tablespoons heavy cream

FILLING:

1 cup light corn syrup
¾ cup packed light brown sugar
3 large eggs
2 large egg yolks
2 teaspoons pure vanilla extract
2 tablespoons unsalted butter
1½ cups pecan halves

■ Special Equipment: 10-inch fluted tart pan with removable bottom

1 Assemble the *mise en place* trays for this recipe.

2 To make the pie pastry, in a food processor fitted with the metal blade, combine the flour, sugar, salt, and butter. Process until the mixture resembles fine meal.

3 Whisk together the egg yolks and 2 tablespoons cream. With the motor running, slowly add to the flour mixture and process until the dough comes together into a ball. Add additional cream if necessary to make a cohesive dough. Transfer the dough to a lightly floured surface. Pat into a circle about ½ inch thick. Wrap in plastic and refrigerate for 2 hours, or until well chilled.

4 Preheat the oven to 375 degrees F.

5 To make the filling, combine the corn syrup, brown sugar, eggs, egg yolks, and vanilla and whisk well.

6 Heat the butter in a small sauté pan over medium heat for 3 minutes, or until it is browned and gives off a nutty aroma. Immediately stir the butter into the corn syrup mixture.

7 On a lightly floured surface, roll out the dough to a 12-inch circle. Carefully fit it into a 10-inch fluted tart pan with removable bottom and trim off the excess. Set the tart pan in a baking sheet lined with foil.

8 Arrange the pecan halves in the bottom of the pastry shell. Carefully ladle the filling mixture over the pecans. Bake in the lower third of the oven for 40 to 45 minutes, or until a cake tester inserted into the center comes out clean. Transfer to a wire rack to cool to room temperature.

▶ The tart pan is set on a foil-lined baking sheet to catch any sugary overflow from the filling, so as to make cleanup easy.

◁ WOLFGANG PUCK: **Pecan Pie**

A MEAL FOR ALL SEASONS

Iced Sweet Pea Soup

*Quail with Coffee and Spice Rub
and White Bean Ragout*

Chocolate Bread Pudding

WINE SUGGESTIONS:

Sparkling Wine *(first course)*
Côtes du Rhône *(second course)*
Ruby Port *(dessert)*

WHAT YOU CAN PREPARE AHEAD OF TIME

Up to 1 week ahead: Prepare the Chicken Stock for the Iced Sweet Pea Soup (if making your own).

The day before: Make the Iced Sweet Pea Soup. Cover and refrigerate. Prepare the White Bean Ragout without adding the kale, parsley, and butter. Cover and refrigerate. Reheat, adding the remaining ingredients, just before serving. Prepare the spice rub for the Quail with Coffee and Spice Rub. Cover and store at cool room temperature.

Early in the day: Bake the Chocolate Bread Pudding. Cover with aluminum foil and reheat at 300 degrees F. for 15 minutes before serving.

Anne Rosenzweig has been teaching at De Gustibus almost as long as she has been Executive Chef at Arcadia, in New York City. According to Anne, De Gustibus was her first teaching experience, but she enjoyed it so much, and we thought her so good, she began to teach all over the country. Chef Rosenzweig loves to experiment with unusual ingredients and techniques. Although the coffee and spice rub for the quail in this menu seems bizarre, the taste is astonishingly delicious. In this dish, she has given us maximum flavor with a minimum of fat. Her dessert combines a traditional technique with contemporary flavor—something all dessert-lovers will appreciate.

◁ ANNE ROSENZWEIG: Iced Sweet Pea Soup

Chocolate Bread Pudding

Here is a simply delicious version of an old-fashioned dessert.

12 one-inch-thick slices brioche (or other richly flavored egg bread such as challah)
3/4 cup unsalted butter, melted
8 ounces bittersweet chocolate, coarsely chopped
3 cups heavy cream
1 cup milk
1 cup granulated sugar
12 large egg yolks
1 teaspoon pure vanilla extract
1/8 teaspoon salt
1 cup heavy cream, softly whipped (optional)

1 Preheat the oven to 425 degrees F. Assemble the *mise en place* trays for this recipe.

2 Brush both sides of the bread slices with the melted butter. Place on a baking sheet and toast in the oven for 7 to 10 minutes, or until golden brown. Set aside.

3 Place the chocolate in a medium-sized bowl set over a saucepan of very hot, not simmering, water. The bottom of the bowl should not touch the water. Stir frequently until melted.

4 In a medium-sized saucepan, heat the cream and milk for about 5 minutes, over medium heat to just under a boil. Do not boil. Remove from the heat.

5 In a large bowl, whisk together the sugar and egg yolks until well blended. Gradually whisk the hot cream and milk mixture. Strain through a fine sieve into a bowl and skim off any foam.

6 Whisk the melted chocolate into the yolk mixture. Stir in the vanilla and salt.

7 Arrange the toasted bread in 2 overlapping rows in a 9-by 13-inch baking pan. Pour the chocolate mixture over the bread. Cover with plastic wrap and place a smaller baking pan on top of the bread so that the slices stay sub-

◁ ANNE ROSENZWEIG: **Quail with Coffee and Spice Rub and White Bean Ragout**

merged. Add weights if necessary. Refrigerate for 1 hour or until the bread is soaked through.

8 Preheat the oven to 325 degrees F.

9 Remove the smaller pan and plastic wrap from the bread pudding. Cover with aluminum foil and punch a few holes in the top to allow the steam to escape. Place in a larger pan and pour in enough water to come 1/2 inch up the sides of the smaller pan. Bake for about 1 hour and 45 minutes, or until all the liquid has been absorbed and the pudding has a glossy look.

10 Cut the pudding into squares and serve warm with whipped cream, if desired.

ANNE ROSENZWEIG: **Chocolate Bread Pudding**

A PASTA PARTY

Smoked Salmon, Salmon Roe, and Pasta Salad

Fusilli with Tomatoes and Bread Crumbs

Apricot and Cherry Tart

WINE SUGGESTIONS:

Sparkling Wine *(first course)*
Pinot Grigio or Sauvignon Blanc *(second course)*
Late Harvest Muscat or Riesling *(dessert)*

WHAT YOU CAN PREPARE AHEAD OF TIME

Early in the day: Prepare all the components for the Smoked Salmon, Salmon Roe, and Pasta Salad. Cover and refrigerate. Prepare the bread crumbs for the Fusilli with Tomatoes and Bread Crumbs. Cover and store at room temperature. Prepare the tomato and herb mixture for the Fusilli. Cover and store at room temperature.

Up to 4 hours ahead: Make the Apricot and Cherry Tart. Cover and set aside in a cool place.

For one of her very rare De Gustibus appearances, Alice Waters spent three days giving classes. Before her arrival, she sent boxes of the most beautiful fruits, vegetables, and herbs from the Chinos Farm in San Diego, California. The colors, textures, and aromas transported us to the sensual Mediterranean.

The influence of the California farmers on Alice most certainly shows in her cooking. With these marvelous ingredients, she created a tempting summer pasta buffet, with only the fusilli requiring last-minute preparation. This was a class that we all remember with all of our senses.

◁ ALICE WATERS: Apricot and Cherry Tart

Smoked Salmon, Salmon Roe, and Pasta Salad

SERVES 6
PREPARATION TIME: ABOUT 30 MINUTES
COOKING TIME: ABOUT 25 MINUTES
CHILLING TIME: ABOUT 4 HOURS

This salad will never seem as delicious to us as it was the first time Alice made it. But, if you use only the best ingredients, you'll come very close!

Juice of 2 limes (about 1/3 cup)
2 teaspoons Dijon mustard
Grated zest of 1 lemon
12 quail eggs (see note)
Salt and freshly ground black pepper to taste
1/2 cup extra-virgin olive oil, or to taste
2/3 pound thin green beans or haricot verts, trimmed
1 bunch fresh cilantro, washed and dried
1 bunch watercress, washed and dried
1 pound dried tubular pasta such as ditali or penne, or small shells
1/2 cup chopped pitted Niçoise olives
1 1/2 cups tiny fresh peas
5 scallions, trimmed and sliced
8 ounces thinly sliced smoked salmon, cut into narrow strips
6 ounces salmon caviar

1 Assemble the *mise en place* trays for this recipe.

2 In a glass or ceramic bowl, whisk together the lime juice, mustard, and lemon zest. Set aside.

3 Put the quail eggs in a medium-sized saucepan and add enough cold water to cover. Bring to a boil over high heat. Immediately remove from the heat, drain, and rinse under cold running water.

4 Peel the quail eggs and slice in half lengthwise. Arrange on a plate and season to taste with salt, pepper, and 2 tablespoons of the olive oil. Cover and refrigerate.

5 In a medium-sized saucepan of boiling salted water, blanch the beans for 2 minutes, or until bright green and crisp-tender. Drain and refresh under cold running water. Pat dry and set aside.

6 Remove the leaves from half of the cilantro and watercress and chop the leaves. Set these aside. Trim the remaining cilantro and watercress sprigs, wrap in damp paper towels, and refrigerate.

7 In a large pot, bring 4 quarts of salted water to a boil over high heat. Cook the pasta until *al dente.* Drain well.

8 Transfer the pasta to a large serving bowl, add the remaining 6 tablespoons of olive oil and toss well. Stir in the lime dressing, chopped cilantro and watercress, beans, olives, peas, and scallions until well mixed. Stir in the salmon and caviar. Wipe the edge of the bowl. Cover and refrigerate for 4 hours, or until well chilled.

9 When ready to serve, garnish the salad with the reserved cilantro and watercress sprigs, and nestle the quail eggs among them. Serve immediately.

▶ **Quail eggs are sold in specialty stores. Hens' eggs are too large to substitute. If you cannot find quail eggs, omit them from the recipe.**

▷ ALICE WATERS: Smoked Salmon, Salmon Roe, and Pasta Salad

SOUTHWEST COOKING

ROBERT DEL GRANDE:
A Cold-Weather Dinner for Close Friends

DEAN FEARING:
Sunny and Bold, A Red and Yellow Dinner

BOBBY FLAY:
A Cocktail Buffet, Southwestern-Style

MARILYN FROBUCCINO:
*A Midweek Dinner—
Light, Fresh, and Fast*

VINCENT GUERITHAULT:
*A Celebratory Dinner for
New Year's Eve*

STEPHEN PYLES:
*An End-of-Summer
Southwestern Dinner*

JIMMY SCHMIDT:
*An Elegant Fall Dinner,
Southwestern-Style*

BRENDAN WALSH:
Casual Cooking for a Crowd

DAVID WALZOG:
A Southwestern Thanksgiving

A COLD-WEATHER DINNER
FOR CLOSE FRIENDS

*Cream Biscuits with Barbecued Crabmeat
and Buttermilk Dressing*

Roasted Pork Loin with Acorn Squash Torte and Red Chile Sauce

Banana Cocoa Cake

WINE SUGGESTIONS:

California Reserve Chardonnay (*first course*)

Beaujolais-Villages (*second course*)

Ruby Port (*dessert*)

WHAT YOU CAN PREPARE AHEAD OF TIME

Up to 1 week ahead: Prepare the Barbecue Spice for the crab. Store in a small screw-top jar (a baby food jar is ideal).

Up to 3 days ahead: Prepare the Chicken Stock (if making your own). Prepare the Red Chile Sauce. Cover and refrigerate.

The night before: Bake the Banana Cocoa Cake.

Early in the day: Wash and dry all the herbs, vegetables, and greens. Wrap separately in wet paper towels, place in a sealed plastic bag, and refrigerate. Toast, stem, and seed all the dried chiles. Toast the pumpkin seeds. Pick over the crabmeat. Cover and refrigerate. Bake the acorn squash. Scrape the flesh into a bowl. Cover and reserve.

In the afternoon: Prepare the Acorn Squash Torte up to the addition of the eggs. Cover and refrigerate.

Just before the party: Mix the dough for the Cream Biscuits and refrigerate it. Do not bake until 10 to 15 minutes before serving. Make the Buttermilk Dressing. Cover and chill in the refrigerator for no longer than 1 hour.

Whenever Robert Del Grande visits the De Gustibus classroom, we prepare for an extraordinary experience. Trained as a biochemist, Robert came to cooking through fate rather than design. Because of this orientation, he is constantly experimenting with combinations of flavors and textures, attempting to create simple foods with maximum taste. His uncommon sense of humor only adds to Robert's prodigious classes—we all laugh a lot as we marvel at his novel path to exuberant meals.

Robert inspired a De Gustibus student, Frank Ball, to create a book and videotape called *Trucs of the Trade.* "Truc" is French for a trick or a shortcut. Robert's "truc" for removing a seed from an avocado without inadvertently making guacamole made Frank realize that many professional chefs must have similar "trucs" that could be shared with home cooks. Frank and I gathered 101 tricks from professional cooks from all over the country. With publication of the book, we were able to support the work of Share Our Strength, a network of food industry and other creative professionals united to fight hunger throughout the world. Thanks, Robert!

The commentary preceding some of the recipes comes directly from the chef's mouth. You'll quickly see that Robert has his own special way of introducing dishes.

◁ **Roasted Pork Loin with Acorn Squash Torte and Red Chile Sauce**

ROBERT DEL GRANDE: Cream Biscuits with Barbecued Crabmeat and Buttermilk Dressing

Cream Biscuits with Barbecued Crabmeat and Buttermilk Dressing

SERVES 6
PREPARATION TIME: ABOUT 30 MINUTES
COOKING TIME: ABOUT 15 MINUTES

"Imagine this: A petite cream biscuit, hot from the oven, its heady aroma of toasted butter and flour startling those quiescent memories of youth. Still hot to the touch, gingerly split equatorially. On the bottom half of such a tender pastry, centered on a huge white plate, is placed some peppery arugula (glistening from a deft treatment with olive oil) and nestled on this, pan-seared crabmeat redolent of barbecued spice and fresh lime. Ah ha…is the picture becoming clearer…le petite biscuit farci?…"

–ROBERT DEL GRANDE

½ pound fresh lump crabmeat
2 tablespoons plus 1½ teaspoons Barbecue Spice (recipe follows)
2 tablespoons unsalted butter
1 bunch arugula, washed, trimmed, and dried
1 tablespoon olive oil
Salt and freshly ground black pepper to taste
6 Cream Biscuits, freshly baked (recipe follows)
Buttermilk Dressing (recipe follows)
Tabasco to taste
6 sprigs fresh cilantro
6 lime wedges

1 Assemble the *mise en place* trays for this recipe.

2 Pick over the crabmeat to remove any shell and cartilage. Set aside 1 tablespoon of the Barbecue Spice for garnish.

3 In a bowl, combine the crabmeat with the remaining 1 tablespoon plus 1½ teaspoons Barbecue Spice and toss to mix. In a medium-sized skillet melt the butter over medium heat. Add the seasoned crabmeat and sauté for 1 minute, or until just heated through. Remove from the heat.

4 In a bowl, toss the arugula leaves with the olive oil. Season to taste with salt and pepper.

5 Split the freshly baked biscuits in half crosswise. Place the bottom halves in the centers of warm plates. Place a few leaves of arugula on each biscuit. Spoon equal portions of the crabmeat on top of the arugula. Drizzle with a little

of the Buttermilk Dressing. Place the biscuit tops over the crabmeat. Lightly dust a little of the reserved Barbecue Spice on each plate. Garnish each biscuit with a drizzle of Tabasco, a sprig of cilantro, and a wedge of lime. Serve immediately.

▶ **Do not dress the arugula more than 5 minutes before serving or it will begin to wilt.**

BARBECUE SPICE
MAKES ABOUT 2½ TEASPOONS

Use the best chile powder you can buy. If possible, buy pure ground chile powder.

1 tablespoon chile powder
2 teaspoons hot paprika
1 teaspoon all-purpose flour
1 teaspoon granulated sugar
¼ teaspoon ground cinnamon
¼ teaspoon coarse salt
Pinch of ground cloves
Pinch of freshly ground black pepper

Combine all ingredients in a small screw-top jar and shake to mix. Store tightly covered until ready to use.

▶ **This recipe multiplies easily. Make lots of extra barbecue spice and store, tightly covered, for up to 3 months. Use it to add zest when roasting poultry or meat.**

ROBERT DEL GRANDE: Banana Cocoa Cake

Red Chile Sauce
MAKES ABOUT 3 CUPS

6 large Ancho chiles, toasted and coarsely
chopped
1 orange, peeled, seeded, and chopped into small pieces
3 cups Chicken Stock
½ cup chopped yellow onion
2 cloves garlic, peeled
Pinch of ground cloves
Pinch of ground cumin
Pinch of of ground cinnamon
2 tablespoons unsalted butter
Coarse salt and freshly ground pepper to taste

1 Put the chiles in a bowl with warm water to cover, and soak for 30 minutes until soft and pliable. Drain.

2 Put the chiles, orange, chicken stock, onion, garlic, and spices in a blender or food processor fitted with the metal blade. Blend or process for 30 seconds, or until smooth.

3 In a medium-sized saucepan, heat the butter over medium heat until it browns slightly. Add the chile puree and bring to a boil, stirring constantly. Lower the heat and simmer for 30 minutes. Taste and adjust the seasoning with salt and pepper. Serve warm.

Banana Cocoa Cake

SERVES 6
PREPARATION TIME: ABOUT 15 MINUTES
COOKING TIME: ABOUT 30 MINUTES

"Here's one for the quick and easy. Sift the dry, mix the liquid, stir it all together and bake. But only if you pass the test that strikes fear in the hearts of doubting cooks: Is a banana dry or liquid, particularly when mashed?…" —ROBERT DEL GRANDE

(Answer according to Del Grande: *liquid*)

1½ cups all-purpose flour
½ cup unsweetened cocoa powder
1 teaspoon baking powder
1 teaspoon baking soda
½ teaspoon salt
1 cup granulated sugar
1½ cups mashed very ripe bananas (about 4 medium bananas)
1 cup milk
8 tablespoons (1 stick) unsalted butter, melted
2 large eggs
1 teaspoon pure vanilla extract
1 cup chopped walnuts or pecans
Confectioners' sugar (optional)
Whipped cream (optional)
Ice cream (optional)

■ Special Equipment: 9-inch square cake pan

1 Preheat the oven to 325 degrees F. Lightly spray a 9-inch square cake pan with non-stick vegetable oil spray. Assemble the *mise en place* trays for this recipe.

2 Sift the flour, cocoa, baking powder, baking soda, and salt into a large bowl. Stir in the sugar.

3 In another bowl, combine the bananas, milk, melted butter, eggs, and vanilla, mixing well. Stir into the flour mixture until just combined. Stir in the nuts. Do not overmix.

4 Pour the batter into the prepared pan and smooth the top. Bake for 30 minutes, or until a cake tester inserted into the center comes out clean. Remove from the oven and allow to cool on a wire rack.

5 To serve, warm the cake in a preheated 275 degree F. oven for 10 minutes, if desired.

6 Cut the cake into squares, dust the tops with confectioners' sugar, if desired, and serve with whipped cream or ice cream.

SUNNY AND BOLD,
A RED AND YELLOW DINNER

Apple-Cheese Soup

Warm Lobster Taco with Yellow Tomato Salsa and Jícama Salad

Grilled Swordfish with Pineapple–Red Chile Salsa

Brown Butter Berry Tart

WINE SUGGESTIONS:

California Sparkling Wine or Loire Valley Sparkling Wine (*first course*)

California Sauvignon Blanc or Italian Pinot Grigio (*second course*)

California Pinot Blanc or Italian Pinot Grigio (*third course*)

Tawny Port, German Riesling Auslese (*dessert*)

WHAT YOU CAN PREPARE AHEAD OF TIME

Up to 1 week ahead: Make the pastry for the Brown Butter Berry Tart. Wrap tightly and freeze. Thaw just before preparing the tart.

Up to 3 days ahead: Prepare the Chicken Stock (if making your own).

The day before: Prepare the Apple-Cheese Soup through step 2. Cover and refrigerate. Finish as directed in the recipe during the afternoon before the meal. Cut up the vegetables for the Jícama Salad. Wrap separately in wet paper towels, place in a sealed plastic bag, and refrigerate.

Early in the day: Prepare the components of the Lobster Taco. Bake the Brown Butter Berry Tart. Put the Jícama Salad together up to 6 hours ahead but do not season until ready to serve. Cover and refrigerate. Make the Pineapple-Red Chile Salsa at least 2 hours ahead of serving. Make the Yellow Tomato Salsa at least 2 hours ahead of serving.

When Dean Fearing walked into the De Gustibus kitchen for the first time, we thought a Texas rock star had arrived. Wearing red lizard cowboy boots and horn rimmed glasses, and radiating enough energy to light up Macy's windows, Dean was accompanied by his fellow Southwestern chef Robert Del Grande and Mimi, Robert's wife. The three of them were going to prep for Dean's class and then go shopping for guitars! In their spare time, these dynamos had created a small country and western band called The Barbwires, and they were ready to rock. We knew then that this would be a spectacular class—and it was. Dean has since come back often, with incredible results each time.

Dean's menu is a riot of brilliant colors and contrasting flavors, light in feeling and zesty in taste. Many of the recipes can be started the day before, with just some quick, last-minute preparation for completion.

◁ Apple-Cheese Soup

DEAN FEARING: Warm Lobster Taco with Yellow Tomato Salsa and Jícama Salad

JÍCAMA SALAD

MAKES ABOUT 2½ CUPS

½ small zucchini, cut into fine julienne about ⅛-inch thick

½ small jícama, peeled and cut into fine julienne about ⅛-inch thick

½ small red bell pepper, seeds and membranes removed, cut into fine julienne about ⅛-inch thick

½ small yellow bell pepper, seeds and membranes removed, cut into fine julienne about ⅛-inch thick

½ small carrot, peeled and cut into fine julienne

¼ cup peanut oil

2 tablespoons fresh lime juice

Salt to taste

Cayenne pepper to taste

In a medium-sized bowl, combine all the vegetables, oil, and lime juice. Season to taste with salt and cayenne pepper. Toss to mix well. Serve immediately.

▶ Although the Jícama Salad may be prepared several hours ahead, covered and refrigerated, do not add the salt until almost ready to serve as it will cause the vegetables to lose their crispness.

▶ A mandoline makes uniform julienne strips from the vegetables.

Grilled Swordfish with Pineapple – Red Chile Salsa

SERVES 6
PREPARATION TIME: ABOUT 25 MINUTES
COOKING TIME: ABOUT 5 MINUTES
CHILLING TIME (SALSA ONLY): AT LEAST 2 HOURS

This is a wonderfully light fish dish, low in fat and really rich in flavor. It's a spectacular warm-weather recipe and great for summer entertaining. Although not necessary, cooking the swordfish on an outdoor grill allows the flavors of the fish to shine.

6 seven-ounce swordfish steaks, trimmed of skin and dark membrane
3 tablespoons sesame oil
Salt to taste
Pineapple-Red Chile Salsa (recipe follows)

1 Prepare a charcoal or gas grill or preheat the broiler. Assemble the *mise en place* trays for this recipe.

2 Brush the swordfish with the sesame oil and season to taste with salt.

3 Put the fish on the preheated grill or under the broiler so that it is 2 to 3 inches from the heat. Cook for 2 minutes, or just long enough to lightly color the side facing the heat. If using a grill, this should be long enough to mark that side with grill marks. Turn the fish over and cook for 2 minutes longer or until the flesh is firm. (To prevent overcooking and keep the fish moist, allow no more than 5 minutes total cooking time for each ½ inch of thickness at the thickest part.)

4 Ladle about ½ cup of the Pineapple-Red Chile Salsa into the centers of 6 warm dinner plates. Place the swordfish steaks on top and serve immediately.

▶ If using an outdoor grill, make sure the grids are very clean. To prevent the fish from sticking, lightly brush the grids with vegetable oil before grilling.

PINEAPPLE-RED CHILE SALSA

MAKES ABOUT 3 CUPS

½ very ripe pineapple, peeled, cored, and coarsely chopped
½ mango or papaya, peeled, seeded, and coarsely chopped
½ red bell pepper, seeds and membranes removed, chopped
½ yellow bell pepper, seeds and membranes removed, chopped
1 small jícama, peeled and chopped
2 teaspoons peeled and grated fresh ginger (from a 3-inch piece)
1 clove garlic, minced
1 serrano chile, seeded and minced
2 dried cayenne chiles, seeded and minced or ⅛ teaspoon ground cayenne pepper
2 teaspoons minced fresh cilantro
2 teaspoons minced fresh basil
2 teaspoons minced fresh mint
1 tablespoon white wine vinegar
1 tablespoon sweet rice vinegar
1 teaspoon soy sauce
1 teaspoon sesame oil
Salt to taste
Juice of 1 lime, or to taste

In a bowl, combine the pineapple, mango, bell peppers, jícama, ginger, garlic, chiles, herbs, vinegars, soy sauce, and sesame oil. Season to taste with salt and the lime juice. Mix well. Cover and refrigerate for at least 2 hours before serving. Bring to room temperature before serving.

▶ The salsa must be made at least 2 hours in advance to allow the flavors to blend. It can be made early in the day and refrigerated until about 1 hour before serving. Allow to come to room temperature before serving so that the flavors are subtle against the swordfish. It does not hold up well for longer than 8 to 12 hours.

▶ For speed, chop the fruit and vegetables—separately—in a food processor using on/off pulses to ensure they remain chunky.

Brown Butter Berry Tart

This luscious dessert is flavored with browned butter scented with vanilla, giving a nutty taste to the berries. After a relatively light dinner, a home-baked fruit tart is always welcome.

TART PASTRY:

1½ cups all-purpose flour

2 tablespoons plus 2 teaspoons granulated sugar

8 tablespoons (1 stick) unsalted butter, chilled and cut into ½-inch pieces

1 large egg yolk

2 to 3 tablespoons heavy cream, chilled

FILLING:

1 pint fresh raspberries, blueberries or blackberries, or a combination of all three

6 tablespoons unsalted butter

1 vanilla bean

3 extra-large eggs

¾ cup granulated sugar

⅓ cup all-purpose flour

■ Special Equipment: 10-inch tart pan with a removable bottom or flan ring

1 Assemble the *mise en place* trays for this recipe.

2 To make the pastry, in a medium-sized bowl, combine the flour and sugar. With your fingers or a pastry blender quickly blend in the butter, a few pieces at a time, until the mixture resembles coarse meal.

3 In a small bowl, blend the egg yolk with 2 tablespoons of cream. Make a well in the center of the flour and pour in the egg mixture. Quickly blend with your fingers to form a soft dough. Add more cream if the dough is dry and crumbly. Do not overmix or the pastry will be tough. Roll the pastry into a ball and flatten slightly. Wrap in plastic wrap and refrigerate for at least 1 hour.

4 To assemble the tart, roll out the pastry on a lightly floured surface or between 2 sheets of plastic wrap to 1/8-inch thick and 14 inches in diameter. Line a 10-inch tart

◁ DEAN FEARING: **Grilled Swordfish with Pineapple-Red Chile Salsa**

DEAN FEARING: **Brown Butter Berry Tart**

pan or flan ring with the pastry so that it overhangs the edges by about 1 inch. Trim the edges and crimp lightly.

5 Preheat the oven to 375 degrees F.

6 To make the filling, wash and dry the berries. Sprinkle half of the berries in the bottom of the pastry-lined pan. Refrigerate the remaining berries.

7 In a small saucepan, melt the butter over low heat. Add the vanilla bean and heat gently for about 10 minutes or until the butter turns golden brown, being careful not to burn it. Immediately remove from heat. Let the butter cool until tepid.

8 In a medium-sized bowl, using an electric mixer set on high speed, whisk the eggs and sugar until pale and creamy and the batter forms a ribbon when the beaters are lifted.

9 Remove the vanilla bean from the browned butter. (Rinse, dry and set aside for future use.) Slowly pour the butter into the batter, beating on low speed, until all the butter is incorporated. Gently fold the flour into the batter, taking care not to overmix.

10 Pour the batter over the berries in the tart shell. Bake for 35 to 40 minutes, or until set. Remove the tart from the oven and set on a rack to cool.

11 Arrange remaining berries on top of the tart. Serve at room temperature.

A COCKTAIL BUFFET, SOUTHWESTERN-STYLE

*Grilled Tuna Tostada with Black Bean-Mango
Salsa and Avocado Vinaigrette*

*Spicy Chicken, Eggplant, and Grilled Red
Onion Quesadilla with Tomatillo Salsa*

*Roast Leg of Lamb with Red Chile Crust
and Jalapeño Preserves*

Sweet Potato Gratin with Chiles

*Red-Pepper Crusted Tenderloin of Beef with Wild Mushroom-
Ancho Chile Sauce and Black Bean-Goat Cheese Torta*

Blue Corn Biscotti

Maple Sugar-Crusted Apple Pie

WINE SUGGESTIONS:

Spanish Cava (sparkling wine)

California Chardonnay

Chilled Valpolicella, Barbera, or Beaujolais

(may be served throughout)

Chef Bobby Flay came to our attention quite by chance. He enrolled in one of our professional classes and then proceeded to query us about the qualifications of the teachers. Bobby was then an unknown chef at the Miracle Grill. Curious about this young man's self-assurance, we went to the Miracle Grill and found that it was, indeed, a miracle. It didn't take long for the rest of New York to discover Bobby's talents. Within three months, he was named the executive chef at the soon-to-be critically acclaimed Mesa Grill, which remains one of the hottest Southwestern restaurants in town.

Since then Bobby has come back to teach many classes at De Gustibus, each one a sellout, each one filled with fans ready to try his tantalizing dishes. We have put together a selection of his recipes to create a really great cocktail buffet for eight people. Bobby has said that no party is worth giving without the host or hostess having to spend a little time in the kitchen to let the guests feel fussed over. We have tried to make this menu as easy as possible, but we think you will still excite your guests with Chef Flay's fabulous creations.

◁ **(From left to right)** Spicy Chicken, Eggplant, and Grilled Red Onion Quesadilla with Tomatillo Salsa; Grilled Tuna Tostada with Black Bean-Mango Salsa and Avocado Vinaigrette

WHAT YOU CAN PREPARE AHEAD OF TIME

Up to 1 week ahead: Make the pastry for the Maple Sugar-Crusted Apple Pie. Wrap tightly and freeze. Thaw early on the day of the party. Make the Jalapeño Preserves. Cover tightly and refrigerate. Prepare the Red Chile Crust for the lamb. Cover tightly and freeze. Prepare the Blue Corn Biscotti. Store in an airtight container.

Up to 3 days ahead: Make the Tomatillo Salsa. Store as directed. Prepare the Chicken Stock (if making your own).

Up to 2 days ahead: Prepare the Wild Mushroom-Chile Sauce. Cover tightly and refrigerate.

The night before: Peel and slice the sweet potatoes. Wrap in damp paper towels, put in a sealed plastic bag and refrigerate. Prepare the ingredients for the Black Bean-Mango Salsa Prepare beans for the Black Bean-Goat Cheese Torta. Cover and refrigerate. Marinate the chicken for the Quesadilla.

Early in the day: Prepare the Black Bean-Mango Salsa. Cover and refrigerate. Bring to room temperature before serving. Prepare the Avocado Vinaigrette. Assemble the Sweet Potato Gratin. Cover and refrigerate until ready to cook. Add 15 minutes to the baking time. Roast the tenderloin of beef. Cool and refrigerate. Bring to room temperature before slicing. Prepare the ingredients for the Black Bean-Goat Cheese Torta. Grill the chicken and vegetables for the Quesadillas.

Up to 3 hours before the party: Assemble the Black Bean-Goat Cheese Torta. Bake the Maple-Sugar Crusted Apple Pie.

Grilled Tuna Tostada with Black Bean-Mango Salsa and Avocado Vinaigrette

SERVES 8
PREPARATION TIME: ABOUT 30 MINUTES
COOKING TIME: ABOUT 8 MINUTES

This is one of Bobby's signature dishes that offers his exciting execution of contrasts in taste, texture, and color. This vibrant dish makes a terrific appetizer.

2 one- to 1¼-pound tuna steaks, trimmed (about 2¼ pounds)
2 tablespoons vegetable oil
Salt to taste
12 four-inch freshly fried Flour Tostadas (see page 13) or store-bought tostadas
Black Bean-Mango Salsa (recipe follows)
Avocado Vinaigrette (recipe follows)
½ cup diced red bell pepper, for garnish
½ cup snipped fresh chives, for garnish

1 Prepare a charcoal or gas grill or preheat the broiler. Preheat the oven to 350 degrees F. Assemble the *mise en place* trays for this recipe.

2 Brush the tuna with the oil and season to taste with salt.

3 Lay the fish on the grill or under the broiler and cook for 1½ to 2 minutes, or just long enough to lightly color the side facing the heat. If using a grill, this should be long enough to mark that side with grill marks. Turn the fish over and cook for 2 minutes more or until the flesh is firm and opaque. (To prevent overcooking and keep the fish moist, allow no more than 5 minutes total cooking time for each ½ inch of thickness at the thickest part.) Cut the tuna into 12 equal slices.

4 Meanwhile, spread the freshly fried tostadas on paper towel-lined baking sheets. Heat them in the oven for 2 to 3 minutes.

5 Arrange the tostadas on a large serving platter. Lightly coat each one with the Black Bean Salsa. Lay a grilled tuna slice in the center. Drizzle the top of each tostada with the Avocado Vinaigrette and then drizzle it in a decorative pattern around the edge of the platter.

6 Sprinkle the bell pepper and chives around the edge of the platter. Serve immediately.

◁ BOBBY FLAY: Grilled Tuna Tostada with Black Bean-Mango Salsa and Avocado Vinaigrette

BLACK BEAN-MANGO SALSA
MAKES ABOUT 2¼ CUPS

1 cup cooked black beans or canned black beans, well drained
1 mango, peeled, seeded, and coarsely chopped (about ½ cup)
1 small red onion, diced
½ jalapeño chile, seeded and finely diced
¼ cup lightly packed, chopped fresh cilantro
¼ cup fresh lime juice
2 tablespoons olive oil
Salt and freshly ground white pepper to taste

In a medium-sized glass or ceramic bowl, combine the black beans, mango, onion, chile, cilantro, lime juice, and oil. Season to taste with salt and white pepper.

AVOCADO VINAIGRETTE
MAKES ABOUT 1½ CUPS

½ avocado, seeded
½ jalapeño chile, seeded
2 tablespoons finely chopped red onion
¼ cup fresh lime juice
1 teaspoon granulated sugar
¾ cup olive oil
Salt and freshly ground black pepper to taste

1 Scoop the flesh from the avocado. In a blender or food processor fitted with the metal blade, combine the avocado, jalapeño, onion, lime juice, and sugar. Blend or process until smooth.

2 With the motor running, slowly add the oil and process until the vinaigrette is quite thick. Season to taste with salt and pepper. Transfer to a squirt bottle or glass ceramic bowl. Cover and refrigerate until ready to use.

▶ To facilitate "painting" a design on the platter, transfer the vinaigrette to a squirt bottle such as those used for ketchup and mustard. Similar squirt bottles can be found in beauty supply stores.

Spicy Chicken, Eggplant, and Grilled Red Onion Quesadilla with Tomatillo Salsa

SERVES 8
PREPARATION TIME: ABOUT 30 MINUTES
COOKING TIME: ABOUT 20 MINUTES
MARINATING TIME: ABOUT 4 HOURS

This quesadilla can be served as a zesty appetizer, a main course for brunch or lunch, or a Sunday night supper. Its greatest appeal is that it can be prepared totally in advance and baked at the last minute.

1½ cups Chicken Stock
⅓ cup fresh lime juice
⅓ cup olive oil
3 jalapeño chiles, seeded and sliced
¼ cup chopped fresh cilantro
1 pound boneless, skinless chicken breast (1 whole breast) sliced on the diagonal into strips about 3 inches long and ¼-inch wide
12 ¼-inch-thick slices red onion
12 ¼-inch thick slices peeled eggplant
9 six- or seven-inch Flour Tortillas or store-bought flour tortillas
¾ cup grated Monterey Jack cheese
¾ cup grated white Cheddar cheese
Salt and freshly ground white pepper to taste
4 tablespoons sour cream
Tomatilla Salsa (recipe follows)

1 Assemble the *mise en place* trays for this recipe.

2 In a blender or food processor fitted with the metal blade, combine the stock, lime juice, olive oil, chiles, and cilantro. Blend until smooth.

3 Put the sliced chicken in a glass or ceramic dish and pour the chicken stock mixture over it. Cover and refrigerate for 4 hours.

4 Prepare a charcoal or gas grill or preheat the broiler. Lightly oil the grid.

5 Remove the chicken from the marinade and discard the marinade. Grill or broil the chicken for 1½ to 2 minutes per side or until cooked through. Remove from the heat and set aside.

6 Grill or broil the onion slices for 2 to 3 minutes on each side. Remove from the heat and set aside. Then grill or broil the eggplant slices for 1½ to 2 minutes on each side. Remove from the heat and set aside.

7 Preheat the oven to 350 degrees F.

8 Place 6 of the tortillas on an ungreased baking sheet and sprinkle with the cheeses. Top each one with an equal portion of chicken, 2 slices of eggplant, and 2 slices of onion. Season to taste with salt and white pepper. Stack one layered tortillas to make 3 stacks of 2 tortillas each. Top each stack with a plain tortilla.

9 Bake for 8 to 12 minutes or until the tortillas are slightly crisp and the cheeses have melted. Remove from the oven and let rest for about 2 minutes. Cut into quarters, and place a dollop of sour cream on the top of each quarter. Serve hot with the Tomatillo Salsa.

TOMATILLO SALSA
MAKES ABOUT 1⅔ CUPS

8 medium tomatillos, husked, washed, and coarsely chopped
2 tablespoons finely diced red onion
1 tablespoon minced jalapeño chile
¼ cup fresh lime juice
¼ cup chopped fresh cilantro
2 tablespoons olive oil
2 teaspoons honey
Salt and freshly ground black pepper to taste

In a glass or ceramic bowl, combine the tomatillos, onion, chile, lime juice, cilantro, olive oil, and honey. Season to taste with salt and pepper. Cover and refrigerate for at least 1 hour. Allow to come to room temperature before serving.

▷ BOBBY FLAY: Spicy Chicken, Eggplant, and Grilled Red Onion Quesadilla with Tomatillo Salsa

Roast Leg of Lamb with Red Chile Crust and Jalapeño Preserves

This is a great dish for a buffet because not only is it good served warm, it is just as tasty at room temperature. Like all the other items on this menu, the lamb makes a wonderful dinner on its own, especially when served with the Sweet Potato Gratin.

1 tablespoon pasilla chile powder
1 tablespoon toasted cumin seeds
2 tablespoons olive oil
Salt and freshly ground black pepper to taste
1 six-pound boned and tied leg of lamb
Jalapeño Preserves (recipe follows)

1 Preheat the oven to 450 degrees F. Assemble the *mise en place* trays for this recipe.

2 In a large bowl, combine the chile powder, cumin, olive oil, and salt and pepper to taste. Rub the meat on all sides with the mixture to coat. Let the meat sit for at least 30 minutes and for as long as 2 hours at cool room temperature.

3 Place the lamb on a rack in a roasting pan. Roast for 15 minutes. Reduce the oven temperature to 350 degrees F. and cook for 30 minutes more, or until a meat thermometer inserted into the center registers 145 degrees F. for rare. Transfer the lamb to a cutting board, cover loosely with aluminum foil, and let rest for about 10 minutes.

4 Slice the lamb against the grain into ¼-inch slices and arrange on a serving platter. Garnish with the Jalapeño Preserves.

JALAPEÑO PRESERVES
MAKES ABOUT 5 CUPS

3 red bell peppers, seeds and membranes removed, diced
6 jalapeño chiles, seeded and diced
4 cups granulated sugar
¼ cup red wine vinegar
¾ cup (6 ounces) liquid pectin

1 In a heavy-bottomed, non-reactive saucepan, combine the bell peppers, jalapeños, sugar, and vinegar. Bring to a boil over medium-high heat, stirring frequently to prevent sticking. Reduce the heat to low and simmer for 20 minutes, stirring every 5 minutes. Take care not to let the mixture boil over.

2 Remove from the heat and stir in the pectin. Return the pan to the heat and bring back to a boil. Immediately remove from the heat and pour into a heatproof glass or ceramic bowl. Allow to cool. Cover and refrigerate for 8 hours or overnight before serving.

▶ You can replace the jalapeños with any other hot chile.

▶ For a thicker consistency, increase the number of bell peppers and chiles by 1 or 2 peppers and chiles each.

▶ These preserves make a great hostess gift, packed in a pretty jar, labeled and tied with a ribbon. The preserves keep for up to 1 month in the refrigerator.

◁ BOBBY FLAY: Roast Leg of Lamb with Red Chile Crust and Jalapeño Preserves and Sweet Potato Gratin with Chiles

Sweet Potato Gratin with Chiles

SERVES 8
PREPARATION TIME: ABOUT 15 MINUTES
COOKING TIME: ABOUT 1 HOUR

Zanne Zakroff, executive food editor of *Gourmet* magazine, enjoyed this dish at a class so much that she has since made it part of her Thanksgiving menu. She especially loved the play of the mild sweet potatoes against the smoky flavor imparted by the chipotle chiles. I think it is much more exciting to serve than the traditional holiday potato casserole, and it's always a smash at a cocktail buffet—holiday time or not. If you'd like to go a little lighter, cut one cup of the cream; however, the volume of the sweet potatoes absorbs the richness of the full amount.

3 tablespoons unsalted butter, at room temperature
2 chipotle chiles in adobo sauce
5 cups heavy cream
9 sweet potatoes, peeled and thinly sliced (about 8 cups)
Salt and freshly ground white pepper to taste

1 Preheat the oven to 350 degrees F. Assemble the *mise en place* trays for this recipe.

2 Generously butter a shallow 4-quart casserole. Set aside.

3 In a blender or food processor fitted with the metal blade, combine the chiles and cream and blend until smooth.

4 Place a layer of sliced sweet potatoes in the casserole. Pour some chile cream over the top and season with salt and pepper. Continue layering until all the potatoes are used, ending with cream.

5 Bake for 1 hour or until the potatoes are tender and the top is lightly browned and bubbling. Serve hot or at room temperature.

Red Pepper-Crusted Tenderloin of Beef with Wild Mushroom-Ancho Chile Sauce and Black Bean-Goat Cheese Torta

SERVES 8
PREPARATION TIME: ABOUT 40 MINUTES
COOKING TIME: ABOUT 1 HOUR AND 20 MINUTES

This is Bobby's Southwestern version of the classic French steak au poivre. When he demonstrated this recipe in class, he made it in individual portions, but we have substituted a whole tenderloin—easier to serve to a buffet crowd.

6 dried New Mexico red chiles
2 tablespoons cracked black peppercorns
1 seven-pound tenderloin of beef, trimmed
1 tablespoon vegetable oil
Salt and freshly ground black pepper to taste
Wild Mushroom-Ancho Chile Sauce (recipe follows)
Black Bean-Goat Cheese Torta (recipe follows)

1 Preheat the oven to 300 degrees F. Assemble the *mise en place* trays for this recipe.

2 Spread the chiles on a rimmed baking sheet and toast in the oven for 1 minute. Remove the stems and seeds, put the cleaned chiles in a blender or food processor fitted with the metal blade and blend or process just until coarsely chopped. The chiles should be approximately the same consistency as the cracked peppercorns. Return the chiles to the baking sheet, add the cracked peppercorns and toss well.

3 Increase the oven temperature to 400 degrees F.

4 Using kitchen twine, tie the tenderloin about every 2

BOBBY FLAY: Red Pepper-Crusted Tenderloin of Beef with Wild Mushroom-Ancho Chile Sauce and Black Bean-Goat Cheese Torta

inches so that it retains its shape while cooking. Rub the tenderloin all over with the oil and season to taste with salt and pepper. Roll the tenderloin in the chile-pepper mixture on the baking sheet.

5 Heat a roasting pan in the oven for 2 minutes, or until very hot. Place the tenderloin in the center of the pan and cook for 12 minutes. Turn the tenderloin over and cook for about 12 minutes more, or until a meat thermometer inserted into the center registers 140 degrees F., for rare. Transfer the tenderloin to a cutting board. Cover loosely with aluminum foil and let rest for 10 minutes.

6 Slice the tenderloin into ⅜-inch-thick slices. Arrange the slices down the center of a serving platter. Top with the Wild Mushroom-Ancho Chile Sauce and garnish the platter with wedges of the Black Bean-Goat Cheese Torta.

▶ Kitchen twine, or any medium-weight untreated cotton thread, is another kitchen necessity. It is used not only for tying up meat and poultry, but also for bouquets garnis, soufflé collars, and many other tasks.

193

Maple Sugar-Crusted Apple Pie

There is nothing particularly Southwestern about this pie. It's just delicious and one of Bobby Flay's favorite desserts.

PIE PASTRY:

¾ cup (1½ sticks) plus 3 tablespoons unsalted butter

2 tablespoons plus 2 teaspoons solid vegetable shortening

2 to 3 teaspoons ice water

3 drops fresh lemon juice

2½ cups all-purpose flour

2 tablespoons plus 2 teaspoons maple sugar

½ teaspoon salt

FILLING:

8 or 9 tart apples, such as Granny Smith, peeled, cored, and sliced

¼ cup granulated sugar

2 teaspoons ground cinnamon

1 teaspoon freshly grated nutmeg

¼ cup cornstarch

2 tablespoons arrowroot

¼ cup maple syrup

1 large egg

2 tablespoons cold water

■ Special Equipment: 10-inch tart pan

1 Assemble the *mise en place* trays for this recipe.

2 To make the pastry, cut the butter and shortening into pea-sized pieces. Place in the freezer for 30 minutes or until frozen.

3 Combine the ice water and lemon juice. Set aside.

4 In the bowl of an electric mixer, whisk together the flour, maple sugar, and salt. With the mixer at its lowest speed, gradually add the frozen butter. Mix for about 3 minutes, or until the butter begins to break up. Add the frozen shortening and mix for 2 minutes more. Drizzle in just enough of the ice water to cause the dough to come together. Gather the dough into a ball and let it rest for 10 minutes.

5 Divide the dough in half and flatten slightly into discs. Wrap in plastic wrap and refrigerate for 30 minutes.

6 Preheat the oven to 400 degrees F.

7 To make the filling, in a large bowl, combine the apples, granulated sugar, cinnamon, nutmeg, cornstarch, and arrowroot. Genty mix in the maple syrup. Set aside.

8 Roll out half of the pastry on a lightly floured surface or between 2 sheets of plastic wrap to a circle about ⅛ inch thick and 14 inches in diameter. Line a 10-inch tart pan with the pastry so that it overhangs the edges by about 1 inch.

9 Spread the apple mixture in the pastry shell, mounding slightly in the center. Roll out the remaining pastry into a circle large enough to cover the apple filling. Lay it over the filling and roll up the edges of the pastry to make a seal. Crimp them together, trimming off any excess dough.

10 In a small bowl, beat the egg with the cold water. Brush this egg wash over the pastry. Sprinkle with half of the maple sugar. Cut a few steam vents in the top. Bake in the center of the oven for 30 minutes.

11 Reduce the oven temperature to 350 degrees F. Sprinkle the remaining maple sugar on top of the pie and bake for about 20 minutes more, or until the pastry is golden and the filling is bubbling. Serve warm.

▷ BOBBY FLAY: Maple Sugar-Crusted Apple Pie and Blue Corn Biscotti

A MIDWEEK DINNER— LIGHT, FRESH, AND FAST

Chipotle-Garbanzo Bean Dip with Blue Corn Tortilla Chips and Salsa Cruda

Seafood Seviche with Summer Greens

Achiote-Fried Catfish with Salsa Fresca

Chilled Minted Melon Soup

WINE SUGGESTIONS:

Sparkling Wine (*first course*)

Chilean Sauvignon Blanc (*second course*)

Sancerre or South African Sauvignon Blanc (*third course*)

Late Harvest Muscat or Fruity Chenin Blanc (*dessert*)

Marilyn Frobuccino first taught at De Gustibus after a two-year stint as executive chef at Arizona 206, New York's first Southwestern restaurant. Her approach to Southwestern food was somewhat different from any we had yet experienced at the school. It was as full of flavor, texture, and color as ever, but lighter and easier for the home cook to execute. Marilyn's class left us all feeling that we could go home and cook these dishes one, two, three! This menu really shines when tomatoes and melons are at summer's ripest, but it is an easy one to put together any time of the year.

WHAT YOU CAN PREPARE AHEAD OF TIME

Up to 3 days ahead: Prepare the Chipotle-Garbanzo Bean Dip. Cover and refrigerate. Bring to room temperature before serving.

The day before: Wash and dry the greens for the Seafood Seviche. Wrap separately in wet paper towels, place in a sealed plastic bag, and refrigerate.

Early in the day: The Seviche can be made in the morning, but it must be well drained after 3 hours, or it will continue to "cook" and become mushy. After draining, cover and refrigerate in a glass or ceramic bowl. Prepare the bean dip if not already made. Cover and refrigerate. Bring to room temperature before serving. Make the Chilled Minted Melon Soup. Fry the tortilla chips for the Bean Dip. Store in a dry place or tightly sealed tin. Prepare the Salsa Cruda, omitting the salt. Cover and refrigerate. Bring to room temperature before serving, and season to taste with salt. Prepare the Salsa Fresca. Prepare the seasoning and coating for the Achiote-Fried Catfish.

Up to 2 hours before the party: Season the catfish strips.

◁ Seafood Seviche with Summer Greens

Achiote-Fried Catfish with Salsa Fresca

SERVES 6
PREPARATION TIME: ABOUT 35 MINUTES
COOKING TIME: ABOUT 40 MINUTES
CHILLING TIME (CATFISH ONLY): AT LEAST 2 HOURS
CHILLING TIME (SALSA ONLY): AT LEAST 30 MINUTES

A southern tradition, catfish is frequently used in South-western and Cajun cooking as it readily takes to a variety of strong seasonings. This mild-flavored, low-fat fish is now farm-raised and available across the country.

4 to 5 six- to seven-ounce catfish fillets (about 2 pounds), cut into 18 long strips
2 tablespoons ground annatto seeds
2 tablespoons plus 2 teaspoons chile powder
2 tablespoons plus 1 teaspoon finely minced garlic
½ cup olive oil
4 large eggs
2 cups coarse-ground yellow cornmeal
1½ teaspoons ground cumin
1 tablespoon salt, or to taste
Vegetable oil, for shallow frying
Salsa Fresca (recipe follows)

■ Special Equipment: deep-fry thermometer

1 Assemble the *mise en place* trays for this recipe.

2 Rinse the catfish strips under cold running water. Pat dry with paper towels.

3 In a glass or ceramic dish, combine the ground annatto, 2 tablespoons of the chile powder, 2 tablespoons of the garlic, and the olive oil. Add the catfish strips and rub the mixture over the fish. Cover and refrigerate for up to 2 hours.

4 Preheat the oven to 200 degrees F.

5 In a shallow bowl, lightly beat the eggs. In another shallow bowl, combine the cornmeal, cumin, salt, and the remaining 2 teaspoons chile powder and 1 teaspoon garlic.

6 One at a time, dip the seasoned catfish strips into the beaten egg, coating well. Then dip into the cornmeal mixture, making sure all sides are well coated. Place the strips on a wire rack.

7 Heat about ½ inch of vegetable oil in a large skillet over medium-high heat to 375 degrees F. on a deep-fry ther-

◁ MARILYN FROBUCCINO: Achiote-Fried Catfish with Salsa Fresca

mometer. Fry the catfish strips, 3 at a time, turning once, for about 6 minutes, or until golden. Drain on paper towels. Put the cooked strips on a wire rack and keep warm in the oven until all strips are cooked.

8 Arrange 3 strips of catfish on each serving plate and spoon the Salsa Fresca on the side. Serve immediately.

SALSA FRESCA
MAKES ABOUT 2 CUPS

1 large, very ripe pineapple, peeled, halved, and cored
¼ cup plus 3 tablespoons extra virgin olive oil
¼ cup fresh lime juice
1 tablespoon jalapeño-flavored vinegar
1 pickled jalapeño chile, seeded and minced
Salt to taste

1 Roughly chop half of the pineapple using a large, sharp knife or a food processor and set aside. Cut the remaining pineapple crosswise into ¼-inch slices. Generously coat the pineapple slices with 3 tablespoons of the oil.

2 Heat a cast-iron skillet over medium-high heat until very hot and smoking. Place the pineapple slices in the skillet and, turning once, sauté for about 2 minutes, or until pineapple darkens. Transfer to paper towels and allow to cool.

3 Meanwhile, put the chopped pineapple in a blender or food processor fitted with the metal blade, and blend or process until thick and smooth. Add the remaining ¼ cup of olive oil and, using 3 to 4 on/off pulses, process until the mixture begins to emulsify. With the machine running, slowly add the lime juice and jalapeño vinegar in a steady stream. Process just to incorporate. Transfer the mixture to a glass or ceramic bowl.

4 Cut the cooked pineapple into ¼-inch pieces. Stir into the pureed pineapple, along with the jalapeños. Season to taste with salt, if necessary. Cover and refrigerate for at least 30 minutes before serving.

Chilled Minted Melon Soup

SERVES 6
PREPARATION TIME: ABOUT 20 MINUTES
CHILLING TIME: AT LEAST 2 HOURS

This dessert soup is immensely refreshing. Made with very ripe melons, it is light, sweet, and the perfect ending to a zesty meal. This soup also serves as a great first course, particularly with the addition of the jalapeño. If you make this in a blender, you will have to do so in batches.

1 five- to six-pound very ripe Crenshaw melon, peeled, seeded, and cubed

1 five- to six-pound very ripe honeydew melon, peeled, seeded, and cubed

3 tablespoons fresh lime juice

2 tablespoons serrano-flavored vinegar

1 tablespoon minced seeded pickled jalapeño (optional)

3 tablespoons chopped fresh cilantro

3 tablespoons chopped fresh mint

¼ teaspoon ground cinnamon

¼ teaspoon freshly grated nutmeg

6 sprigs fresh mint

1 Assemble the *mise en place* trays for this recipe.

2 Put the melon cubes in a food processor fitted with the metal blade, or a blender. Add the lime juice, vinegar, jalapeño, if using, the cilantro, chopped mint, cinnamon, and nutmeg. Process or blend for 30 to 45 seconds, or until smooth, adding about 2 tablespoons of cold water if necessary to thin to a soupy consistency.

3 Transfer to a glass or ceramic bowl. Cover and refrigerate for at least 2 hours to allow the flavors to develop.

4 Serve in chilled soup bowls, garnished with the fresh mint sprigs.

◁ MARILYN FROBUCCINO: **Chilled Minted Melon Soup**

A CELEBRATORY DINNER FOR NEW YEAR'S EVE

Smoked Salmon Quesadillas

Sea Scallops with Potato Cakes and Sherry-Vinegar Dressing

Roast Rack of Veal with Parsnip Puree and Chipotle Beurre Blanc

Chocolate Walnut Tarte

WINE SUGGESTIONS:

Full-bodied vintage Champagne:
Taittinger Brut Millesiné (*served throughout*)

WHAT YOU CAN PREPARE AHEAD OF TIME

Up to 1 week ahead: Make the pastry for the Chocolate Walnut Tarte. Wrap tightly and freeze. Thaw at least 1 hour before preparing the tarte.

Early in the day: Make the horse-radish cream for the Smoked Salmon Quesadillas. Cover and refrigerate. Bring to room temperature before using. Wash, trim, and dry all the herbs and greens. Wrap separately, in wet paper towels, place in a sealed plastic bag and refrigerate. Make the vinaigrette for the Potato Cakes. Prepare the Potato Cakes up to cooking. Cover and refrigerate. Prepare the Parsnip Puree. Cool, cover, and refrigerate. Reheat in the top half of double boiler before serving. Bake the tart shell for the Chocolate Walnut Tarte.

In the afternoon: Complete the Walnut Tarte up to 3 hours in advance. Cook the Potato Cakes up to 1 hour before serving. Keep warm in a preheated 350 degree F. oven. (These are best when made right before serving.)

I first met Vincent Guerithault in his adopted home state of Arizona. After working as a chef in cold and wintry Chicago, Vincent yearned for the sunny flavors and warmth of his boyhood in the South of France. During his travels in the United States, he had discovered Arizona. He also "discovered" the unfamiliar ingredients of the foods of the Southwest and immediately got hooked. Teamed with his classical French training, these ingredients offered a whole new way to interpret the traditional recipes he knew so well.

Vincent came to De Gustibus when he arranged a press trip to introduce cynical New Yorkers to his passion: cooking in the classical French manner using the whole range of Southwestern ingredients. We all got hooked on Vincent's new-found style of cooking and on his outgoing personality!

When Vincent joined us at De Gustibus, his fervor excited the classroom. His refined style and use of up-to-the-minute ingredients were all designed to work for the home cook. He made us want to review the classic French recipes—and then be adventurous in adapting them to our favorite flavors.

The menu that Vincent devised for this festive dinner is extravagant yet perfect for a quiet New Year's Eve with good friends, or those times when you want to display how much you care. Much of the prep work for the dinner can be done well in advance, with only a few last-minute cooking requirements for each of the dishes.

◁ Chocolate Walnut Tarte

Smoked Salmon Quesadillas

This is Vincent's innovative way of pairing succulent yet conventional smoked salmon with the bread of the Southwest. This recipe can easily be doubled or tripled. Traditionally, quesadillas are folded tortillas. Vincent plays with the concept by serving them unfolded.

2 ounces mild goat cheese
1 tablespoon grated fresh horseradish or well-drained prepared horseradish
1 tablespoon sour cream
1 tablespoon plus 1 teaspoon chopped fresh dill
Salt to taste (optional)
Freshly ground white pepper to taste
3 tablespoons extra-virgin olive oil
3 seven- or eight-inch fresh flour tortillas or store-bought flour tortillas
6 thin slices smoked salmon (about 4 ounces)
1 tablespoon fresh lemon juice

1 Assemble the *mise en place* trays for this recipe.

2 In a small bowl, combine the goat cheese, horseradish, sour cream, 1 teaspoon of the chopped dill, salt, if desired, and white pepper to taste. Beat with a wooden spoon until smooth and well blended. Set aside.

3 In a small skillet, heat the oil over medium-high heat for 1 minute. Fry the tortillas, one at a time, turning once, for 2 minutes, or until lightly browned. Drain on paper towels.

4 Spread about 2 generous teaspoons of the horseradish cream on each tortilla. Arrange the smoked salmon over the cheese. Sprinkle with the remaining chopped dill and drizzle with the lemon juice.

5 Cut each tortilla into 6 wedges and serve immediately.

Sea Scallops with Potato Cakes and Sherry-Vinegar Dressing

On its own, this appetizer can become a quick mid-week supper for two or three when served with a crisp green salad.

DRESSING:
3 teaspoons sherry vinegar
1½ teaspoons honey
3 tablespoons extra-virgin olive oil

POTATO CAKES:
3 baking potatoes, peeled and cut into ½-inch chunks
1½ tablespoons unsalted butter
2 tablespoons plus 2 teaspoons extra-virgin olive oil
2 tablespoons chopped fresh cilantro
Salt and freshly ground black pepper to taste

SEA SCALLOPS:
6 large sea scallops, about 2 inches in diameter
1 tablespoon olive oil
1 head frisée (curly endive), trimmed, washed, and dried

1 Assemble the *mise en place* trays for this recipe.

2 To make the dressing, whisk the vinegar and honey together in a glass or ceramic bowl. Slowly add the olive oil, whisking until thick and emulsified. Set aside.

3 Preheat the oven to 350 degrees F.

4 To make the potato cakes, in a large saucepan, cover the potatoes by several inches with salted, cold water and bring to a boil over high heat. Boil for 20 minutes, or until tender when pierced with a fork. Drain well. Put the potatoes in a medium-sized bowl and add the butter and 2 table-spoons of the olive oil. Mash with a fork or potato masher until smooth. Stir in cilantro, salt and pepper to taste, and mix well. Divide the mixture into 12 equal portions and form each into a patty about 3 inches in diameter.

5 Heat a nonstick griddle over medium-high heat. Brush

◁ VINCENT GUERITHAULT: Smoked Salmon Quesadillas

209

VINCENT GUERITHAULT: Sea Scallops with Potato Cakes and Sherry-Vinegar Dressing

the griddle with 1 teaspoon of oil. Place 4 to 6 of the potato patties on the griddle and cook, turning once, for 6 minutes, or until golden brown. Transfer to a wire rack set on a baking sheet and keep warm in the oven. Cook the remaining potato patties in the same way, brushing the griddle with a teaspoon of the oil before cooking the next batch. Keep warm.

6 To prepare the scallops, brush them with the olive oil. Heat a nonstick skillet over medium-high heat. Add the scallops and sauté, turning once, for 3 to 5 minutes, or until firm and opaque. Drain on paper towels.

7 Arrange the frisée on serving plates. Arrange 2 potato cakes so that they overlap slightly in the center of each plate. Place a scallop on top, drizzle with the Sherry-Vinegar Dressing and serve immediately.

▶ Keep olive oil in a spray bottle and use it to spray skillets when sautéing. You will use much less oil than when you pour it directly into or even brush it onto the pan.

▶ If holding the potato cakes for longer than 1 hour, reduce the oven temperature to 300 degrees F. to prevent them from drying out.

Roast Rack of Veal with Parsnip Puree and Chipotle Beurre Blanc

SERVES 6
PREPARATION TIME: ABOUT 30 MINUTES
COOKING TIME: ABOUT 1 HOUR AND 30 MINUTES

Rack of veal is a truly spectacular cut of meat, perfect for special occasions. The beurre blanc adds a bit of smoky taste and a tinge of amber color to the mellow, juicy meat.

RACK OF VEAL:

1 four-pound rack of veal
Salt and freshly ground black pepper to taste
1 tablespoon extra-virgin olive oil

PARSNIP PUREE:

2 pounds parsnips, peeled and cut into 1-inch pieces
1½ cups heavy cream
2 tablespoons unsalted butter, softened
Salt and freshly ground black pepper

CHIPOTLE BEURRE BLANC:

2 chipotle chiles in adobo, well drained
1 cup dry white wine
1 cup white wine vinegar
1 tablespoon minced shallots
1 cup (2 sticks) unsalted butter, softened

■ Special Equipment: steamer; meat thermometer or instant-read thermometer; double boiler

1 Preheat the oven to 350 degrees F. Assemble the *mise en place* trays for this recipe.

2 Wipe the veal rack with a paper towel and season with salt and pepper to taste.

3 In an ovenproof skillet or roasting pan, heat the oil over medium-high heat until almost smoking. Add the veal and sear the meat on all sides for 4 to 6 minutes, or until well browned.

4 Roast the veal, rib side down, for 1½ hours, or until a meat thermometer or instant-read thermometer registers 150 degrees F. when inserted into the center. Transfer to a cutting board, cover loosely with aluminum foil and allow to rest for 15 minutes before slicing.

5 Meanwhile, to make the parsnip puree, steam the parsnips in a covered steamer basket set over boiling water for 20 minutes, or until tender when pierced with a fork. Transfer the parsnips to a blender or food processor fitted with the metal blade.

6 In a small saucepan, heat the cream over medium heat until small bubbles begin to appear around the edges. Do not boil. Add to the parsnips. Add the butter and salt and pepper to taste, and blend or process for 15 to 20 seconds until smooth. Transfer the puree to the top half of a double boiler over simmering water. Cover and keep warm.

7 To make the beurre blanc, put the chipotles in a blender or food processor fitted with the metal blade and blend or process until smooth.

8 In a small, heavy, nonreactive saucepan, bring the wine, wine vinegar, and shallots to a boil over medium heat. Reduce the heat to low and simmer, uncovered, for 20 to 30 minutes, or until the liquid has evaporated. Whisking vigorously, add the butter, 2 tablespoons at time, making each addition just before the previous one has been totally incorporated. When all the butter has been incorporated, whisk in the chipotle puree. Remove from the heat, cover and keep warm.

9 Slice the veal into chops. Place a mound of parsnip puree in the center of each warm dinner plate. Arrange one or two chops on top. Spoon the Chipotle Beurre Blanc over the meat. Serve immediately.

▶ Because it usually has to be special-ordered from the butcher, replace the rack of veal with a more economical rolled veal roast weighing about 3½ pounds, if you prefer.

▶ If you have difficulty pureeing the small amount of chipotle chiles in the blender or food processor, chop them very fine with a sharp knife.

Chocolate Walnut Tarte

SERVES 6
PREPARATION TIME: ABOUT 30 MINUTES
BAKING TIME: ABOUT 25 MINUTES
CHILLING TIME (PASTRY ONLY): ABOUT 2 HOURS AND 30 MINUTES

When Vincent Guerithault made this dessert in class, we could hardly keep the audience in its seats. Chef Vincent suggests serving this tart with a scoop each of banana and chocolate ice cream drizzled with chocolate sauce. Talk about a sweet death!

TART PASTRY:

1 cup all-purpose flour
1 teaspoon granulated sugar
8 tablespoons (1 stick) unsalted butter, chilled and cut into pieces
2 to 3 tablespoons ice water

FILLING:

1½ cups semisweet chocolate chips
1½ ounces semisweet chocolate, chopped
1 cup walnut halves
1 tablespoon plus 1 teaspoon dark rum
2 teaspoons pure vanilla extract
2 tablespoons unsalted butter
½ cup dark brown sugar
1 large egg, lightly beaten
4 firm bananas

■ Special Equipment: 10-inch tart pan with removable bottom; pie weights or dried beans, peas, or rice

1 Assemble the *mise en place* trays for this recipe.

2 To make the pastry, in a medium-sized bowl, combine the flour and sugar. With your fingertips or a pastry blender, quickly blend in the butter, a few pieces at time, until the mixture resembles coarse meal. Add the water, a tablespoon at time, and quickly blend with your hands to form a soft dough. Do not overmix, or the pastry will be tough. You may need additional water, but take care not to allow the dough to get sticky. Roll the pastry into a ball and flatten slightly. Wrap in plastic wrap and refrigerate for at least 2 hours.

3 To make the tart, roll out the pastry on a lightly floured surface or between 2 sheets of plastic wrap to a circle about 14 inches in diameter and ⅛ inch thick. Line a 10-inch tart pan with the pastry so that it overhangs the edges by about 1 inch. Trim the edges and crimp lightly. Prick the bottom of the pastry with a fork. Refrigerate for at least 30 minutes.

4 Preheat the oven to 450 degrees F.

5 Line the pastry with lightly buttered parchment paper or aluminum foil, buttered side down. Fill with pie weights, dried beans, or rice. Bake about 15 minutes or until the edges of the pastry are golden and the bottom is set. Remove the weights and parchment and return the tart shell to the oven for 3 to 4 minutes until lightly browned. Cool completely on a wire rack before filling. (Leave the oven on.)

6 To make the filling, in a medium-sized bowl, combine the chocolate chips, chopped chocolate, walnuts, rum, and vanilla extract. Set aside.

7 In a small saucepan, melt the butter and sugar over medium heat, stirring frequently. Bring the mixture just to a boil. Remove from the heat and pour over chocolate mixture, stirring continously until smooth and cooled slightly.

8 Mix in the egg, stirring until incorporated.

9 Peel and slice the bananas and arrange them evenly in the baked tart shell. Spoon the chocolate mixture over the bananas, forming a slight mound in the center. Bake for about 4 minutes, or until the top is slightly crumbly. Do not overbake. Allow to cool completely on a wire rack before serving.

▶ **Be sure to let the chocolate mixture cool slightly before stirring in the egg to prevent the egg from "cooking."**

◁ VINCENT GUERITHAULT: **Roast Rack of Veal with Parsnip Puree and Chipotle Beurre Blanc**

AN END-OF-SUMMER SOUTHWESTERN DINNER

*Red Snapper with Mexican Oregano Pesto Sauce
and Jícama-Melon Relish*

*Chipotle Lamb Chops with Creamed Corn Pudding
and Three Tomato Salsas*

*Cranberry-Mango Cobbler
with Cinnamon-Pecan Cream*

WINE SUGGESTIONS:

Sauvignon Blanc (*first course*)

Merlot (*second course*)

Muscat de Beaumes-de-Venise (*dessert*)

WHAT YOU CAN PREPARE AHEAD OF TIME

Up to 1 week ahead: Make the Mexican Oregano Pesto. Store in tightly sealed jar and refrigerate. Make the Fish Stock (if making your own).

The day before: Scrape the corn kernels from the cobs for the Creamed Corn Pudding. Store in covered container and refrigerate.

Early in the day: Prepare the Jícama-Melon Relish. Prepare the three different salsas. Cover and refrigerate. Bring to room temperature before serving. Bake the Cranberry-Mango Cobbler. Reheat in a preheated 300 degree F. oven for 15 minutes before serving. Store loosely covered in a cool place. Prepare the Cinnamon-Pecan Cream. Cover and refrigerate.

Up to 2 hours before the party: Make the chile sauce for the lamb chops up to the point of adding the butter.

1 hour before the party: Make the butter sauce for the snapper. Keep warm in a double boiler over gently simmering water.

Just before the party: Reheat the chile sauce for the lamb chops. Incorporate the butter as instructed in the recipe. Keep warm over gently simmering water. Measure and assemble the ingredients for the Creamed Corn Pudding.

While organizing cooking classes in Dallas, Texas, a number of years ago, I had the good fortune to eat at two of the most acclaimed restaurants in the city at that time: Routh Street Cafe and Baby Routh. I was immediately struck by the creativity of Stephan Pyles, the chef at both. He brought together a startling combination of ingredients and mixed them with techniques of cooking and presentation that had helped turn Dallas into a food mecca. We enticed Stephan east for teaching demonstration classes at De Gustibus. We quickly found that he was not only a great chef but also a passionate and dedicated teacher more than willing to share his culinary expertise with his students.

The menu he presents here is, in many ways, as elaborate and complicated as the most exalted French meal, but with a very definite Southwestern flair. Color and flavor are dependent on the lushness and succulence of the end-of-summer tomatoes, corn, peppers, and melons. The lamb chops are only heightened by outdoor grilling. What a great way to celebrate Labor Day—or any late-summer weekend!

As delicious as the meal is when served in its entirety, each course can stand on its own so that you can create your own menu if you have less time than this one demands.

◁ **Chipotle Lamb Chops with Creamed Corn Pudding and Three Tomato Salsas**

Red Snapper with Mexican Oregano Pesto Sauce and Jícama-Melon Relish

Mexican oregano (found in Hispanic markets), with a somewhat sharper flavor than the traditional Mediterranean oregano, perfectly complements the mild fish.

SAUCE:

⅔ cup Fish Stock
⅓ cup dry white wine
2 tablespoons white wine vinegar
1 tablespoon minced shallots
1 sprig fresh parsley
½ cup heavy cream
1 cup (2 sticks) unsalted butter, softened
1 tablespoon Mexican Oregano Pesto (recipe follows)
1 teaspoon fresh lime juice
Salt and freshly ground white pepper to taste

SNAPPER:

6 seven-to-eight-ounce red snapper fillets, rinsed and patted dry
Salt and freshly ground black pepper to taste
1 cup all-purpose flour
Vegetable oil for shallow frying
Jícama-Melon Relish (recipe follows)

1 Assemble the *mise en place* trays for this recipe.

2 To make the sauce, in a medium-sized saucepan, combine the stock, wine, vinegar, shallots, and parsley. Bring to a boil over medium heat and cook for about 10 minutes or until the liquid is reduced to 2 tablespoons. Add the cream and boil for 4 to 5 minutes longer, until reduced by one third.

3 Remove the pan from the heat and whisk in 2 tablespoons of the butter. Return the pan to very low heat and whisk in the remaining butter, a tablespoon at a time. Do not add the next tablespoon of butter until the one before it is incorporated. If drops of melted butter appear on the surface, remove the pan from the heat and whisk to reincorporate the butter. Then return to the heat and continue adding the butter.

4 Strain the sauce through a fine sieve into the top half of a double boiler. Whisk in the pesto and lime juice. Season to taste with salt and white pepper. Set over gently simmering water and keep warm until ready to serve. (You should have about 1½ cups of sauce.)

5 To prepare the fish, season the fillets with salt and pepper to taste. Place the flour in a shallow bowl and lay the fillets in it, one at a time, turning to coat on both sides. Shake off the excess flour.

6 Heat about ½ inch of vegetable oil in a large skillet over medium heat. When the oil is hot, add the fish fillets and cook, turning once, for about 5 minutes, or until golden. Do not crowd the pan; fry the fish in batches if necessary.

7 Drain the fish fillets on paper towels. Place on plates, spoon a little of the sauce around the fish and garnish with Jícama-Melon Relish. Serve immediately.

MEXICAN OREGANO PESTO
MAKES ABOUT 1 CUP

1 cup tightly packed fresh Mexican oregano leaves
2 teaspoons toasted pine nuts
1 clove garlic
¼ cup olive oil

In a blender or food processor fitted with the metal blade, combine the oregano, nuts, and garlic. Blend or process, using quick on/off pulses, until minced. With the motor running, slowly add the oil, processing until smooth. Transfer the pesto to a glass or ceramic bowl. Cover and refrigerate. Bring to room temperature before using.

▶ **Store leftover pesto in the refrigerator in a tightly sealed glass jar or bowl for up to 2 weeks. Use it to flavor mayonnaise-based salad dressings, vinaigrettes, and pasta dishes.**

▶ **If you can't find Mexican oregano use any fresh oregano available**

▷ STEPHAN PYLES: Red Snapper with Mexican Oregano Pesto Sauce and Jícama-Melon Relish

RED TOMATO SALSA
MAKES ABOUT 1½ CUPS

4 small, ripe tomatoes, cored, seeded, and cut into ¼-inch dice
2 cloves garlic, roasted, peeled and mashed
⅓ cup finely diced red onion
2 tablespoons finely diced red bell pepper
1 teaspoon fresh lime juice
Salt to taste

Put the tomatoes in a medium-sized glass or ceramic bowl. Stir in the garlic, onion, pepper, and lime juice. Season to taste with salt. Let stand for at least 30 minutes before serving.

YELLOW TOMATO SALSA
MAKES ABOUT 2 CUPS

4 small yellow tomatoes or 1½ to 2 cups yellow cherry tomatoes, cored, seeded, and cut into ¼-inch dice
2 serrano chiles, seeded and finely diced
3 tablespoons finely diced mango
2 tablespoons finely diced yellow bell pepper
2 to 3 teaspoons fresh orange juice
Salt to taste

In a medium-sized glass or ceramic bowl, combine the tomatoes, chiles, mango, bell pepper, and 2 teaspoons of orange juice. Season to taste with salt. Add more juice, if necessary. Let stand for at least 30 minutes before serving.

Cranberry-Mango Cobbler with Cinnamon-Pecan Cream

SERVES 6
PREPARATION TIME: ABOUT 30 MINUTES
BAKING TIME: ABOUT 1 HOUR
INFUSING AND COOKING TIME (CINNAMON-PECAN CREAM ONLY): ABOUT 50 MINUTES

If the end of summer is too early for the usual fall arrival of cranberries, check the freezer section of the supermarket, where cranberries are available all year long.

CRUMB TOPPING:

1 cup all-purpose flour
½ cup granulated sugar
½ cup packed light brown sugar
⅛ teaspoon freshly grated nutmeg
8 tablespoons (1 stick) cold, unsalted butter, cut into ½-inch pieces

COBBLER:

4 cups fresh or frozen cranberries, washed
1 cup plus ⅓ cup granulated sugar
2 cups all-purpose flour
2 teaspoons baking soda
½ teaspoon salt
1 cup (2 sticks) unsalted butter
1 large egg, lightly beaten
1 cup buttermilk
3 ripe mangoes, peeled, seeded, and diced (about 3½ cups)
Cinnamon-Pecan Cream (recipe follows)

■ Special Equipment: candy thermometer

1 Preheat the oven to 350 degrees F. Butter and flour a 9 x 12 x 2-inch baking dish. Assemble the *mise en place* trays for this recipe.

2 To make the crumb topping, in a medium-sized bowl, combine the flour, granulated sugar, brown sugar, and nutmeg. With your fingers or a pastry blender, quickly blend in the butter until the mixture resembles coarse meal. Set aside.

3 To make the cobbler, in a bowl, combine the cranberries with 1 cup of the granulated sugar and set aside.

4 Sift together the flour, baking soda, and salt. Set aside.

5 In the bowl of an electric mixer, beat the butter and the remaining ⅓ cup sugar at high speed until light and fluffy. Beat in the beaten egg. Finally, stir in the flour mixture and the buttermilk, alternating the dry and liquid ingredients.

6 Spoon the batter into the prepared baking dish and smooth the top.

7 Gently toss the mangoes with the cranberries and spoon the fruit over the batter in an even layer. Sprinkle the reserved crumb topping over the fruit. Bake for 1 hour, or

until the topping is crisp and light brown and the center is cooked through.

8 Remove the cobbler from the oven and allow to set for 10 minutes. Cut into squares and serve with the Cinnamon-Pecan Cream.

CINNAMON-PECAN CREAM
MAKES ABOUT 3 CUPS

2 cups milk
1 vanilla bean, split lengthwise
1 cup chopped toasted pecans
2 cinnamon sticks
6 large egg yolks
2/3 cup granulated sugar
2/3 cup heavy cream, whipped to soft peaks

1 In a large saucepan, combine the milk, vanilla bean, pecans, and cinnamon sticks. Bring to a boil over medium-high heat. Remove from the heat and set aside for 30 minutes to infuse.

2 In a large bowl, using an electric mixer set on high speed, beat the egg yolks and sugar until thick and pale.

3 Return the milk to the heat and bring to a boil. Strain through a fine sieve into the egg mixture, stirring constantly. Return the mixture to the pan and place over simmering water. Cook, stirring frequently, for about 20 minutes, or until the custard has thickened and a candy thermometer inserted into the center registers 180 degrees F.

4 Fill a very large bowl or pan with ice cubes. Set the pan of custard in the ice and stir in the whipped cream just until mixed. Allow to cool then pour into a bowl, cover and refrigerate until ready to serve.

STEPHAN PYLES: **Cranberry-Mango Cobbler with Cinnamon-Pecan Cream**

AN ELEGANT FALL DINNER, SOUTHWESTERN-STYLE

Chanterelles with Blue Corn Chips

Escalope of Salmon with Pepper-Ginger Medley

Grilled Beef Tenderloin with Tomatillo Sauce and Blue Corn Crêpes

Passion Fruit Ice Cream with Raspberry Puree and White Chocolate Sauce

WINE SUGGESTIONS:

Champagne or Sparkling Wine (*first course*)

Dry Riesling, Alsatian or German (*second course*)

Zinfandel or California Rhône-Style Wine (*third course*)

J immy Schmidt became a chef when he found himself enamored with the variety of colors and textures in the food combinations available throughout the United States. He is particularly fascinated by the flavors of foods served at the peak of their seasonality. This menu takes some time and effort to prepare, but many of the recipes can be done in stages—and the results will be well worth your work. This dinner really looks like fall, with the many hues of the ingredients reminiscent of the leaves changing into their autumnal glory.

WHAT YOU CAN PREPARE AHEAD OF TIME

One week ahead: Make the ginger sauce for the salmon. Cover and refrigerate. Make the Achiote Paste. Prepare the Blue Corn Crêpes and layer between pieces of wax paper. Wrap tightly in aluminum foil and freeze. To reheat, place on a baking sheet in a preheated 325 degree F. oven for 30 minutes. Make the Beef Stock. Make the Fish Stock.

Up to 2 days ahead: Make the Blue Corn Tortillas for the chips. Wrap in plastic wrap and refrigerate. Make the Passion Fruit Ice Cream. Make the Raspberry Puree. Cover and refrigerate.

Early in the day: Prepare the vegetables, herbs, and greens as instructed in the recipes. Make the White Chocolate Sauce.

In the afternoon: Chop the herbs. Prepare the cheese mixture for the Chanterelles with Blue Corn Chips. Cover and refrigerate. Bring to room temperature before using. Fry the Blue Corn Tortilla Chips.

Up to 2 hours before the party: If not already made, make the ginger sauce for the salmon. Keep warm. Marinate the salmon. Bring to room temperature before cooking.

◁ Chanterelles with Blue Corn Chips

Chanterelles with Blue Corn Chips

These have got to be the world's most elegant nachos! With these as hors d'oeuvres and a glass of bubbly, you are on your way to a great party.

½ cup sour cream
¼ cup mild goat cheese, such as a Bucheron
Tabasco to taste
4 tablespoons unsalted butter
2 cups trimmed and cleaned chanterelles
24 fresh blue corn tortilla chips (see page 13) or store-bought, unsalted blue corn chips
¼ cup chopped fresh mint
¼ cup snipped fresh chives

1 Preheat the oven to 400 degrees F. Assemble the *mise en place* trays for this recipe.

2 In a bowl, beat the sour cream and goat cheese until smooth. Season to taste with Tabasco. Set aside.

3 In a large skillet, melt the butter over high heat. Add the chanterelles and sauté for about 3 minutes, or until golden. Drain on paper towels and keep warm.

4 Spread the corn chips on an ungreased baking sheet. Generously spread the sour cream mixture on each chip. Bake on the lower rack of the oven for about 4 minutes, or until hot.

5 Sprinkle the chips with the mint and chives. Top with the chanterelles and serve immediately.

▶ **Always cook chanterelles quickly over high heat, or they will toughen. Substitute any cultivated "wild" mushrooms for the chanterelles if you cannot find them in the market.**

Escalope of Salmon with Pepper-Ginger Medley

The mildly spicy, marinated salmon resting on a bed of crisp greens, with its slightly acidic sauce, is a zinging rendition of the traditionally sedate fish course.

1½ cups chopped fresh ginger
½ cup fresh lemon juice
2 tablespoons granulated sugar
2 cups water
12 three-ounce salmon fillets, trimmed of dark flesh
⅓ cup Achiote Paste
2 tablespoons olive oil
½ cup finely julienned chayote squash (about ½ chayote)
1½ cups fish stock
1½ cups Chardonnay or other dry white wine
1½ cups heavy cream
1 red bell pepper, seeds and membranes removed, cut into fine julienne
1 yellow bell pepper, seeds and membranes removed, cut into fine julienne
Salt and freshly ground black pepper to taste
Juice of 1 lime
1 poblano chile, roasted , peeled, seeded and diced
2 heads frisée (curly endive), trimmed, washed and dried
⅓ cup chopped fresh Italian parsley

1 Assemble the *mise en place* trays for this recipe.

2 In a small saucepan, combine the ginger, lemon juice, sugar, and water. Bring to a boil over high heat. Reduce the heat and simmer, partially covered, for about 30 minutes, until slightly thickened. Transfer the mixture to a blender or food processor fitted with the metal blade. Blend or process until smooth. Strain through a fine sieve into a glass or ceramic bowl and discard the solids. Set aside.

▷ JIMMY SCHMIDT: Escalope of Salmon with Pepper-Ginger Medley

Passion Fruit Ice Cream with Raspberry Puree and White Chocolate Sauce

SERVES 6
PREPARATION TIME: ABOUT 25 MINUTES
CHILLING AND FREEZING TIME: ABOUT 10 HOURS

This dessert is a true indulgence with the tropical perfume of the passion fruit enhanced by the rich white chocolate sauce and delicate raspberry puree—certainly an exotic end to a most cosmopolitan meal.

ICE CREAM:

2½ cups passion fruit puree
½ cup granulated sugar
8 large egg yolks
1 teaspoon pure vanilla extract
⅛ teaspoon salt
2 cups heavy cream

RASPBERRY PUREE:

1 pint fresh raspberries

SAUCE:

1 cup half-and-half
1 tablespoon chopped cassia buds (or 2 three-inch cinnamon sticks, broken into pieces)
3 large egg yolks
2 tablespoons granulated sugar
1 teaspoon pure vanilla extract
⅛ teaspoon salt
5 ounces white chocolate, finely chopped
½ cup heavy cream
6 sprigs fresh mint

■ **Special Equipment: ice cream maker**

1 Assemble the *mise en place* trays for this recipe.

2 To make the ice cream, in a medium-sized saucepan, combine the passion fruit puree, sugar, egg yolks, vanilla extract, and salt. Cook over medium-low heat, stirring continuously, for 10 minutes, or until the mixture is thick enough to coat the back of a spoon. Do not allow to boil.

3 Remove from the heat and add the cream. Strain through a fine sieve into a bowl. Cool until tepid, cover and refrigerate for at least 2 hours until cold.

4 Pour the passion fruit mixture into an ice cream maker and process according to the manufacturer's directions. When frozen, scrape into a freezer container with a lid,

cover, and freeze for at least 8 hours for a firm texture.

5 To make the raspberry puree, put the berries in a blender or food processor fitted with the metal blade. Puree and strain through a fine sieve into a small bowl. Cover and refrigerate.

6 To make the white chocolate sauce, heat the half-and-half in a small saucepan over medium heat until bubbles form around the edges. Do not boil. Remove from the heat and add the cassia. Allow to cool.

7 In a bowl, whisk together the egg yolks, sugar, vanilla, and salt.

8 Strain the half-and-half, return it to the saucepan and heat again until bubbles form around the edges. Remove from the heat and whisk a few tablespoons into the egg mixture. Add the rest of the hot half-and-half to the egg mixture, whisking continuously. Transfer the mixture to the saucepan and cook over medium heat for about 5 minutes, or until thick enough to coat the back of a spoon. Do not boil.

9 Remove the pan from the heat, add the chopped chocolate, and stir continuously until melted. Stir in the cream, and strain through a fine sieve into a bowl. Cool until tepid, cover and refrigerate until ready to use.

10 To serve, spoon a little of the sauce into the center of each of 6 small dessert plates or shallow bowls. Drizzle with the raspberry puree. Place a scoop of ice cream in the center of the sauce. Garnish with the mint sprigs and serve immediately.

▶ **Passion fruit puree is available in the frozen food section of specialty food stores. It is also sold through restaurant supply companies. According to Chef Schmidt, one fresh passion fruit will yield only about 2 tablespoons of puree, so the frozen is the most economical.**

▶ **Leftover white chocolate sauce will keep in a tightly sealed jar in the refrigerator for up to 2 days. Leftover ice cream will keep in the freezer for up to 2 weeks.**

▷ JIMMY SCHMIDT: Passion Fruit Ice Cream with Raspberry Puree and White Chocolate Sauce

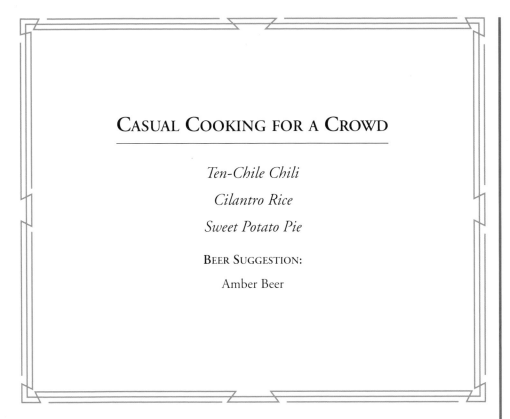

CASUAL COOKING FOR A CROWD

Ten-Chile Chili

Cilantro Rice

Sweet Potato Pie

BEER SUGGESTION:

Amber Beer

WHAT YOU CAN PREPARE AHEAD OF TIME

Up to 1 week ahead: Make the Beef or Chicken Stock. Make the Chili. Cool, transfer to a freezer container, cover well and freeze. Partially thaw at room temperature, and then gently reheat in a large Dutch oven. Prepare the pie shell and freeze.

Up to 3 days ahead: If not already made, make the Chili. Cool, cover, and refrigerate.

Early in the day: Dice the peppers for the Cilantro Rice. Cover and refrigerate. Prepare the puree for the Sweet Potato Pie. Bake the pie shell.

In the afternoon: Cook the Cilantro Rice. Cover and let stand at room temperature. Bake the Sweet Potato Pie.

B rendan Walsh was the pioneer of Southwestern cooking in New York City at the legendary Arizona 206. Brendan grew up in the Bronx, a far cry from the deserts of Arizona and New Mexico, but when his love of cooking led him to study French cooking with an emphasis on the foods of the South of France, it seemed a logical step to investigate the lively cuisine of America's Southwest. As with everything he does, Brendan plunged into this style of cooking with exuberant enthusiasm. He has had such a good time learning that he especially enjoys teaching—give him a crowd of food enthusiasts and he will share all his culinary secrets!

This menu brings a taste of the Southwest to a football weekend crowd or any large group you have gathered for informal entertaining. The chili is, without question, the Super Bowl of chilies, especially when teamed with cilantro-flavored rice and a down-home Sweet Potato Pie. All you need to add is a big green salad and plenty of Mexican beer to score a cook's touchdown.

◁ Ten-Chile Chili and Cilantro Rice

Ten-Chile Chili

Brendan's chili calls for 10 chiles, with each one imparting its own special aromatic scent to the final dish. The chef says that this is one instance when more is better! I agree. However, if you cannot find all of the chiles, don't panic. Simply up the quantity of those you can find. The dish will still taste very good. This recipe serves at least 12 hungry people, so it is the perect chili to make when you are expecting a crowd.

3 pounds Spanish onions, chopped
¾ pound slab bacon, diced
5 pounds lean beef chuck, trimmed and cut into ¼-inch by 1½-inch strips
¾ cup diced celery
½ cup chopped dried mulato chiles
½ cup chopped dried pasilla chiles
½ cup chopped dried ancho chiles
5 dried chiles pequín
1 cup ancho chile powder
⅓ cup ground toasted coriander seeds
⅓ cup ground cumin seeds
1 tablespoon plus 2 teaspoons cayenne pepper
5 bay leaves
4 cups peeled, seeded, and chopped ripe plum tomatoes
2 cups Beef or Chicken Stock
½ cup tequila, such as Cuervo Gold
¼ cup seeded, minced serrano chiles
¼ cup seeded, minced jalapeño chiles
3½ ounces canned chipotle chiles in adobo, chopped (half of a seven-ounce can)
1 smoked ham hock
1 sprig fresh rosemary
1 sprig fresh sage
1 sprig fresh oregano
Salt to taste

GARNISH:

1 tablespoon olive oil
1 cup seeded, julienned red bell peppers
1 cup seeded, julienned yellow bell peppers
1 cup seeded, julienned poblano chiles
1 cup seeded, julienned Anaheim chiles
1 jalapeño chile, seeded and julienned

■ Special Equipment: large Dutch oven

1 Assemble the *mise en place* trays for this recipe.

2 In a large Dutch oven, cook the bacon, stirring frequently, over medium-high heat for 5 minutes, or until the fat is rendered. Using a slotted spoon, remove the bacon and drain on paper towels. Drain off all but 2 to 3 tablespoons of bacon fat.

3 Add a quarter of the beef to the pot and cook, stirring, for 2 to 3 minutes. Remove the meat and drain on paper towels. Repeat with the remaining meat, cooking in batches.

4 When all the meat has been browned, add the onions to the pot. Lower the heat and cook, stirring frequently, for 15 to 20 minutes, or until caramelized. Add the celery and cook for 4 to 5 minutes, or until tender.

5 Return the meat to the pot. Stir in the chopped dried chiles, chiles pequín, chile powder, ground coriander, ground cumin, cayenne, and bay leaves. Add the tomatoes, stock, and tequila and stir to blend. Stir in the minced chiles, chipotle chiles, ham hock, rosemary, sage, and oregano. Raise the heat and bring to a simmer. Reduce the heat to medium-low and cook, partially covered, for 6 hours, stirring occasionally, or until the chili is thick and the flavors are intensely blended. Taste and add salt, if necessary.

6 To prepare the garnish, about 20 minutes before the chili is ready, heat the olive oil in a large saucepan over medium-high heat. Add the julienned bell peppers and chiles and sauté for 4 to 5 minutes, or until just softened. Remove from the heat, cover to keep warm, and set aside.

7 To serve, remove the ham hock, bay leaves, and herb sprigs from the chili. Serve the chili in bowls, topped with a spoonful of julienned peppers. Serve the Cilantro Rice on the side.

▶ Fresh tomatoes can be replaced with chopped, canned Italian plum tomatoes. The ham hock can be replaced with 1 smoked turkey leg.

Cilantro Rice

Brendan's method for cooking rice should yield perfectly cooked rice every time. His addition of pungent cilantro adds a whole new dimension to plain boiled white rice while giving it a flavor readily associated with Southwestern cooking. This rice can be served warm or at room temperature as a well-seasoned salad.

8 cups cold water
4 cups long-grain white rice
1 tablespoon plus 1 teaspoon coarse salt
3 cups chopped fresh cilantro
2 cups diced red bell peppers
2 cups diced yellow bell peppers
1 cup olive oil
⅔ cup white wine vinegar
Freshly ground black pepper to taste

1 Assemble the *mise en place* trays for this recipe.

2 In a large saucepan, bring the water to a boil over high heat. Add the rice and salt and bring back to a boil. Immediately lower the heat, cover the pan, and cook for 20 minutes. Remove from the heat and let rest, covered, for 10 minutes.

3 Transfer the rice to a large bowl. Stir in the cilantro, bell peppers, olive oil, vinegar, and pepper to taste. Serve immediately or cover and let stand at room temperature.

▶ This recipe can be easily tripled for a large crowd.

▶ Fresh basil or parsley may be substituted for cilantro.

BRENDAN WALSH: Cilantro Rice

233

Sweet Potato Pie

Borrowing from the cooking of America's South, Chef Walsh prepares Sweet Potato Pie as the perfect ending to a winning meal. Cut this rich pie into thin wedges and serve with a generous scoop of vanilla ice cream alongside, or, if you want more dessert, bake two pies.

PIE PASTRY:

1½ cups all-purpose flour
¼ teaspoon salt
½ cup solid vegetable shortening, chilled
3 to 4 tablespoons ice water

FILLING:

2 pounds sweet potatoes, peeled and cubed
¼ teaspoon salt
2 tablespoons unsalted butter
½ cup honey
¼ cup packed light brown sugar
1 tablespoon dark rum
1 teaspoon ground cinnamon
⅛ teaspoon freshly grated nutmeg
3 large eggs, lightly beaten
½ cup heavy cream, whipped to soft peaks

■ Special equipment: 9-inch pie plate; pie weights

1 Assemble the *mise en place* trays for this recipe.

2 To make the pastry, in a medium-sized bowl, combine the flour and salt. With your fingertips or a pastry blender, blend in the shortening until the mixture resembles coarse meal. Add the water, a tablespoon at a time, blending lightly after each addition, until the dough just holds together. Roll the pastry into a ball and flatten slightly. Wrap in plastic wrap and refrigerate for at least 2 hours.

3 Meanwhile, to make the filling, put the sweet potatoes and salt in a saucepan and add enough cold water to cover by several inches. Bring to a boil, lower the heat, and simmer for about 15 minutes, until the potatoes are very tender when pierced with a fork. Drain well.

4 Transfer the drained potatoes to a blender or a food processor fitted with the metal blade. Blend or process until smooth. Transfer the puree to a bowl and allow to cool for 5 minutes.

5 Stir the butter, honey, brown sugar, rum, and spices into the sweet potato puree until well blended. Cover and set aside.

6 Preheat the oven to 425 degrees F.

7 To continue making the pie pastry, roll out the pastry on a lightly floured surface or between 2 sheets of plastic wrap to circle about 12 inches in diameter and ⅛-inch thick. Line a 9-inch pie plate with the pastry so that it overhangs the edges by about 1 inch. Trim the edges and crimp lightly. Prick the bottom of the pastry with a fork.

8 Line the pastry with cooking parchment or aluminum foil and fill with pie weights, dried beans, or rice. Bake for 5 minutes. Remove the weights and parchment and bake for 4 minutes more. The pastry will barely begin to brown. Remove from the oven and cool on a wire rack. Lower the oven temperature to 350 degrees F.

9 Finish making the filling by putting the eggs in the top half of a double boiler over gently simmering water. Using a hand-held electric mixer set on high speed, or a whisk, beat the eggs for 5 minutes, or until very pale and thick. Do not let the water boil or the eggs may scramble.

10 Fold the eggs into the sweet potato puree until well incorporated. Gently fold in the whipped cream.

11 Pour the filling into the partially baked pie shell. Bake for approximately 1 hour and 15 minutes, or until the filling is golden brown on top and set. Transfer to a wire rack and cool before serving.

▷ BRENDAN WALSH: Sweet Potato Pie

A SOUTHWESTERN THANKSGIVING

*Guajillo-Maple Glazed Turkey
with Sautéed Greens, Beets and Yams*

Apricot-Peach Chutney

Black Pepper-Scallion Cornbread

Lemon Anise Churros

WINE SUGGESTIONS:

Sparkling Wine

Cru Beaujolais

Zinfandel

(may be served throughout)

WHAT YOU CAN PREPARE AHEAD OF TIME

Up to 1 week ahead: Make the Apricot-Peach Chutney. Cover and refrigerate.

Up to 2 days ahead: Make the Guajillo-Maple Glaze. Cover and refrigerate. Reheat before using.

The day before: Wash and trim the beet greens. Wrap in wet paper towels, place in a sealed plastic bag, and refrigerate. Cook and cool beets and yams. Cover and refrigerate.

Early in the day: Make the Black Pepper-Scallion Cornbread. Reheat in a preheated 200 degrees F. oven for 10 minutes before serving.

David Walzog is the latest in our list of most impressive chefs from Arizona 206 in New York City. His intense infatuation with Southwestern cooking is infectious. This is deliciously illustrated in his Thanksgiving menu, which emphasizes the use of traditional ingredients in a very contemporary way. Turkey and all the trimmings—beets, yams, and cornbread—are here but the meal is designed to incorporate the best of the lively ingredients we associate with the sun-drenched flavors of western Texas, New Mexico, and Arizona. The meal does not turn its back on New England and the familiar fare, it simply rejoices in the great diversity of our expansive and always inventive country.

◁ (From left to right) Black Pepper-Scallion Cornbread; Lemon Anise Churros; Guajillo-Maple Glazed Turkey with Sautéed Greens, Beets, and Yams; and Apricot-Peach Chutney

Guajillo-Maple Glazed Turkey with Sautéed Greens, Beets, and Yams

SERVES 6
PREPARATION TIME: ABOUT 45 MINUTES
COOKING TIME: ABOUT 5 HOURS AND 30 MINUTES

The sweet-and-spicy glaze keeps the turkey moist and adds enormous zest to the mild-flavored bird. The beautiful color of the glazed skin is further accentuated by the rich red and gold of the vegetables.

GLAZE:
2 large turkey legs
3 heads garlic, halved crosswise
2½ cups pure maple syrup
1 cup chopped white onions
5 sprigs fresh thyme
5 sprigs fresh rosemary
4 cups chicken stock
½ cup guajillo chile puree
1 cup water

TURKEY:
1 fourteen-pound fresh turkey
4 heads garlic, halved crosswise
About 10 sprigs fresh thyme
About 10 sprigs fresh rosemary
Salt and freshly ground black pepper to taste

VEGETABLES:
5 large yams, washed
6 large beets, washed
3 bunches beet greens, trimmed, washed, and dried
4 tablespoons unsalted butter

■ Special Equipment: **small melon-baller**

1 Preheat the oven to 425 degrees F. Assemble the *mise en place* trays for this recipe.

2 To make the glaze, split the turkey legs open with a sharp knife and pull apart to butterfly them. Place in a roasting pan and cook for about 1 hour, or until very brown, draining off the fat periodically.

3 Add the garlic, maple syrup, onion, and thyme and rosemary sprigs, and continue to roast for 20 minutes. Reduce the oven temperature to 325 F.

4 Transfer the contents of the roasting pan to a large, heavy saucepan. Stir in the stock, chile puree, and water. Bring to a boil over medium-high heat. Reduce the heat and simmer for 30 minutes.

5 Strain the glaze through a fine sieve into a smaller saucepan. Set aside and keep warm.

6 To roast the turkey, rinse it and pat it dry with paper towels. Put the halved garlic heads, thyme, and rosemary into the cavity. Sprinkle, inside and out, with salt and pepper. Press the legs against the breast and tie in place using kitchen twine. Tuck the wings under the back. Set the turkey on a rack in the roasting pan. Cover the turkey with aluminum foil and roast for 1 hour and 30 minutes.

7 Remove the foil and continue to roast the turkey, basting every 15 minutes with the glaze, for about 2 hours longer, or until the juices run clear when the thigh is pierced with a fork. Remove from the oven and let rest for about 15 minutes before carving.

8 Meanwhile, prepare the vegetables: In separate saucepans, cook the yams and beets in boiling, salted water to cover by several inches for about 20 minutes, or until tender when pierced with a fork. Drain well and allow to cool.

9 Carefully peel the vegetables. Using a small melon-baller, scoop out balls from each vegetable, using as much of the flesh as you can. Set the balls aside in separate bowls.

10 Just before serving, in a large saucepan, melt 2 tablespoons of the butter over medium heat. Add the beet greens, cover and cook for about 2 minutes, or until wilted. Remove from the pan and keep warm.

11 Add the remaining 2 tablespoons of butter and 1 tablespoon of water to the saucepan. When the butter melts, add the reserved vegetable balls. Cook for 1 minute, or until the vegetables are heated through.

12 Place the turkey on a warm serving platter and surround with the vegetables. Reheat and pass the remaining glaze on the side.

▶ If you don't have a melon-baller, cut the beets and yams into 1-inch cubes.

▷ DAVID WALZOG: Guajillo-Maple Glazed Turkey with Sautéed Greens, Beets, and Yams

Lemon Anise Churros

These are David's version of traditional folk fare snacks, with the lemon and anise adding a refreshing light-ness. Since these have to be made at the last minute, allow some time between the end of the meal and dessert.

1¼ cups all-purpose flour
⅛ teaspoon salt
1 cup water
8 tablespoons (1 stick) unsalted butter
2 teaspoons ground star anise
Grated zest of 1 lemon
4 large eggs
1 cup granulated sugar
1 cup confectioners' sugar
Vegetable oil, for deep-frying

■ Special Equipment: deep-fat fryer, deep-fry thermometer, pastry bag with a medium star tip

1 Assemble the *mise en place* trays for this recipe.

2 Sift together the flour and salt into a medium-sized bowl.

3 In a medium-sized saucepan, combine the water, butter, anise, and lemon zest. Bring to a boil over high heat. Immediately stir in the flour mixture and cook, beating constantly with a wooden spoon, until the mixture forms a ball and pulls away from the sides of the pan. Remove the pan from the heat.

4 Beat in the eggs, one at a time until they are well incor-porated and the batter is smooth.

5 Combine the sugars in a plastic bag and set aside.

6 Spoon the batter into a pastry bag fitted with a medium-sized star tip.

7 Heat the oil in a deep-fat fryer to 375 degrees F. on a deep-fry thermometer. Or pour enough oil into a large heavy pan to reach a depth of 3 inches and heat to 375 degrees F.

8 Pipe the batter into the hot oil in 5- to 6-inch lengths, being careful not to crowd the pan. Fry for about 3 min-utes, or until golden brown, turning once with tongs. Remove from the oil with a long-handled slotted spoon or tongs and drain well on paper towels. Continue frying until all the batter is used. Make sure the oil reaches the correct frying temperature between batches.

9 While they are still warm, drop the churros into the bag of sugar. Shake the bag to coat the churros generously with sugar. Serve warm.

▶ These are also great breakfast treats served with a steaming cup of Mexican coffee.

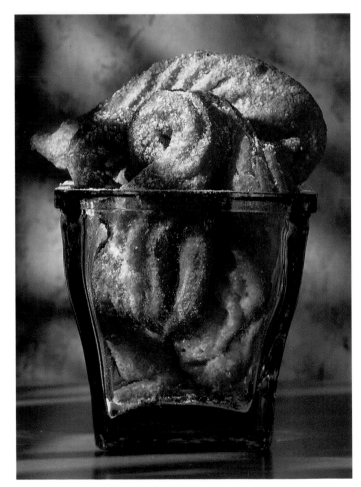

DAVID WALZOG: Lemon Anise Churros

ITALIAN COOKING

FRANCESCO ANTONUCCI:
*A Truly Delicious Dinner
for Friends*

LIDIA BASTIANICH:
An Early Fall Dinner

GIULIANO BUGIALLI:
*From Parma to Tuscany to Liguria
for Dinner*

BIBA CAGGIANO:
A Trip to a Trattoria

Roberto Donna:
A Festive Meal

Johanne Killeen and George Germon:
Two Americans Create "Al Forno"

Carlo Middione:
A Perfect Spring Dinner

Marta Pulini:
A Meal from Modena

Claudio Scadutto:
Casual Dining at Its Best

A DELICIOUS DINNER FOR FRIENDS

Fried Parmesan Cups and Prosciutto
COPPE DI PARMIGIANO FUSO CON PROSCIUTTO

Red Snapper in a Salt Crust with Herb Dressing
PAGELLO AL SALE ALL'ERBETTE

Mascarpone with Fruit
MASCARPONE CON FRUTTA

WINE SUGGESTIONS:

Prosecco or Champagne *(first course)*

Sauvignon Blanc *(second course)*

Asti Spumante or St. Francis Muscat Canelli *(dessert)*

WHAT YOU CAN PREPARE AHEAD OF TIME

Early in the day Make the Fried Parmesan Cups. Store at room temperature in a dry spot. (If the day is very humid, do not make these ahead of time.) Prepare the Red Snapper for baking. Stuff it with the herbs and garlic and wrap in plastic wrap. Refrigerate until ready to lay in the salt and bake.

Francesco Antonucci first taught at De Gustibus when he was at the Remi restaurant on Manhattan's East Side. His food was so outstanding and the restaurant so popular that he was forced to move to larger premises across town on the West Side. The crowds and the kudos followed!

When Chef Antonucci teaches, he always keeps the home kitchen in mind. Even though his food is very sophisticated, home cooks find it easy to prepare. This particular menu was wildly popular—each course had the classroom shouting "More!" The Parmesan Cups add a crispy, savory crunch to the beginning of the meal (and lend themselves to a variety of other uses). And wait until you bring the red snapper to the table—your guests will be impressed by this special dish that is as dramatic as it is delicious. The snapper will be the highlight of the dinner party, and so we have decided to end the meal in a typically Italian fashion: wonderful cheese and beautifully ripe fruit.

◁ FRANCESCO ANTONUCCI: **Mascarpone with Fruit**

Fried Parmesan Cups and Prosciutto

SERVES 6
PREPARATION TIME: ABOUT 5 MINUTES
COOKING TIME: ABOUT 10 MINUTES

Coppe di Parmigiano Fuso con Prosciutto

Once you get the knack of these cups, you'll make them regularly. The rich cheese taste is completely unadulterated and quite addictive! For success in creating these gems, start with a perfectly smooth, nonstick pan and the best imported Parmigiano-Reggiano you can find.

3 cups (about ¾ pound) freshly grated Parmigiano-Reggiano cheese
18 two-and-a-half-inch-by-two-and-a-half-inch, very thin slices prosciutto (from about 6 whole slices)
6 sprigs fresh herb, such as oregano, parsley, or rosemary

■ Special Equipment: 8-to-10-inch nonstick skillet or griddle; 3 to 6 custard cups

1 Assemble the *mise en place* trays for this recipe. Position 3 to 6 six-ounce custard cups upside down on a work surface. The diameter of the upturned cups should be no greater than 2 to 3 inches.

2 Heat an 8- or 10-inch nonstick skillet or small, smooth griddle over medium heat for about 5 minutes, until very hot. Sprinkle 2 tablespoons of the grated cheese into the center of the pan and, gently shaking the pan in a back-and-forth motion or spreading the cheese with a spatula, evenly distribute it to form a thin, lacy circle. Cook for 30 seconds, or until the cheese has melted and turned pale golden. (Do not turn the cheese circles over.) Using a spatula, carefully lift the cheese circle and place onto an inverted cup, letting it bend down over the sides of the cup. Allow to cool completely and harden before gently lifting the cheese cup off the custard cup. Continue making cheese circles until you have at least 18 cups.

3 Arrange 3 Parmesan cups on each serving plate, rounded side up. Drape a square of prosciutto over the top of each one.
Garnish the plates with the fresh herb sprigs, and serve immediately.

▶ Three measured cups of cheese should make as many as 24 cooked Parmesan Cups. This amount allows for a couple of "practice" cups, breakage, and nibbling.

▶ If the air is humid, the cups may collapse if made in advance and left at room temperature. Even slight humidity will make them chewy.

▷ FRANCESCO ANTONUCCI: Fried Parmesan Cups and Prosciutto

Red Snapper in a Salt Crust with Herb Dressing

SERVES 6
PREPARATION TIME: ABOUT 15 MINUTES
COOKING TIME: ABOUT 60 MINUTES

Pagello al Sale all'Erbette

The salt crust sounds overpowering but in actuality it holds in moisture while imparting a delicate and pleasing salty flavor. You can use this method to cook any whole fish with scales. Splash a bit of citrus on before serving to heighten the flavor even more. This is wonderful with sautéed greens.

SNAPPER:

1 bunch fresh rosemary, rinsed and patted dry
1 bunch fresh sage, rinsed and patted dry
1 bunch fresh thyme, rinsed and patted dry
3 cloves garlic
2 three-to-four-pound red snappers or 1 six-to-eight-pound red snapper, scales, skin, and tail intact, rinsed and patted dry
4 pounds coarse sea salt or kosher salt
1/4 cup all-purpose flour
2 tablespoons water

HERB DRESSING:

Juice of 1/2 lemon
Salt and freshly ground white pepper to taste
1 cup extra-virgin olive oil
1/2 cup water
1 teaspoon minced fresh rosemary
1 teaspoon minced fresh flat-leaf parsley
1 teaspoon dried oregano
1/2 teaspoon minced garlic

1 Preheat the oven to 400 degrees F. Assemble the *mise en place* trays for this recipe.

2 Divide each bunch of herbs into 4 equal portions. Combine these portions to make 4 bunches of mixed herbs. Using kitchen twine, tie each bunch together. Place 2 bunches of herbs and 1 1/2 cloves of garlic in the cavity of each fish. If using 1 fish, make 2 bunches of herbs and put all 3 cloves of garlic in the cavity.

FRANCESCO ANTONUCCI: **Red Snapper in a Salt Crust with Herb Dressing**

3 In a large bowl, combine the sea salt, flour, and water. Mix to make a rough dough. Spread evenly in a 3-inch-deep baking pan large enough to hold the fish flat. Lay the fish in the center of the salt mixture and generously cover them with salt mixture gathered up from the sides of the pan, patting the mixture firmly with your fingertips to help it adhere. Bake, uncovered, for 1 hour. (As it bakes the salt will form a compact crust.)

4 Meanwhile, make the dressing. In a small bowl, combine the lemon juice and salt and white pepper to taste.

Slowly whisk in the olive oil. When emulsified, whisk in the water, minced fresh herbs, oregano, and garlic.

5 Remove the fish from the oven. Gently crack the salt crust open and carefully remove the crust along with the fish skin. Use kitchen shears to cut through the crust and skin, if necessary. Brush any loose salt off the fish. Using 2 spatulas, lift the fish onto a warm serving platter. Pour the herb dressing over the top, and serve immediately.

▶ **For a more elaborate Italian dinner, serve pasta before the fish course and a simple grilled poultry or meat afterwards. Vegetables can be served as a separate course or with the main course.**

Mascarpone with Fruit

Mascarpone con Frutta

Mascarpone is a double-to-triple-cream cow's milk cheese from Italy's Lombardy region, and frequently sweetened and served with fresh or dried fruit as a dessert. It ranges in texture from very soft, almost runny, to the consistency of room-temperature cream cheese or butter. Its delicate flavor blends well with a wide variety of both savory and sweet seasonings. A small portion of rich, buttery mascarpone requires only a piece of sweet fruit as enrichment to make a most satisfying dessert.

3/4 pound mascarpone cheese
6 ripe large fruits, such as peaches, pears, or apples
12 ripe, small fruits, such as figs, apricots, or small bunches of grapes, or an assortment of dried fruits

Place the mascarpone cheese on a platter. Serve it with a bowl of the fruit. Let the guests peel and cut the fruit themselves.

▶ **Serve whatever fruit is in season, either by the piece or in a large, overflowing centerpiece, allowing your guests to choose whatever they wish.**

▶ **For the best mascarpone, buy the cheese from a cheese shop or an Italian market.**

▶ **Instead of fresh fruit, you can serve dried fruit. Or bring white wine or water seasoned with pungent spices to a boil and pour this over the dried fruit. Let it soak for at least 8 hours. The soaking gives the fruit time to absorb the flavors of the wine or spiced water and to plump up.**

251

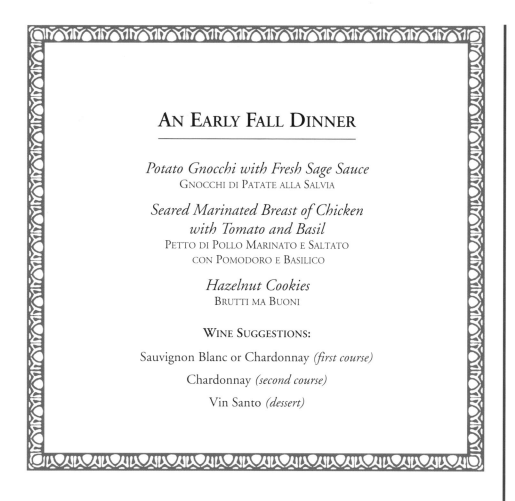

AN EARLY FALL DINNER

Potato Gnocchi with Fresh Sage Sauce
GNOCCHI DI PATATE ALLA SALVIA

Seared Marinated Breast of Chicken
with Tomato and Basil
PETTO DI POLLO MARINATO E SALTATO
CON POMODORO E BASILICO

Hazelnut Cookies
BRUTTI MA BUONI

WINE SUGGESTIONS:

Sauvignon Blanc or Chardonnay *(first course)*

Chardonnay *(second course)*

Vin Santo *(dessert)*

WHAT YOU CAN PREPARE AHEAD OF TIME

Up to 1 week ahead: Prepare the Chicken Stock (if making your own). Bake the Hazelnut Cookies. Store tightly covered in an airtight container in a cool place. Make and freeze the Potato Gnocchi. Do not thaw before cooking; add 2 to 4 minutes to the cooking time.

The day before: Marinate the chicken for the Seared Breast of Chicken.

Early in the day: Make the Tomato and Basil Sauce for the Seared Breast of Chicken, up to the point of adding the basil. Reheat over low heat and add the basil just before serving.

Up to 3 hours before: Make the Fresh Sage Sauce. Keep warm in the top half of a double boiler over hot water.

Up to 1 1/2 hours before: Make the gnocchi and allow to stand at room temperature until ready to cook (if not already made and frozen).

Lidia Bastianich is the epitome of earth mother. When she teaches at De Gustibus, we are all embraced by her warmth. She has great knowledge of the history, the chemistry, and the taste of food and combines her understanding with a caring empathy with the home cook.

Chef Bastianich grew up on a farm in Istria, Italy, where she learned to cook. Her simple origins meshed with her intellectual curiosity have translated into a teaching style that keeps the classroom mesmerized. In the menu we have chosen, you can really taste each ingredient, providing the cook with a more complete understanding of Lidia's style of cooking. Many of the dishes can be prepared in advance, which makes for a very relaxing evening with friends.

◁ LIDIA BASTIANICH: **Hazelnut Cookies**

Potato Gnocchi with Fresh Sage Sauce

Gnocchi di Patate alla Salvia

Gnocchi are Italian dumplings made from flour, farina, or, as in this case, potatoes. Sometimes they are made with the addition of either eggs and cheese, or both. When Lidia makes them, they are silky and light as a feather. With her recipe, yours should be also.

6 large Idaho or russet potatoes, peeled and cut into quarters
2 large eggs, beaten
1 tablespoon salt
Freshly ground white pepper to taste
About 4 cups sifted, unbleached all-purpose flour
Fresh Sage Sauce (recipe follows)
1 cup freshly grated Parmigiano-Reggiano cheese

1 Assemble the *mise en place* trays for this recipe.

2 Place the potatoes in a large saucepan with enough cold water to cover by several inches. Bring to a boil over high heat, lower the heat, and simmer for 15 minutes, or until tender. Drain well. Push the potatoes through a ricer or a food mill into a medium-sized bowl, or mash with an old-fashioned potato masher and allow to cool thoroughly, about 30 minutes.

3 Mound the potatoes on a cool work surface, such as a marble slab. Make a well in the center, and add the beaten eggs, 1 teaspoon of the salt, and white pepper to taste. Using both hands, work the mixture together, slowly adding 3 cups flour. Scrape the dough up from the surface with a pastry scraper or knife and keep blending until you have a smooth dough that is still sticky on the inside. The whole process should take no longer than 10 minutes (the more you work this dough, the more flour it absorbs). Sprinkle the dough with a little flour.

4 Cut the dough into 8 equal pieces. Sprinkle your hands with flour and using both hands, roll each piece on a lightly floured surface into a 1/2-inch-thick rope, continuously sprinkling flour on the work surface and your hands as you work the dough. Cut each rope into 1/2-inch pieces and set the pieces on an ungreased baking sheet. Indent each gnocchi with your thumb or score with the tines of fork. (The texture on the gnocchi will help the sauce adhere.)

5 Meanwhile, bring a 6-quart saucepan of water to a boil over high heat. Just as it comes to a boil, add the remaining 2 teaspoons salt.

6 Drop the gnocchi into the boiling water a few at a time, stirring the water continuously with a wooden spoon. Boil for 2 to 3 minutes, until the gnocchi rise to the top. Using a slotted spoon, transfer the gnocchi to a warm serving platter. Let the water return to a boil before adding each new batch of gnocchi.

7 Pour the Fresh Sage Sauce over the gnocchi, stir in the grated cheese and pepper to taste, and serve immediately.

■ **Special Equipment: Potato ricer, food mill, or old-fashioned potato masher**

FRESH SAGE SAUCE
Salsa alla Salvia

MAKES ABOUT 4 CUPS

1 cup unsalted butter
8 to 10 large fresh sage leaves, quartered
2 cups heavy cream
1 cup Chicken Stock
Salt and freshly ground white pepper to taste

In a medium-sized saucepan, melt the butter over medium heat. Add the sage and sauté for 2 minutes. Stir in the cream and stock, bring to a simmer, and simmer for 5 minutes. Season to taste with salt and pepper. Serve warm.

▶ **Although the sauce is not particularly thick when it's finished, it thickens nicely when mixed with the potato gnocchi and the grated cheese.**

▷ LIDIA BASTIANICH: **Potato Gnocchi with Fresh Sage Sauce**

Seared Marinated Breast of Chicken with Tomato and Basil

SERVES 6
PREPARATION TIME: ABOUT 40 MINUTES
COOKING TIME: ABOUT 25 MINUTES
MARINATING TIME: AT LEAST 8 HOURS

Petto di Pollo Marinato e Saltato Con Pomodoro e Basilico

Simple but full of flavor, this dish is a home cook's dream. The chicken can marinate overnight and the sauce can be made early in the day. It could be served over pasta for a less formal meal, or at room temperature for an easy summer lunch.

MARINADE AND CHICKEN:

1/2 cup olive oil
4 cloves garlic, crushed
1 tablespoon minced fresh rosemary
1 tablespoon minced fresh sage
Salt and freshly ground black pepper to taste
2 pounds skinless, boneless chicken breasts, split and trimmed

SAUCE:

1/4 cup olive oil
8 cloves garlic, crushed
1 pound ripe plum tomatoes, cored, peeled, seeded, and thinly sliced, juices reserved
Red pepper flakes to taste
Salt and freshly ground black pepper to taste
1/2 cup shredded fresh basil leaves

1 Assemble the *mise en place* trays for the marinade and chicken.

2 To make the marinade, in a small bowl, combine the olive oil, garlic, rosemary, sage, and salt and pepper to taste.

3 Slice the chicken breasts on the diagonal into thirds. Using a large knife or cleaver, lightly pound each piece to flatten slightly. Place in a shallow glass or ceramic dish. Pour the marinade over the chicken, cover, and refrigerate for at least 8 hours, turning occasionally.

4 Assemble the *mise en place* trays for the sauce.

5 To make the sauce, in a medium-sized saucepan, heat 3 tablespoons of the olive oil over moderate heat. Add the garlic and sauté for about 4 minutes, or until lightly browned. Stir in the tomatoes with their juices, the red

LIDIA BASTIANICH: **Seared Marinated Breast of Chicken with Tomato and Basil**

pepper flakes, and salt and pepper to taste. Simmer for 5 minutes. Stir in half of the basil leaves. Remove from the heat and cover to keep warm.

6 Heat a large sauté pan over medium-high heat until very hot. Drain the chicken, discarding the marinade. Add the chicken to the hot pan, without crowding, and sauté for 5 to 10 minutes, or until golden brown on both sides and just cooked through. (Cook the chicken in batches or in 2 pans if necessary.) Transfer to a large, warm serving platter.

7 Drizzle the remaining 1 tablespoon olive oil over the tomato sauce and pour over the chicken. Sprinkle the remaining basil over the top and serve.

256

Hazelnut Cookies

MAKES 20 TO 30 COOKIES
PREPARATION TIME: ABOUT 20 MINUTES
COOKING TIME: ABOUT 30 MINUTES

Brutti ma Buoni

Here is a simple cookie to dip into Vin Santo or a frothy cappuccino. These are good keepers, so make a couple of batches to have on hand.

1 cup finely chopped toasted and skinned hazelnuts
1 cup confectioners' sugar, sifted
1/8 teaspoon ground cinnamon
4 large egg whites

1 Assemble the *mise en place* trays for this recipe. Preheat the oven to 400 degrees F. Line 2 baking sheets with parchment paper.

2 In a heavy saucepan, combine the nuts, confectioners' sugar, and cinnamon.

3 In a large bowl, using an electric mixer set on medium-high speed, beat the egg whites until stiff. Gently stir the whites into the nut mixture. Cook over medium heat, stirring constantly, for 8 to 10 minutes, or until golden brown and the mixture pulls away from the sides of the pan. Remove from the heat.

4 Using 2 teaspoons, scoop out rough 1 1/2- to 2-inch mounds of the mixture and place them about 1 1/2 inches apart on the prepared baking sheets. Bake for 10 minutes, or until lightly browned. Lifting the paper by both ends, transfer the cookies, still on the paper, to a wire rack to cool and set. Repeat with the other sheet of parchment paper.

5 Lift the cookies from the paper with a spatula. Store, tightly covered, until ready to serve.

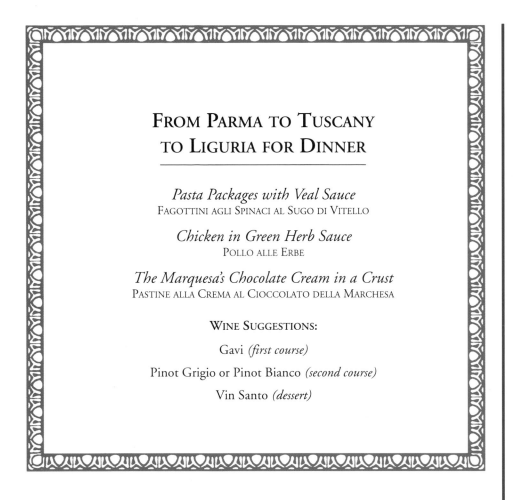

FROM PARMA TO TUSCANY
TO LIGURIA FOR DINNER

Pasta Packages with Veal Sauce
FAGOTTINI AGLI SPINACI AL SUGO DI VITELLO

Chicken in Green Herb Sauce
POLLO ALLE ERBE

The Marquesa's Chocolate Cream in a Crust
PASTINE ALLA CREMA AL CIOCCOLATO DELLA MARCHESA

WINE SUGGESTIONS:

Gavi *(first course)*

Pinot Grigio or Pinot Bianco *(second course)*

Vin Santo *(dessert)*

WHAT YOU CAN PREPARE AHEAD OF TIME

Up to 1 week ahead: Prepare the Chicken or Veal Stock (if making your own).

Up to 3 days ahead: Make the Veal Sauce for the Pasta Packages. Cover and refrigerate. Reheat just before serving.

Up to 1 day ahead: Cook the Chicken in Green Herb Sauce. Cover and refrigerate. Reheat, covered with foil, in a preheated 325 degree F. oven for 20 minutes before serving.

Early in the day: Assemble the Pasta Packages up to the addition of the balsamella sauce. Cover and refrigerate the pasta and balsamella sauce separately. Remove from the refrigerator 1 hour before baking, and whisk the sauce before pouring it over the pasta. Make the Chocolate Cream. Bake the cookie shells for the Chocolate Cream. Store in a cool, dry place. Assemble The Marquesa's Chocolate Cream in a Crust at least 30 minutes before serving.

Giuliano Bugialli is the De Gustibus Grand Master of Italian cooking. Over the years, he has introduced us to the art of preparing authentic and historically correct Italian meals. The admiration we all feel for his professional quest just grows and grows.

Always dazzled by Chef Bugialli's fresh pasta, veteran students are still attempting to recreate the perfectly light pasta texture at which he excels. Since much of this menu can be prepared in advance, your travels through Italy shouldn't be too tiring. Giuliano is a cook who prefers recipes in their classic form, so you should feel a real sense of accomplishment when you offer this meal.

◁ GIULIANO BUGIALLI: **Pasta Packages with Veal Sauce**

Chicken in Green Herb Sauce

Pollo alle Erbe

An interesting chicken recipe from Tuscany, using the underutilized leg and thigh meat. The intense, fresh herb taste permeates the flavorful meat for a complex yet simple-to-prepare dish.

1½ ounces (2 to 3 slices) white bread, crusts removed
7 tablespoons fresh rosemary leaves
45 large fresh sage leaves
3 large cloves garlic, peeled
7 tablespoons Chicken Stock
6 tablespoons olive oil
6 boneless chicken legs, skin on, trimmed of excess fat (from 3½-pound chickens, if possible)
6 boneless chicken thighs, skin on, trimmed of excess fat (from 3½-pound chickens, if possible)
Salt and freshly ground black pepper to taste
1 cup dry white wine
2 scant tablespoons fresh lemon juice
Grated zest of 2 lemons

1 Preheat the oven to 250 degrees F. Assemble the *mise en place* trays for this recipe.

2 In a food processor fitted with the metal blade, combine the bread, rosemary, sage, garlic, and stock and pulse until finely ground. Set aside.

3 In a large sauté pan, heat the oil over low heat. Add the chicken, increase the heat to medium, and cook for about 15 minutes, turning once, until lightly golden on both sides and the juices run clear when the meat is pierced with the tip of a knife. Remove the pan from the heat. Season the chicken with salt and pepper to taste, and transfer to a large, ovenproof serving platter. Cover with aluminum foil and put in the oven to keep warm.

4 Scrape the bread and herb mixture into the sauté pan, and season with salt and pepper. Set the pan over medium heat and cook the mixture for about 4 minutes, continuously scraping the bottom of the pan with a wooden spoon. Combine the wine and lemon juice and pour into the pan. Cook for about 3 minutes, stirring continuously to deglaze the pan and make a smooth sauce. Strain the sauce through a fine sieve into a bowl, pushing on the solids with the back of a wooden spoon; discard the solids. Taste and adjust the seasonings. Pour the sauce over the chicken and sprinkle the lemon zest over all. Serve immediately.

▶ To grate the lemon peel (or any citrus fruit) with ease, Chef Bugialli suggests covering the side of a grater with a piece of parchment paper. Rubbing the citrus fruit back and forth, turn the fruit as the peel is scraped off. Lift the parchment paper off the grater. Instead of being stuck in the grater, the tiny bits of peel remain on the paper and can be scraped into a bowl. The unwanted, bitter, white pith is left behind.

▷ GIULIANO BUGIALLI: **Chicken in Green Herb Sauce**

The Marquesa's Chocolate Cream in a Crust

SERVES 6
PREPARATION TIME: ABOUT 1 HOUR
COOKING TIME: ABOUT 30 MINUTES
CHILLING TIME (CHOCOLATE CREAM AND FILLED MOLDS):
ABOUT 1 HOUR TOTAL

Pastine alla Crema al Cioccolato della Marchesa

A spectacularly delicious chocolate dessert from Liguria—and all the components can be made in advance.

COOKIE MOLDS:

2 extra-large egg whites
1 cup confectioners' sugar
1/4 cup plus 2 tablespoons sifted, unbleached all-purpose flour
1/4 cup milk
1 teaspoon pure orange extract

CHOCOLATE CREAM:

2 ounces bittersweet chocolate, coarsely chopped
8 tablespoons unsalted butter, cut into pieces, at room temperature
1 tablespoon unflavored gelatin
1/4 cup cold water
3/4 cup hot milk
1 tablespoon brandy
5 extra-large eggs, separated
1/4 cup plus 1 tablespoon granulated sugar
2 tablespoons confectioners' sugar
1/2 cup bittersweet chocolate shavings

1 Preheat the oven to 400 degrees F. Assemble the *mise en place* trays for this recipe. Butter 4 baking sheets. Set 6 four-ounce custard cups on a work surface.

2 To make the cookie molds, using a fork, lightly beat the egg whites in a small bowl until foamy. Sift the confectioners' sugar over the whites, mixing with a wooden spoon until the sugar is completely absorbed. Add the flour a tablespoon at a time, mixing with the wooden spoon until incorporated. Combine the milk and orange extract, and stir into the batter until well blended.

3 For each cookie mold, spoon 1 tablespoon of batter onto a prepared baking sheet to form a thin circle about 5 inches in diameter. Place only 3 or 4 circles on each sheet, allowing at least 1 inch between them so that they do not run into each other during baking. Bake 1 sheet of cookies at a time for 4 to 5 minutes, or until the edges of the circles are lightly golden.

4 Using a thin-edged metal spatula, lift the cookies from the baking sheets, one at a time, and immediately fit each one into a custard cup, gently pressing it into the bottom for a neat fit. (If the cookies become too firm to mold, put the baking sheet back in the oven for about 1 minute.) Allow the cookies to cool in the cups for at least 5 minutes, or until firm, and then carefully remove them from the cups and set on a wire rack to cool completely. When cool, set on an ungreased baking sheet or tray. You will need 12 cups, and there is enough batter for a couple of practice cups.

5 To make the chocolate cream, put the chocolate in a medium-sized bowl or the top of a double boiler and melt it over very warm, but not simmering, water. Add the butter and, using a wooden spoon, beat vigorously for about 2 minutes, until well incorporated.

6 Meanwhile, in a small bowl, sprinkle the gelatin over the water. Let it soften for about 5 minutes. Add the hot milk and stir until the gelatin is completely dissolved.

7 Pour the gelatin mixture into the chocolate mixture, stirring continuously with a wooden spoon. Remove the chocolate mixture from the pan of water. Stir in the brandy and then the egg yolks, one at a time. Let cool for about 20 minutes.

8 In a large bowl, using an electric mixer set on medium-high speed, whip the egg whites until foamy. Add the granulated and confectioners' sugar and continue to beat until stiff, about 3 to 4 minutes. Gently fold the meringue into the cooled chocolate mixture. Cover and refrigerate for 30 minutes.

9 Spoon 2 heaping tablespoons of the chocolate mixture into each cooled cookie mold and refrigerate for at least 30 minutes. When ready to serve, sprinkle chocolate shavings over each filled cup.

▶ **The cookie shells do not hold up well if made on a humid day.**

◁ GIULIANO BUGIALLI: **The Marquesa's Chocolate Cream in a Crust**

A Trip to a Trattoria

*Onion and Zucchini Frittata
with Balsamic Vinegar*
FRITTATA DI CIPOLLE E ZUCCHINE ALL'ACETO BALSAMICO

*Shells with Shrimp, Broccoli,
Bread Crumbs, and Chile Pepper*
CONCHIGLIE CON SCAMPI, BROCCOLI E PEPERONCINO

Tirami-sù

WINE SUGGESTIONS:

Prosecco or Champagne *(first course)*

Pinot Grigio *(second course)*

Espresso *(dessert)*

What You Can Prepare Ahead of Time

The day before: Make the Tirami-sù.

Up to 6 hours ahead: If you plan to serve it at room temperature, make the Onion and Zucchini Frittata.

Biba Caggiano lives in Sacramento, California, where she is the chef-owner of the restaurant that bears her name. She travels frequently and whenever we are able to schedule a class with her, we have a great time getting reacquainted with her no-nonsense approach to food. Practicality seems to be her middle name! Just before Biba's last class, she had visited trattorias throughout Italy and she came loaded with many of their homey Italian recipes, reworked for the American home cook.

The menu we have chosen is easy, full of flavor, and jam-packed with savory taste combinations. Especially inviting is Biba's recipe for tirami-sù, everyone's favorite Italian dessert.

◁ BIBA CAGGIANO: Onion and Zucchini Frittata with Balsamic Vinegar on a terrace in Tuscany

Onion and Zucchini Frittata with Balsamic Vinegar

SERVES 6
PREPARATION TIME: ABOUT 20 MINUTES
COOKING TIME: ABOUT 25 MINUTES

Frittata di Cipolle e Zucchine all'Aceto Balsamico

A frittata is an easy-to-make Italian omelet in which the flavors are mixed into the eggs. This frittata is incredibly versatile. Try serving it at brunch or lunch as a light entrée by making individual frittatas in a nonstick five- or six-inch crêpe pan; prepare it for a picnic; or slice and serve it as an hors d'oeuvre.

9 large eggs
3/4 cup freshly grated Parmigiano-Reggiano cheese
1 1/2 tablespoons chopped fresh parsley
8 fresh basil leaves, finely shredded
Salt to taste
3 tablespoons olive oil
1 large onion, thinly sliced
2 medium zucchini, trimmed and thinly sliced
2 tablespoons balsamic vinegar

1 Assemble the *mise en place* trays for this recipe.

2 In a medium-sized bowl, lightly beat the eggs. Stir in the Parmigiano, parsley, and basil. Season to taste with salt.

3 In a 12-inch, nonstick skillet, heat the oil over medium heat. Add the onion and cook, stirring continuously, for 3 to 5 minutes. Add the zucchini and cook, stirring, for 5 to 8 minutes, until both vegetables are lightly golden. Stir in 1 1/2 tablespoons of the balsamic vinegar and immediately remove from the heat. Using a slotted spoon, transfer the vegetables to the egg mixture, draining them against the side of the skillet and leaving what liquid there is in the pan. Mix vegetable and egg mixture well.

4 Return the skillet to medium heat and add the vegetable-egg mixture. Cook for about 6 minutes, or until the bottom of the frittata is set and lightly browned.

5 Invert a large, flat plate over the skillet and invert the frittata onto it. Slide the frittata back into the skillet and cook for 3 to 4 minutes more, until set in the center and lightly browned on the bottom. Slide the frittata onto a warm serving dish. Immediately drizzle the remaining 1/2 tablespoon balsamic vinegar over the top. Serve warm or at room temperature, cut into 6 wedges.

▶ **The amount of balsamic vinegar required really depends on the strength of the vinegar. The stronger the vinegar, the less you need to use. It's worth it to taste different brands of balsamic vinegar and choose those that you particularly like. Not all taste the same.**

▷ BIBA CAGGIANO: Onion and Zucchini Frittata with Balsamic Vinegar

Shells with Shrimp, Broccoli, Bread Crumbs, and Chile Pepper

SERVES 6
PREPARATION TIME: ABOUT 20 MINUTES
COOKING TIME: ABOUT 20 MINUTES

Conchiglie con Scampi, Broccoli, e Peperoncino

This simple seafood pasta dish requires only three-quarters of a pound of shrimp to feed six nicely—an economy that pays off handsomely in the cholesterol department, too.

2 pounds broccoli, stalks removed and florets separated
1/3 cup extra-virgin olive oil
3/4 pound medium shrimp, shelled, deveined, rinsed, and well drained
2 tablespoons fresh white bread crumbs
4 anchovy fillets, separated from one another
3 cloves garlic, minced
Generous pinch of red pepper flakes, or more to taste
Salt to taste
1 pound dried pasta shells, orecchiette, or penne

1 Assemble the *mise en place* trays for this recipe.

2 In a steamer basket, steam the broccoli over boiling water for 4 minutes, or until tender. Refresh under cold running water and set aside.

3 In a large skillet, heat the oil over medium heat until nearly smoking. Add the shrimp and cook, stirring continuously, for 1 to 2 minutes, or until opaque. Using a slotted spoon, transfer the shrimp to a plate.

4 Immediately stir the bread crumbs into the skillet, and stir for 10 seconds, or until the crumbs are lightly golden. (The pan is very hot and the bread crumbs will brown in no time at all.) Stir in the anchovies and garlic. Cook for 15 to 20 seconds, stirring, until the garlic is browned and cooked. Return the shrimp to the skillet and add the broccoli florets and red pepper flakes. Season to taste with salt and cook, stirring continuously, for 1 minute. Remove from the heat.

5 Bring a large pot of water to a boil. When it boils, add salt and cook the pasta for about 10 minutes, or until *al dente*. Drain well, reserving some of the cooking water.

6 Add the pasta to the skillet and set over medium heat. Cook for 1 to 2 minutes, stirring continuously, until the pasta, shrimp, and vegetables are well combined. If the pasta looks dry, add 2 to 3 tablespoons of the reserved cooking water. Taste and adjust the seasoning with salt and red pepper flakes. Serve immediately.

▶ **If you have organized your *mise en place* well, this recipe will come together in minutes.**

◁ BIBA CAGGIANO: **Shells with Shrimp, Broccoli, Bread Crumbs, and Chile Pepper**

Tirami-sù

SERVES 6
PREPARATION TIME: ABOUT 20 MINUTES
COOKING TIME: ABOUT 15 MINUTES
CHILLING TIME: AT LEAST 4 HOURS

Tirami-sù, literally translated as "pick me up," needs no introduction. In the last ten years, this dessert has become more popular in America than in Italy. It is served in one version or another in all types of restaurants. Apparently, the dessert originated in Tuscany in the early 1900s, but many regions claim it as their own.

A true tirami-sù is always made with mascarpone, a delicious, sweet, soft Italian cheese, not unlike a very thick, slightly acidic whipped cream—never with any other cheese or with whipped cream.

Biba's generously portioned recipe is based on a tirami-sù from the fancy Osteria Trattoria Laguna in Cavallino, near Venice, Italy, which she found had a particular extra-light texture that made it simply irresistible. She uses a creamy zabaglione as the custard to avoid using uncooked eggs.

ZABAGLIONE:

8 large egg yolks
1/2 cup granulated sugar
1/3 cup brandy

FILLING AND CAKE:

1 1/2 pounds mascarpone cheese
4 large egg whites
2 tablespoons granulated sugar
2 cups Italian espresso, at room temperature
1/4 cup brandy
40 high-quality ladyfingers, preferably imported from Italy
1/2 cup unsweetened cocoa powder
1/2 cup semisweet chocolate curls, optional

1 Assemble the *mise en place* trays for this recipe.

2 To make the zabaglione, put the egg yolks and sugar in a large bowl or the top of a double boiler set over slowly simmering water. Beat with a whisk or hand-held electric mixer set at medium speed until thick and pale yellow. Beat in the brandy and cook for about 10 minutes, whisk-ing constantly, until the zabaglione doubles in volume, is soft and fluffy, and feels hot to the touch. Immediately set the zabaglione over a bowl of ice water and let cool.

3 To make the filling, combine the mascarpone and the cooled zabaglione in the bowl of an electric mixer and beat at low speed to blend.

4 In a large bowl, using clean beaters, beat the egg whites on medium-high speed until foamy. Add the sugar and beat until stiff peaks form. Fold the egg whites into the mascarpone mixture.

5 In a medium-sized bowl, combine the espresso and brandy. One at a time, quickly dip half the ladyfingers into the coffee mixture. Lay them very close together in a 13-by-9-inch baking dish. Spread half the mascarpone mixture evenly over the ladyfingers.

6 Using a fine-mesh strainer, sprinkle half the cocoa powder evenly over the mascarpone. Dip the remaining ladyfingers in the espresso mixture and place side by side on the mascarpone, making another layer. Spread the remaining mascarpone mixture evenly over the ladyfingers, and sprinkle with the remaining cocoa powder. Cover the dish with plastic wrap and refrigerate for at least 4 hours, or overnight.

7 Just before serving, sprinkle semisweet chocolate curls over the tirami-sù, if desired.

▶ **American ladyfingers are more spongy than their Italian counterpart, and since real Italian tirami-sù requires a slightly harder cookie, Biba suggests using ladyfingers imported from Italy.**

▷ BIBA CAGGIANO: Tirami-sù

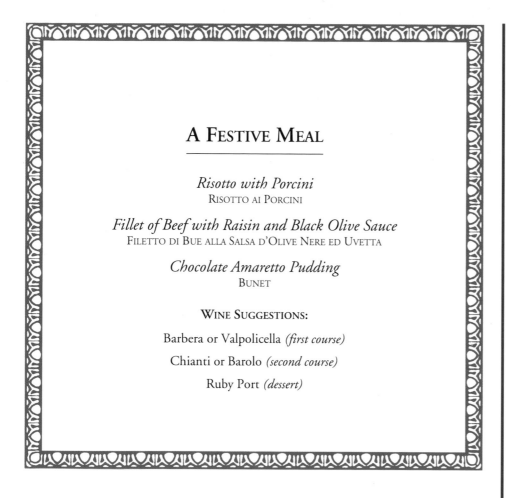

A FESTIVE MEAL

Risotto with Porcini
RISOTTO AI PORCINI

Fillet of Beef with Raisin and Black Olive Sauce
FILETTO DI BUE ALLA SALSA D'OLIVE NERE ED UVETTA

Chocolate Amaretto Pudding
BUNET

WINE SUGGESTIONS:

Barbera or Valpolicella *(first course)*

Chianti or Barolo *(second course)*

Ruby Port *(dessert)*

WHAT YOU CAN PREPARE AHEAD OF TIME

Up to 1 week ahead: Prepare the Chicken Stock (if making your own). Prepare the Veal Stock (if making your own).

Up to 3 days ahead: Make the veal reduction for the Fillet of Beef. Cover and refrigerate.

Up to 1 day ahead: Make the Chocolate Amaretto Pudding. Cover and refrigerate until ready to serve.

Early in the day: Marinate the beef and the raisins for the Fillet of Beef.

Roberto Donna came to teach at De Gustibus on the recommendation of Jean Louis Palladin of the famed Washington, D.C. restaurant, Jean-Louis at the Watergate. Jean-Louis told us that Roberto was a truly great chef who would shine in our classroom. This was no exaggeration! Roberto came, we saw, and he conquered!

The results of the menu we have chosen from Chef Donna make it worth the effort. The excitement he conveyed to his students is here in each recipe. His recipe for risotto is creamy and rich with the flavor of porcini. The contrast of the sweet raisins and tart olives offers a new dimension to the fillet of beef. And the chocolate pudding explodes with caloric goodness—it is delicious!

◁ **A home along Appia Antica, Italy**

Risotto with Porcini

Risotto ai Porcini

Risotto can be a home cook's nightmare, only because it must be made at the last minute and stirred constantly while the rice absorbs the liquid. But, with its rich, creamy taste, it's a fantastic dream to eat. And like any dream, it is worth a little effort.

1 cup Veal Stock
6 porcini mushroom caps, wiped clean, plus 7 ounces fresh porcini mushrooms, trimmed and wiped clean
1 bulb garlic
1/4 cup olive oil
6 cups Chicken Stock
6 tablespoons unsalted butter
1/2 large onion, minced
1/2 teaspoon minced fresh sage
1/2 teaspoon minced fresh rosemary
1 pound Arborio rice (see note)
3/4 cup dry white Italian wine, such as Pinot Grigio
Salt and freshly ground black pepper to taste

1 Preheat the oven to 375 degrees F. Assemble the *mise en place* trays for this recipe.

2 In a small saucepan, bring the veal stock to a boil over medium heat. Reduce the heat and simmer for about 20 minutes, or until reduced to 2 tablespoons. Remove from the heat, cover, and set aside.

3 Put the porcini caps in a small baking pan. Cut the garlic bulb in half crosswise and add to the pan. Drizzle 3 tablespoons of the olive oil over the mushrooms and garlic. Set aside.

4 Cut the remaining mushrooms into 1/4-inch pieces and set aside.

5 In a medium-sized saucepan, bring the chicken stock to a simmer over medium heat. Reduce the heat to low and keep hot.

6 In a medium-sized saucepan, melt 4 tablespoons of the butter with remaining 1 tablespoon olive oil over low heat. Add the onion and cook, stirring, for about 10 minutes, or until translucent. Raise the heat to medium-high and stir in the sage, rosemary, and diced porcini. Sauté for 2 minutes. Stir in the rice, reduce the heat to medium, and toast, stirring occasionally, for 3 minutes, or until the rice is glistening. Add the wine and cook, stirring continuously, for about 1 minute, or until all the liquid has been absorbed by the rice.

7 As soon as the wine has been absorbed, begin adding the hot chicken stock to the rice 1/2 cup at a time, cooking and stirring until each addition is absorbed. This should take no more than 15 to 20 minutes, as you want the rice to be creamy but still *al dente.*

8 Meanwhile, roast the porcini caps for 10 minutes, or until just tender. Turn off the oven and open the door or remove and cover to keep warm.

9 Remove the risotto from the heat. Add the remaining 2 tablespoons butter and salt and pepper to taste, and stir until the rice is very creamy. Spoon into a warm serving bowl. If necessary, reheat the reduced veal stock. Place the porcini caps on top, and drizzle with the warm veal stock. Serve immediately.

NOTE: Arborio rice is Italian, medium-grain rice that is especially good for risotto. Buy it in specialty shops, the gourmet section of the supermarket, or an Italian grocery.

▶ **Even though risotto must be made at the last minute, this dish will all come together easily if you are well organized.**

▶ **You can buy frozen veal stock in gourmet or specialty shops.**

◁ ROBERTO DONNA: **Risotto with Porcini**

Fillet of Beef with Raisin and Black Olive Sauce

Filetto di Bue alla Salsa d'Olive Nere ed Uvetta

Profoundly concentrated flavors heighten the taste of the tender fillet. I think that this dish could also be done with pork or tender lamb loins with the same aromatic result.

4 cups Veal Stock
1 one-and-a-half-pound beef tenderloin, trimmed and cut crosswise into 6 pieces
1/3 cup olive oil
3 cloves garlic, sliced
3 fresh rosemary sprigs
1/2 cup raisins
1/4 cup Cognac
1 tablespoon prepared black olive puree

1 Assemble the *mise en place* trays for this recipe.

2 Put the beef in a shallow dish. Add the olive oil, garlic, and rosemary, and toss to coat. Cover with plastic wrap and refrigerate at least 2 hours.

3 Meanwhile, in a small bowl combine the raisins and Cognac. Set aside at room temperature to macerate for 2 hours.

4 In a medium-sized saucepan, simmer the veal stock over medium heat for 45 minutes to 1 hour, or until reduced to 1 1/2 cups. Set aside.

5 Remove the beef from the marinade and pat dry with paper towel. Discard the garlic and reserve the oil and rosemary separately.

6 Drain the raisins, reserving the Cognac.

7 Preheat the oven to 175 degrees F.

8 In a large sauté pan, heat the reserved oil over high heat. Add the reserved rosemary and then add the beef and cook, turning once, for 4 to 5 minutes, until it has a nice crispy crust. Remove the rosemary from the pan as soon as it starts to darken. Add the Cognac and continue to cook for 30 seconds to 1 minute, until the Cognac has evaporated. Transfer the beef to a warm serving dish and keep warm in the oven. Spoon off any fat from the pan.

9 Add the veal reduction to the sauté pan, stir in the olive puree, and cook over medium-high heat for 2 minutes, or until reduced to a rich sauce. Stir in the raisins. Place beef on warmed dinner plates. Pour the sauce over the beef, and serve.

▶ **Black olive puree, which is sometimes called olivata, is available at Italian groceries, specialty markets, and many supermarkets.**

▷ ROBERTO DONNA: Fillet of Beef with Raisin and Black Olive Sauce

Chocolate Amaretto Pudding

Bunet

This rich, chocolate "bread pudding" uses delicate amaretti cookies for the bread, providing just a hint of one of Italy's favorite flavors.

10 amaretti cookies, crumbled
1½ cups granulated sugar
¼ cup unsweetened cocoa powder
6 large eggs
1 quart milk
1 cup Marsala wine
1 tablespoon plus 1 teaspoon Cognac
1 tablespoon water

1 Preheat the oven to 350 degrees F. Assemble the *mise en place* trays for this recipe.

2 In a heatproof bowl, combine the amaretti with 1 cup plus 2 tablespoons of the sugar, the cocoa, and eggs and stir to blend.

3 In a medium-sized saucepan, bring the milk to a boil over medium heat. Immediately stir into the amaretti mixture. Stir in the Marsala and Cognac, remove from the heat, and set aside.

4 In a small saucepan, combine the water with the remaining ¼ cup plus 2 tablespoons sugar and cook over medium heat, stirring continuously, for 10 minutes, or until dark gold and caramelized. Remove from the heat and carefully pour into the bottom of a 2-quart soufflé dish or mold. Using caution, pour the milk mixture into the mold (it may splatter).

5 Place the soufflé dish into a large baking pan and add enough hot water to come about halfway up the sides of the dish. Bake for 45 minutes to 1 hour, until the center of the pudding is set. Cool completely on a wire rack. When cool, cover and refrigerate for at least 3 hours or overnight.

6 When ready to serve, place a serving plate on top of the soufflé dish and invert to unmold the pudding. Serve immediately, spooning any caramel remaining in the dish over the pudding.

▶ **Before boiling milk, wet the bottom of the saucepan with water to prevent the milk from sticking to the bottom of the pot.**

◁ ROBERTO DONNA: **Chocolate Amaretto Pudding**

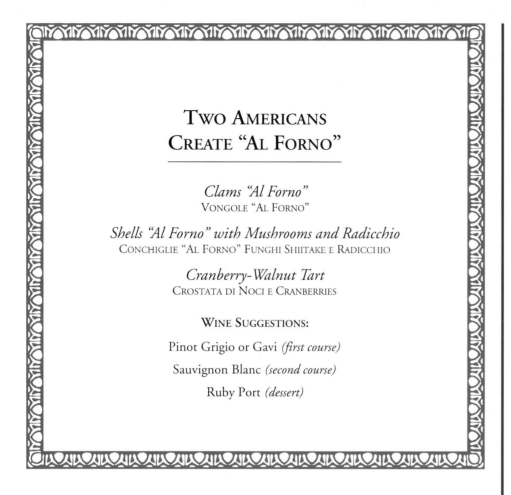

TWO AMERICANS CREATE "AL FORNO"

Clams "Al Forno"
VONGOLE "AL FORNO"

Shells "Al Forno" with Mushrooms and Radicchio
CONCHIGLIE "AL FORNO" FUNGHI SHIITAKE E RADICCHIO

Cranberry-Walnut Tart
CROSTATA DI NOCI E CRANBERRIES

WINE SUGGESTIONS:

Pinot Grigio or Gavi *(first course)*

Sauvignon Blanc *(second course)*

Ruby Port *(dessert)*

WHAT YOU CAN PREPARE AHEAD OF TIME

Up to 1 week ahead: Make the pastry for the Cranberry Walnut Tart. Wrap tightly and freeze. Defrost, still wrapped, for 45 minutes, or until pliable but still cold.

Early in the day: Scrub the clams for the Clams "Al Forno." Prepare the Conchiglie "Al Forno." Cover and refrigerate. Bring to room temperature before baking. Bake just before serving.

Johanne and George were students at the Rhode Island School of Design when they fell in love with each other—and with the foods of Italy. They decided to forego careers in the world of design and devote their lives, together, to exploring the Italian menu. Much to the delight of lovers of great food, these two Americans have opened a great Italian restaurant in Providence, which draws diners from all over the world.

Although the dishes we have chosen from Johanne and George do not really come together as a complete menu, they each give a sense, in their recreation, of some of Italy's great recipes. And the Cranberry-Walnut Tart is perfect for the American holiday table.

◁ Picnic on a hillside in Tuscany

Clams "Al Forno"

Vongole "Al Forno"

This aromatic appetizer could easily be served as a main course in larger portions, with crusty bread and a tossed salad.

42 littleneck clams
1 1/2 cups cored, peeled, seeded, and chopped ripe plum tomatoes
2 onions, halved and thinly sliced
2 tablespoons minced garlic
1 tablespoon minced jalapeño, or to taste
1/2 teaspoon red pepper flakes
3/4 cup dry white Italian wine, such as Pinot Grigio
1/2 cup water
8 tablespoons unsalted butter, cut into pieces
3 scallions, trimmed and cut into 1-inch julienne
6 lemon wedges

1 Preheat the oven to 450 degrees F. Assemble the *mise en place* trays for this recipe.

2 Wash the clams under cold running water, scrubbing them with a stiff brush. Lay in a single layer in 2 nine-by-twelve-inch shallow baking dishes. Cover with the tomatoes, onions, garlic, jalapeño, pepper flakes, wine, water, and butter.

3 Bake the clams for 6 to 7 minutes. Turn the clams and stir them to move those in the center to the sides of the pans. Bake for 10 to 15 minutes longer, or until the clams open. Discard any unopened clams.

4 Spoon the clams into shallow soup bowls. Using tongs, distribute the tomatoes and onions evenly among the bowls. Pour the broth into the bowls, sprinkle with the scallions, and garnish with the lemon wedges. Serve immediately.

▶ Although we call for more clams than you will need, to allow for any that do not open, if none stay closed, serve them all.

▶ You can use canned imported Italian plum tomatoes in place of the fresh tomatoes.

▷ JOHANNE KILLEEN AND GEORGE GERMON: Clams "Al Forno"

Shells "Al Forno" with Mushrooms and Radicchio

SERVES 6
PREPARATION TIME: ABOUT 30 MINUTES
COOKING TIME: ABOUT 45 MINUTES

Conchiglie "Al Forno" Funghi Shiitake e Radicchio

Here is a richly delicious "make ahead" casserole filled with the flavors of earthy mushrooms, sharp radicchio, and pungent cheeses. Johanne and George recommend a good imported dried pasta, such as De Cecco or Del Verde, or any pasta that is 100-percent semolina.

6 tablespoons unsalted butter
6 ounces shiitake mushrooms, wiped clean, stemmed and cut into 1/4-inch slices
Salt to taste
1 pound medium-sized dried conchiglie (pasta shells)
2 1/2 cups heavy cream
1/2 cup freshly grated Parmigiano-Reggiano cheese
1/2 cup shredded Bel Paese cheese
1/2 cup crumbled Gorgonzola cheese
2 heads (about 1 pound) radicchio, halved, cored, and shredded
6 fresh sage leaves, shredded

1 Preheat the oven to 450 degrees F. Assemble the *mise en place* trays for this recipe. Generously butter a 9-inch square baking dish.

2 In a medium-sized sauté pan, melt 4 tablespoons butter over medium heat. Add the mushrooms and sauté for 5 minutes, or until tender. Add salt to taste. Remove from the heat and set aside.

3 Bring a large pot of water to a boil over high heat. When the water boils, add a little salt. Cook the pasta for about 10 minutes, until *al dente*. Drain well.

4 In a large bowl, combine the cream, Parmigiano-Reggiano, Bel Paese, Gorgonzola, mushrooms, and radicchio. Add the drained pasta and toss to combine. Add the sage leaves and season to taste with salt.

5 Transfer the pasta to the prepared dish. Dot with the remaining 2 tablespoons butter. Bake for 30 minutes, or until bubbly and golden brown on top. Serve immediately.

▶ The mushroom stems not needed for this recipe can be used to enrich soups, stocks, and sauces.

▶ Conchiglie is a shell-shaped pasta available in many sizes, from very small (generally for soup) to large (for stuffing).

▷ JOHANNE KILLEEN AND GEORGE GERMON: Conchiglie "Al Forno" with Mushrooms and Radicchio

Cranberry-Walnut Tart

Crostata di Noci e Cranberries

This easy-to-make dessert is perfect for the Thanksgiving and Christmas table. The dough is fail-safe and can be used for any tart or pie.

TART PASTRY:

2 cups unbleached, all-purpose flour
1/4 cup superfine sugar
1/2 teaspoon coarse salt
1 cup unsalted butter, cut into 1/2-inch cubes and chilled
1/4 cup ice water

FILLING:

2 cups fresh cranberries, rinsed and dried
1/2 cup chopped walnuts
2 tablespoons superfine sugar
2 tablespoons light brown sugar
2 tablespoons confectioners' sugar
1 cup whipped cream (optional)

1 Preheat the oven to 450 degrees F. Assemble the *mise en place* trays for this recipe.

2 To make the tart pastry, combine the flour, sugar, and salt in a food processor fitted with the metal blade. Pulse on and off a few times to combine.

3 Add the chilled butter, tossing quickly with your fingers to coat with flour (this prevents the butter cubes from adhering together and helps them to combine more evenly with the flour). Pulse on and off about 15 times, until the mixture resembles small peas.

4 With the motor running, add the ice water all at once through the feed tube and process for about 10 seconds, stopping the machine before the dough becomes a solid mass.

5 Turn the dough out onto a sheet of aluminum foil, pressing any loose particles into the ball of dough. Form

6 On a lightly floured surface, roll out the dough to an 11-inch circle. Transfer to a baking sheet and trim the edges.

7 To make the filling, combine the cranberries, walnuts, superfine sugar, and brown sugar in a bowl. Toss to distribute the sugar evenly.

8 Spoon the cranberry mixture into the center of the dough round, leaving a 1 1/2-inch border all around the edge. Lift the dough border up over the filling, letting it drape gently over the fruit. Some of the filling will be exposed. Press down on the edges of the dough, snugly securing the sides and the bottom, being careful not to mash the fruit. Gently pinch together the pleats that have formed from the draping.

9 Bake the tart for 15 to 20 minutes, or until the crust is golden. Cool on a wire rack for about 10 minutes. Dust with confectioners' sugar and serve warm, with whipped cream, if desired.

▶ **The tart dough works best when made with very cold butter. This dough recipe makes enough for 2 nine-inch tart shells or 4 four-inch tartlet shells.**

◁ JOHANNE KILLEEN AND GEORGE GERMON: Cranberry-Walnut Tart

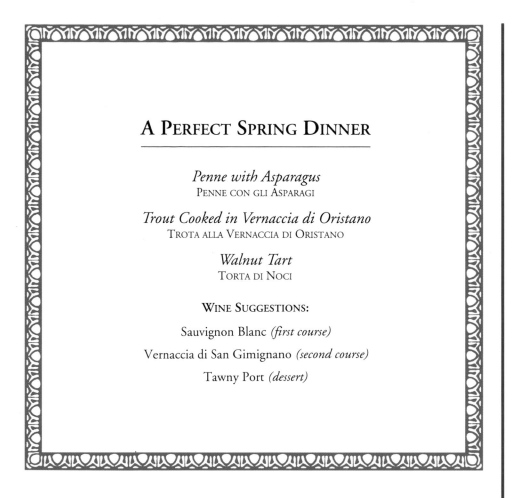

A PERFECT SPRING DINNER

Penne with Asparagus
PENNE CON GLI ASPARAGI

Trout Cooked in Vernaccia di Oristano
TROTA ALLA VERNACCIA DI ORISTANO

Walnut Tart
TORTA DI NOCI

WINE SUGGESTIONS:

Sauvignon Blanc *(first course)*

Vernaccia di San Gimignano *(second course)*

Tawny Port *(dessert)*

WHAT YOU CAN PREPARE AHEAD OF TIME

Up to 5 days ahead: Make the Walnut Tart. Cool, wrap tightly in aluminum foil, and refrigerate. Bring to room temperature before serving.

Early in the day: Prepare all the components for the Penne with Asparagus. Prepare all the components for the Trout Cooked in Vernaccia di Oristano.

Carlo Middione is the owner of Vivande restaurant and take-out food shop in San Francisco. His ancestors came from southern Italy, a region he clearly favors in his cooking—this sunny heritage virtually shines in all he teaches. Meals are always light and flavorful and, for the home cook, easy to prepare. I know that the recipes we have selected to represent Carlo's repertoire will become old standards in your kitchen.

◁ Springtime in Bellagio, Italy

Penne with Asparagus

Penne con gli Asparagi

Spring bursts forth with sweet asparagus peeking through this rich pasta dish. If you prefer, substitute another green vegetable.

1 pound thin asparagus stalks, trimmed and cut into 2-inch pieces
¼ cup extra-virgin olive oil
2 cloves garlic, minced
1½ pounds ripe Italian plum tomatoes, cored, peeled, seeded, and finely chopped
14 ounces dried penne
1 cup freshly grated Pecorino Romano cheese, plus extra for serving, if desired
2 large eggs, lightly beaten
Salt and freshly ground black pepper to taste

1 Assemble the *mise en place* trays for this recipe.

2 Bring a large saucepan of water to a boil. When it boils, add salt and cook the asparagus for 4 minutes. Turn off the heat and, using a slotted spoon or tongs, transfer the asparagus to a bowl and cover to keep warm. Reserve the water for cooking the pasta.

3 In a large saucepan, heat the olive oil over medium heat. Add the garlic and cook for 2 to 3 minutes, until golden. Stir in the tomatoes and cook for about 10 minutes.

4 Meanwhile, return the asparagus water to a boil. Add the pasta and cook for 7 minutes, or until just barely *al dente.* Drain, leaving a little water clinging to the pasta.

5 Put the pasta in a large, heated casserole or a ceramic serving bowl set over a pan of simmering water. Stir in the asparagus and cheese. Add the beaten eggs and stir gently for 3 to 4 minutes, until the pasta is well coated and glossy. Stir in the tomato sauce and season to taste with salt and pepper. Serve immediately on warm dinner plates, with extra grated cheese passed at the table if desired.

▶ To heat the casserole, set it in a warm (250 degree F.) oven while you prepare the rest of the dish.

▶ The heat of the penne actually cooks the eggs. Adding the cheese before the eggs creates an insulation that keeps the eggs from getting too hot too quickly and curdling.

▷ CARLO MIDDIONE: Penne with Asparagus

Trout Cooked in Vernaccia di Oristano

Trota alla Vernaccia di Oristano

Vernaccia di Oristano wine from Sardegna is as different as night from day from the better-known Vernaccia di San Gimignano, a Tuscan wine. It is not yet readily available in American markets, and Carlo Middione suggests approximating the taste of Vernaccia di Oristano by mixing three parts California golden sherry with one part dry white vermouth. For that essential undertaste of bitterness so characteristic of the wine, Carlo adds a well-crushed kernel from the pit of a peach or apricot per quart of the wine mixture. This, he says, adds just enough of the amaro taste, which gives "ballast" to the flavor of the finished dish.

⅓ cup extra-virgin olive oil
2 cloves garlic, minced
1 large carrot, peeled and finely chopped
1 large yellow onion, finely chopped
2 ribs celery, finely chopped
1 large, ripe tomato, cored, peeled, seeded, and finely chopped
1 lemon, washed and thinly sliced
⅓ cup chopped fresh parsley
½ teaspoon ground oregano
Salt and freshly ground black pepper to taste
6 eight-ounce trout, cleaned
About 2 cups Vernaccia de Oristano, or a mixture of sherry and dry vermouth (see above)

1 Assemble the *mise en place* trays for this recipe.

2 In a sauté pan large enough to hold all the trout, heat the olive oil. Add the garlic and sauté oven medium heat for 3 minutes, or until deep gold. Stir in the carrots, onions, celery, tomatoes, lemon, parsley, and oregano. Add salt and pepper to taste. Cook, stirring, for about 10 minutes, or until all the vegetables are lightly browned.

3 Reduce the heat and spread the vegetables evenly over the bottom of the pan. Arrange the trout snugly on top of the vegetables. Add enough wine to come halfway up the trout. Cover loosely with a lid or foil and cook for 5 minutes. Carefully turn the trout with a slotted spatula and cook for about 5 minutes more, or until cooked through. Remove the trout to a warm platter and cover with aluminum foil to keep warm.

4 Strain the vegetables and pan liquid through a fine sieve, pushing down on the solids to extract all the juices. Discard the solids. Pour the cooking liquid into a medium-sized saucepan and simmer over medium heat for about 10 minutes, or until reduced to 1 cup.

5 Place the trout on serving plates and spoon the sauce over the top. Serve immediately.

▶ Since this dish must be cooked at the last minute, organize your *mise en place* trays well to speed preparation.

▶ You may need to use 2 sauté pans, particularly if you decide to leave the heads on the trout for presentation purposes.

▶ California golden sherry is made by such wineries as Christian Brothers and Almaden. Good dry white vermouth is made by Cinzano and Martini and Rossi. Vermouth has a higher alcohol content than a dry white wine and, therefore, is more in keeping with the spirit of the Vernaccia di Oristano.

◁ CARLO MIDDIONE: Trout cooked in Vernaccia di Oristano

Walnut Tart

Torta di Noce

The key elements here are the walnuts and the *mosto cotto*, a jelly-like substance made from wine must. A good substitution for *mosto cotto* in this recipe is tart, lemony-tasting, red currant jelly.

PASTRY:

2 cups all-purpose unbleached flour, or more if necessary
1/3 cup granulated sugar
1/4 cup lard or solid vegetable shortening
1/4 cup unsalted butter
Grated zest of 1 lemon
1 large egg
3 to 4 large egg yolks

FILLING:

2 cups coarsely chopped walnuts
1/2 cup raisins
1/4 cup finely chopped candied orange peel
1 1/3 cups *mosto cotto* or 1 cup red currant jelly
1 large egg, beaten, for egg glaze

■ Special Equipment: Special equipment: 9-inch fluted tart pan with a removable bottom

1 Preheat the oven to 350 degrees F. Assemble the *mise en place* trays for this recipe.

2 To make the pastry, combine the flour, sugar, lard, butter, and lemon zest in a food processor fitted with the metal blade. Pulse on and off 8 to 10 times, until the mixture resembles coarse crumbs. Add the egg and 3 egg yolks, and process until the dough just comes together. If the dough seems too wet, add additional flour, 1 teaspoon at a time. If the dough is too dry and won't hold together, add 1 more egg yolk.

3 Scrape the dough onto a lightly floured work surface and knead for 1 minute, or until quite soft. Form into a ball, wrap in plastic wrap, and refrigerate for 1 hour.

4 Meanwhile, make the filling. Stir together the walnuts, raisins, orange peel, and *mosto cotto* or jelly. Set aside.

5 Divide the dough in half. On a lightly floured surface, roll out half the dough to a 12-inch circle. Fit it into a 9-inch fluted tart pan with a removable bottom, leaving about a 1 1/2-inch overhang.

6 Spoon the filling into the tart pan, spreading it evenly.

7 Roll out the remaining piece of dough to a 12-inch circle. Lay the circle on top of the filling. Press the 2 layers of overhanging dough together and then roll up and over to make a raised edge, using your thumb and index finger to flute the edge. Make sure the edge is well sealed.

8 Using a pastry brush, coat the top of the tart with the egg glaze. Insert a small pastry tip into the center of the tart for a steam vent, or cut a cross-hatch in the center of the pastry. Then cut several 1/2-inch slashes in a decorative pattern over the surface to help steam escape. Set the tart on a baking sheet to catch any juices that escape during baking.

9 Bake for 55 to 60 minutes, or until nicely browned. Transfer to a wire rack to cool for 10 minutes. Remove the tart ring, cut the tart into wedges and serve warm. Or let cool before serving.

▶ **To facilitate removing the tart from the pan, place it, while still hot, on a bowl that is smaller than the tart pan, or on a large can. The ring will slip down and the tart will be supported by the metal bottom. If the ring does not slide down of its own accord, apply gentle pressure to the edges to loosen it.**

▶ **You may be able to buy *mosto cotto* in an Italian market or from a winery. Or, if you live near a winery, you may be able to buy wine must, which is juice freshly squeezed from grapes. If so, make *mosto cotto* by boiling the must in a heavy pan until it reduces to a thick, jelled consistency. Cool and use as you would any jelly.**

▷ CARLO MIDDIONE: Walnut Tart

A MEAL FROM MODENA

Parmesan Ice Cream
GELATO AL PARMIGIANO

Spinach Tart
ERBAZZONE

Fillet of Beef in the Modena Manner
FILETTO DI MANZO ALL'ACETO BALSAMICO TRADIZIONALE DI MODENA

Sour Cherry Tart
CROSTATA DI AMARENE

WINE SUGGESTIONS:

Champagne *(first course)*

Champagne *(second course)*

Chianti Classico *(third course)*

Ruby Port *(dessert)*

WHAT YOU CAN PREPARE AHEAD OF TIME

Up to 2 days ahead: Make the Parmesan Ice Cream.

Early in the day: Assemble the Spinach Tart. Cover and refrigerate until 1 hour before baking. Brush with the egg wash just before baking. Prepare the Fillet of Beef for roasting. Cover and refrigerate until 1 hour before roasting. Bake the Sour Cherry Tart. Warm just before serving, if desired.

Marta Pulini first taught at De Gustibus when she was the chef at Le Madri restaurant in New York City. Now executive chef at mad.61, the restaurant located in New York's famed Barney's uptown store on Madison Avenue, Marta has a most direct way of explaining her style of cooking. Not surprisingly, she favors the foods from the region around Modena, where she grew up, often giving favorite family recipes cosmopolitan flair. Exuding love for food, Marta reflects her long time passion for the kitchen. Attending her class, you feel as though you have been embraced by a storybook Italian mother. This menu is a taste of some of the dishes with which Marta Pulini grew up.

◁ MARTA PULINI: **Parmesan Ice Cream**

to 5 minutes, until the spinach has wilted. Transfer to a large bowl and stir in the parsley and cheese. Season to taste with pepper. Allow to cool for about 15 minutes.

6 Add the eggs and bread crumbs to the spinach mixture and stir to combine.

7 Divide the dough into 2 pieces, one slightly larger than the other. On a well-floured surface, roll out the larger piece to a 14-inch circle. Carefully fit into the prepared tart pan. Spoon the spinach filling into the tart shell, spreading it evenly and smoothing the top.

8 Roll out the remaining dough to a thin, 12-inch circle. Lay the circle on top of the filling and pull the overhanging dough up over it. Press the edges of dough together and pinch them to make a raised edge, using your thumb and index finger to flute the edge. Prick the top with a fork. Using a pastry brush, coat the top of the tart with the egg wash.

9 Bake the tart for 30 minutes, or until the top is golden. Remove from the oven and let rest for 5 minutes. Remove the tart ring, cut into wedges, and serve.

▶ **If time is an issue, substitute 1¾ pounds (3 ten-ounce boxes) frozen chopped spinach. Thaw it and squeeze as much moisture as possible from it before proceeding with the recipe. (This eliminates at least 30 minutes of preparation time, as cleaning and stemming fresh spinach is tedious work.)**

▶ **The tart dough is fragile. Take care when working with it, but if it rips, simply smooth it together again. The dense filling does not require a flawless crust.**

Fillet of Beef in the Modena Manner

Filetto di Manzo All'Aceto Balsamico Tradizionale di Modena

This is an easy-to-prepare dinner party main course. Use the absolute best Aceto Balsamico Tradizionale Di Modena (balsamic vinegar) to finish, for the authentic taste.

2 pounds beef tenderloin, trimmed of all fat
1 bunch fresh sage
1 bunch fresh thyme
4 sprigs fresh rosemary
2 cloves garlic, peeled
Salt and freshly ground black pepper to taste
2 tablespoons unsalted butter
2 tablespoons olive oil
3 tablespoons fine-quality balsamic vinegar

1 Preheat the oven to 400 degrees F. Assemble the *mise en place* trays for this recipe.

2 Using a very sharp knife, butterfly the tenderloin by cutting it almost in half down its entire length. Open out and flatten slightly.

3 Chop all the herbs and the garlic very fine and mix together. Add salt and pepper to taste and chop again to mix. Sprinkle half the mixture over the cut side of the meat. Reshape the fillet and, using kitchen twine, tie in 6 or 8 places along the length. Rub the outside with the remaining herb mixture.

4 In a large roasting pan, melt the butter with the olive oil over medium-high heat. Add the meat and sear until well browned on all sides. Transfer to the oven and roast for 12 minutes. Turn the meat and cook for 12 minutes more for rare meat; for medium-rare meat, cook for 18 minutes on each side. Remove from the oven and allow to rest for a few minutes.

5 Slice the meat crosswise into ¼-inch slices, discarding the twine, and fan out on a warm serving platter. Drizzle with the balsamic vinegar and serve immediately.

MARTA PULINI: Fillet of Beef in the Modena Manner

303

Sour Cherry Tart

Crostata di Amarene

The sour cherry tart with its pretty latticed top is an appealing dessert to serve at the end of a special meal.

DOUGH:

1¾ cups plus 2 tablespoons all-purpose flour
½ cup plus 2 tablespoons granulated sugar
1½ teaspoons baking powder
Grated zest of 1 lemon
1 large egg plus 1 large egg yolk, lightly beaten
9 tablespoons unsalted butter, chilled

FILLING:

4 cups pitted fresh sour cherries
¾ cup granulated sugar
Grated zest of 1 orange
1 vanilla bean, split
1 tablespoon all-purpose flour
1 large egg yolk beaten with 1 tablespoon milk, for egg wash

■ Special Equipment: 9-inch fluted tart pan with a removable bottom

1 Assemble the *mise en place* trays for this recipe.

2 To make the dough, combine the flour, sugar, baking powder, and lemon zest and mound on a clean work surface. Make a well in the center. Add the beaten egg and butter and, using your fingertips, rub into the flour until the dough just holds together. Form into a ball, wrap in plastic wrap, and refrigerate for at least 30 minutes.

3 Preheat the oven to 375 degrees F. Generously butter a 9-inch fluted tart pan with a removable bottom.

4 To make the filling, combine the cherries, sugar, orange zest, and vanilla bean in a medium-sized saucepan set over low heat. Cook over low heat, stirring frequently, for 35 to 50 minutes, until the mixture resembles chunky preserves (the time depends on the type of cherries). Remove from the heat and allow to cool for 15 minutes. Remove the vanilla bean.

5 Cut off about a quarter of the dough, rewrap the smaller piece, and refrigerate it. On a lightly floured surface, roll the larger piece of dough to a 12-inch circle. Fit it into the prepared tart pan. Trim the overhanging dough and combine trimmings with reserved dough.

6 Sprinkle the flour over the bottom of the tart shell. Spoon the cherry filling into the shell, smoothing the top.

7 Divide the reserved dough into 8 to 10 pieces and form into long strips by rolling them between the floured palms of your hands. Use the strips to make a widely spaced lattice top, pushing the ends of the ropes into the edges of the bottom shell. Trim off the excess dough.

8 Using a pastry brush, lightly coat the latticework and the edge of the tart with the egg wash. Bake for 30 to 35 minutes, until the crust is golden. Cool for 5 to 10 minutes on a wire rack. Then remove the tart ring, cut the tart into wedges, and serve warm.

▶ **Sour cherries are in season in midsummer. If you cannot find frozen or dried cherries, use canned. For this recipe, you will need 2 16-ounce cans unsweetened sour cherries packed in water. Drain them well. (Do not use cherry pie filling or sweet cherries!) You can also substitute dried cherries by reconstituting them in warm water for about 30 minutes.**

▷ MARTA PULINI: **Sour Cherry Tart**

CASUAL ITALIAN FARE

ANTIPASTI:

Broccoli Rabe, Garlic, and Pignoli Nuts
CIME DI RAPE AGLIO OLIO CON PIGNOLI

Roasted Carrots, Oregano, Rosemary, and Fontina Cheese
CAROTE ARROSTITE ALLA PIEMONTESE

Roasted Fennel, Thyme, and Parmigiano
FINOCCHIO ARROSTITO AL PARMIGIANO E TIMO

White Pizza with Arugula
PIZZA BIANCA CON RUCOLA

Walnut Biscotti
BISCOTTI ALLE NOCI

WINE SUGGESTIONS:

Champagne *(Antipasto course)*

Champagne *(second course)*

Vin Santo *(dessert)*

WHAT YOU CAN PREPARE AHEAD OF TIME

Up to 1 week ahead: Make the Walnut Biscotti. Store in an airtight container in a cool, dry place.

Early in the day: Prepare the antipasto. Cover and refrigerate. Bring to room temperature before serving. Make the dough for the White Pizza with Arugula. Wrap in plastic wrap and refrigerate. Bring to room temperature before baking. Prepare the arugula and garlic for the pizza topping.

Claudio Scadutto's De Gustibus class was pure joy! We had been dazzled by the tantalizing antipasto bar at his home base, Trattoria dell'Arte in New York City, and he brought a sampling of these inviting vegetable antipasto recipes with him to share with the students. Each one was more delicious than the one before, and, when served together, provided a feast of colors, shapes, and textures. Add Chef Scadutto's pizza for the perfect casual meal. To complete the De Gustibus experience, however, you need Claudio singing opera as he works. What an Italian event!

◁ CLAUDIO SCADUTTO: **Walnut Biscotti**

Antipasto

This selection is only the beginning. Use your imagination and let your creativity fly. An antipasto platter can be filled with any variety of cold meats, vegetables, and condiments.

The following recipes are designed to serve 6 people. If one recipe particularly appeals to you, the ingredients can easily be doubled to increase your antipasto bounty.

BROCCOLI RABE, GARLIC, AND PIGNOLI NUTS
Cime di Rape Aglio Olio con Pignoli

2 pounds broccoli rabe (about 2 bunches)
4 cloves garlic, minced
1/4 cup toasted pignoli nuts
1/4 cup extra-virgin olive oil
Salt to taste

1 Assemble the *mise en place* trays for this recipe.

2 Soak the broccoli rabe in cold water to cover for about 15 minutes. Drain well. Trim off any large leaves and the tough stem ends. Using a small sharp knife, cut slashes into the stalks. Using the kitchen twine, tie the broccoli rabe into bunches.

3 In a large deep saucepan of boiling, salted water, cook the broccoli rabe, standing it upright so that the heads are covered by about 1 inch of water for 4 to 5 minutes, until just tender and bright green. Drain well and remove the twine.

4 Arrange the broccoli rabe on a serving platter or in a shallow bowl. Gently toss with the garlic, nuts, olive oil, and salt to taste. Serve at room temperature.

▶ **This is also delicious served over pasta for a quick dinner.**

◁ CLAUDIO SCADUTTO: Antipasto: Broccoli Rabe, Garlic, and Pignoli Nuts; Roasted Carrots, Oregano, Rosemary, and Fontina Cheese; Roasted Fennel, Thyme, and Parmigiano

ROASTED CARROTS, OREGANO, ROSEMARY, AND FONTINA CHEESE
Carote Arrostite alla Piemontese

8 carrots, peeled and sliced diagonally into 1/2-inch thick slices
3 tablespoons extra-virgin olive oil
Salt and freshly ground black pepper to taste
2 teaspoons minced fresh oregano
2 teaspoons minced fresh rosemary
1/2 cup freshly shredded Fontina cheese

1 Preheat the oven to 350 degrees F. Assemble the *mise en place* trays for this recipe.

2 In a shallow baking dish, combine the carrots with the olive oil and salt and pepper to taste, and toss lightly to coat. Roast for 35 minutes, or until just slightly crisp.

3 Transfer the carrots to a serving platter. Sprinkle with the minced herbs and cheese. Serve at room temperature.

ROASTED FENNEL, THYME, AND PARMIGIANO
Finocchio Arrostito al Parmigiano e Timo

3 small fennel bulbs, washed, trimmed, cored, and quartered lengthwise
1/4 cup extra-virgin olive oil
Salt and freshly ground black pepper to taste
2 teaspoons minced fresh thyme
1 three-ounce piece Parmigiano-Reggiano cheese

1 Preheat the oven to 350 degrees F. Assemble the *mise en place* trays for this recipe.

2 In a shallow baking dish, combine the fennel with the olive oil and salt and pepper to taste, and toss lightly to coat. Roast for 30 to 35 minutes, or until light golden brown.

3 Transfer the fennel to a serving platter. Sprinkle with the thyme. Using a vegetable peeler or cheese slicer, shave the Parmigiano over the top. Serve at room temperature.

White Pizza with Arugula

SERVES 6
PREPARATION TIME: ABOUT 30 MINUTES
COOKING TIME (FOR ALL 6 PIZZAS AT 15 MINUTES PER
INDIVIDUAL PIZZA): 1 HOUR AND 30 MINUTES
RESTING TIME (DOUGH ONLY): ABOUT 2 HOURS

Pizza Bianca con Rucola

These delightfully crisp pizzas bear no resemblance to the soggy, fast-food variety. They are wonderfully fresh-tasting, with no tomato sauce or cheese. These little pizzas are best eaten directly from the oven. Serving them this way turns your party into an informal affair, as you continue to cook pizzas while others are being happily devoured.

PIZZA DOUGH:

3 cups water
¼ cup sugar
One ¼-ounce package active dry yeast
¼ cup vegetable oil
1 tablespoon salt
1½ cups plus 3 tablespoons bread flour
1½ cups plus 3 tablespoons semolina flour

TOPPING:

3 cups packed finely shredded arugula
¼ cup finely chopped garlic
¾ to 1 cup extra-virgin olive oil

▪ Special Equipment: Pizza stone.

1 Assemble the *mise en place* trays for this recipe.

2 In a large, warm bowl, combine the water, sugar, and yeast. Stir to dissolve. Let rest for 15 minutes.

3 Stir the vegetable oil and salt into the yeast mixture. Add both the flours and mix with a wooden spoon or your hands to combine. Put the dough in a bowl, cover with a kitchen towel, and let stand for 20 minutes in a warm, draft-free place.

4 Turn the dough a few times in the bowl. Let stand 20 minutes longer.

5 Again, turn the dough and let stand 20 minutes.

6 Turn the dough out onto a lightly floured surface and knead dough for about 3 minutes, until smooth and elastic. Divide into 6 pieces and shape into balls. Leaving the balls on the floured surface, cover them with kitchen towels, and let rest for about 1 hour.

7 Put a pizza stone on the center rack of the oven and preheat the oven to 450 degrees F.

8 Flatten each piece of dough into a round, pushing it into a 6-inch circle with your fingertips. Place 1 pizza on the hot pizza stone and bake for about 15 minutes, or until golden. Remove from the oven and sprinkle with ½ cup of the arugula and 2 teaspoons of the garlic. Drizzle with olive oil and serve. Continue baking the remaining pizzas, serving each one as soon as it is assembled.

▶ If you have 2 pizza stones, raise the oven temperature to 500 degrees F. and bake 2 pizzas at a time. If you don't have a pizza stone, you can bake the pizzas on a preheated heavy baking sheet, but the crusts will not be as crispy. Pizza stones are sold in kitchenware shops. You can also use unglazed ceramic tiles, found in kitchenware shops, instead of a pizza stone.

▶ You can make 2 large pizzas with the dough and the same amount of topping and serve them cut into wedges.

◁ CLAUDIO SCADUTTO: White Pizza with Arugula

Walnut Biscotti

Biscotti alle Noci

Crisp biscotti are perfect for dunking in a cup of strong, rich espresso. Great keepers, they are a boon to have on hand for unexpected guests.

3 3/4 cups all-purpose flour
2 tablespoons baking powder
5 large eggs
1 1/2 cups sugar
1 vanilla bean or 1 teaspoon pure vanilla extract
1 1/2 cups chopped walnuts
1 1/2 cups vegetable oil

1 Preheat the oven to 350 degrees F. Assemble the *mise en place* trays for this recipe. Line 2 baking sheets with parchment paper.

2 In a medium-sized bowl, whisk together the flour and baking powder. Set aside.

3 In a large bowl, using an electric mixer set on medium-high speed, beat the eggs and sugar together until light and creamy. Split the vanilla bean, if using, in half and scrape the seeds into the batter. Or add the vanilla extract, if using, and stir to combine. Add the walnuts and stir just to combine.

4 Stir the flour mixture into the batter, alternating it with the oil and mixing gently until incorporated.

5 Scrape about a quarter of the dough into a pastry bag fitted with a #2 plain tip, and pipe long cylinders of dough about 1 inch thick and about the width of the baking sheet onto the prepared sheets, leaving about 2 inches between each one. Refill the pastry bag and repeat with the remaining dough. Bake for 15 minutes, or until golden brown. Remove the baking sheets and leave the oven on.

6 Let the biscotti rest for about 5 minutes. Cut each cylinder on the diagonal into cookies about 3 inches long. The cookies are about 1/4 inch thick. Lay the cookies on the baking sheets and bake for 2 to 3 minutes longer. Transfer to wire racks to cool completely.

MEDITERRANEAN COOKING

COLMAN ANDREWS:
A Spanish Repast

CHARLES BOWMAN:
A Taste of Greece

TERRANCE BRENNAN:
Flavors of the Sun

DOMINICK CERRONE:
Great Sunny Flavors

ANDREW D'AMICO:
A Magical Mediterranean Buffet

ALAIN DUCASSE:
Tribute to the South of France

JOYCE GOLDSTEIN:
California on the Mediterranean

MATTHEW KENNEY:
A Night in Morocco

TOM VALENTI:
A Robust Winter Dinner

PAULA WOLFERT:
A World of Food

A SPANISH REPAST

Catalan Tomato Bread
PA AMB TOMAQUET

Swordfish with Pine Nuts and Raisins
PEIX ESPASA EN CASSOLA

Banana Fritters
TORTITAS DE PLATANOS

Champagne *(first course)*
Rioja or Rias Baixas *(second course)*
Dry Rosé such as Tavel *(dessert)*

Early in the day: Soak and drain the anchovies for the Catalan Tomato Bread. Toast the bread for the same recipe. Prepare the ingredients for the Swordfish with Pine Nuts and Raisins. Pulverize the almonds for the swordfish.

Up to 3 hours ahead: Make the Banana Fritters.

Colman Andrews is one of America's most distinguished food writers. When he introduced himself to the De Gustibus classroom he said, "I am not a chef, just a lover of the foods of Catalan. I want to share with you the ingredients and cooking methods of this ancient land, which has been influenced as much by its geographical proximity to the Mediterranean as by its roots in Spain." He proceeded to demonstrate that although we might all be familiar with the basic ingredients, such as tomatoes, garlic, parsley, pine nuts, raisins, and wonderfully fresh fish, the Catalans use them by giving them a different twist. The ease with which he prepared these recipes made this almost undiscovered cuisine deliciously inviting and exciting to the students.

◁ COLMAN ANDREWS: *Ingredients for Catalan Tomato Bread*

Catalan Tomato Bread

Pa amb Tomaquet

This simple combination of country-style bread and lush, ripe tomatoes is a fantastic introduction to casual Mediterranean dining. For a relaxed meal *al fresco*, you might want to place all the ingredients on the table and let your guests assemble their own plates. Colman told us that ham, sardines, herring, or sausage are all welcome additions.

24 large anchovy fillets
Six 1½-inch-thick slices country-style French or Italian bread (see Note)
3 medium-sized very ripe tomatoes, halved
About ½ cup mild Spanish extra-virgin olive oil (preferably a Catalan brand, such as Siurana, Verge de Borges, or Lerida)
Salt to taste

1 Assemble *mise en place* trays for this recipe.

2 Place the anchovy fillets in a small bowl and add enough cool water to cover. Allow to soak for 1 hour. Drain and pat dry.

3 Prepare a charcoal or gas grill or preheat the broiler.

4 Lightly toast the bread on both sides over the fire or under the broiler.

5 Squeezing gently, rub the tomatoes over both sides of each slice of toast, leaving a thin film of tomato flesh and seeds on the surfaces. Drizzle olive oil to taste evenly over both sides of each toast. Sprinkle both sides with salt to taste. Place 1 toast slice on each plate. Arrange 4 anchovy fillets on top of each toast and serve immediately.

NOTE: You will need a large round or oval dense hearty bread. Do not use a baguette, as it will not be of the right consistency to absorb the tomato juices and oil properly.

COLMAN ANDREWS:
Catalan Tomato Bread

Swordfish with Pine Nuts and Raisins

Peix Espasa en Cassola

Relying on an unusual combination of sweet and sour flavors, Colman has created a unique way to cook fish. The sauce works equally well with chicken breasts.

2 pounds swordfish, about 1 inch thick, cut into 2 x 3-inch pieces
1/4 cup all-purpose flour
2 tablespoons Spanish olive oil
1 1/2 cups dry white wine
3/4 cup fresh orange juice
1 1/2 tablespoons fresh lemon juice
24 toasted blanched almonds
2 sprigs fresh flat-leaf parsley, minced
2 sprigs fresh mint, leaves only, minced
2 sprigs fresh marjoram or oregano, leaves only, minced
1/2 cup golden raisins, plumped in water and drained
1/2 cup toasted pine nuts
Coarse salt and freshly ground black pepper to taste

1 Assemble *mise en place* trays for this recipe.

2 Dredge the swordfish pieces in the flour. In a large non-stick skillet, heat the oil over medium heat. Add the fish and cook for about 5 minutes, or until lightly browned on all sides. Drain on paper towels and set aside.

3 Return the skillet to the heat, add the wine and citrus juices, bring to a boil, and boil, stirring frequently, for about 15 minutes, or until the liquid is reduced to 3/4 cup.

4 While the liquid is reducing, pulverize the almonds in a mortar and pestle. Add the herbs and about 1 tablespoon of the reducing liquid and work into the almonds to form a thick paste. This is called a *picada*.

5 Add the raisins, pine nuts, and *picada* to the skillet and stir to combine. Return the fish to the skillet and cook, stirring gently, for about 3 minutes, or until the fish is hot and opaque throughout and the flavors are well blended. Season to taste with coarse salt and pepper. Serve immediately, with rice or a green salad if desired.

NOTE: Unless you use a mortar and pestle to pulverize the almonds, the sauce will be chunky rather than smooth. If you don't have one, use a food processor fitted with the metal blade and pulse just until the nuts are smooth, taking care not to overprocess them.

COLMAN ANDREWS: *Swordfish with Pine Nuts and Raisins*

Banana Fritters

Tortitas de Platanos

These simple doughnut-like treats are easy to make and always draw raves. They are also a marvelous way to use overripe bananas. What's more, you can make them several hours before serving.

1 pound very ripe bananas, peeled and mashed
6 large eggs
1/2 cup milk
2 to 3 tablespoons dark rum, or to taste
Grated zest of 1 lemon
1/2 teaspoon ground cinnamon
Pinch of salt
1 teaspoon active dry yeast
3 to 4 cups all-purpose flour
4 cups corn oil
4 large pieces orange peel
About 1/2 cup confectioners' sugar

1 Assemble *mise en place* trays for this recipe.

2 In a bowl, combine the bananas and eggs. Add the milk, rum, lemon zest, cinnamon, and salt and whisk until well blended. Add the yeast, whisking, then add just enough flour to make a smooth batter that is the consistency of softly whipped cream. Cover and set aside to rest for 30 minutes.

3 In a large heavy nonstick frying pan, heat the oil over medium-high heat until hot (see Note). Add the orange peel and cook for about 2 minutes, or until the peel begins to brown. Remove and discard the peel, and heat the oil until it registers 360 degrees F on a candy thermometer. Use a soup spoon to form the batter into small ovals, drop the ovals into the oil, a few at a time, and fry for about 3 minutes, or until golden and crisp. Using a slotted spoon, remove the fritters and drain on paper towels. Continue until all the batter has been used.

4 Using a fine sieve or sugar shaker, lightly dust the warm fritters with confectioners' sugar. Serve warm or at room temperature.

NOTE: The oil must be deep enough for the fritters to float freely, or they will brown too quickly and still be raw in the center.

◁ COLMAN ANDREWS: *Banana Fritters*

A TASTE OF GREECE

Spanakopita

Almond Skordalia

White Beans with Garlic

Fillet of Snapper with Tomato, Onion, and Garlic

Baklava

WINE SUGGESTIONS:

Sparkling Wine, Champagne, or Greek White Wine such as
Mantinia or Anhialos *(first course)*

Sauvignon Blanc or Pinot Blanc *(second course)*

Muscat de Patras (Greek dessert wine) or Tawny Port *(dessert)*

WHAT YOU CAN PREPARE AHEAD OF TIME

Up to 1 week ahead: Prepare and freeze the Spanakopita. (See recipe note.) Make the Clarified Butter.

Up to 2 days ahead: Make the Skordalia and White Beans with Garlic.

Up to 1 day ahead: Prepare the tomato sauce for the Fillet of Snapper. Cover and refrigerate. Prepare the Baklava. Cover and store at room temperature.

Charles Bowman came to De Gustibus on the wave of the popularity of the New York City restaurant, Periyali, owned by Nicola Kotsoni and Steve Tzolis. Although he had worked with Charles Palmer at the very American River Café in Brooklyn, he had always had a special love for Greek food. His enthusiasm and knowledge helped the Greek owners of Periyali create a fine restaurant featuring classic Greek cooking tempered by memories of their mothers' kitchens. For his class, Charles prepared a plate of typical *meze*, tempting appetizers that form a complete meal when served with his signature fillet of snapper.

◁ CHARLES BOWMAN: *Spanakopita, Almond Skordalia,* and *White Beans with Garlic*

Spanakopita

This crispy spinach-filled appetizer can be made well in advance, frozen, and the eheated.

1/2 cup plus 1 tablespoon extra- gin olive oil
1/2 cup shredded onions
1/2 cup shredded leeks
Three 10-ounce packages frozen chopped spinach, thawed, drained, and squeezed of all excess liquid
2 tablespoons chopped fresh dill
1 teaspoon salt, or to taste
1/4 teaspoon freshly ground white pepper
2 large eggs
3/4 cup crumbled feta cheese
1/4 cup small-curd cottage cheese
1 tablespoon freshly grated Parmesan cheese
1 tablespoon dry bread crumbs
20 sheets phyllo dough, thawed according to the package directions
2 cups Clarified Butter, melted

■ Special Equipment: Pizza cutter (optional)

1 Assemble *mise en place* trays for this recipe.

2 In a large skillet, heat 1 tablespoon of the oil over medium heat. Add the onions and leeks and sauté for about 5 minutes, or until lightly browned. Stir in the spinach and the remaining 1/2 cup oil and cook, stirring constantly, for about 4 minutes. Add the dill, salt, and white pepper and stir to blend. Transfer to a large bowl. Cover and refrigerate for 1 hour, or until well chilled.

3 Preheat the oven to 400 degrees F.

4 Stir the eggs, cheeses, and bread crumbs into the spinach mixture. Set aside.

5 Lay the phyllo sheets on a dry work surface with a long side toward you. Using a ruler and a pizza cutter or a very sharp knife, cut the sheets crosswise into three 5 1/2-inch-wide strips. Lift off 12 strips and fold crosswise in half. Cut at the fold to make 24 pieces. Again fold the strips in half and cut to make 48 pieces in all. Set aside, covered with a well-wrung-out damp kitchen towel. These will be used as patches to reinforce the phyllo under the filling.

6 Lay 2 strips of dough side by side on the work surface.

(Keep the strips that you are not actually working with covered with a well-wrung-out damp kitchen towel so that the pastry doesn't dry out.) Using a pastry brush, lightly and completely coat both strips with clarified butter, starting at the center and working out toward the ends. Position a phyllo patch lengthwise about an inch up from the bottom and in the center of each strip. Butter the patches.

7 Working quickly, place 1 rounded measuring teaspoon of the filling in the center of 1 patch. Fold the sides of the strip over the filling. Brush the folds with clarified butter. Fold the bottom of the strip up over the filling to form a triangular point, then continue folding, making sure that with each fold you align the bottom edge with the alternate side of the pastry strip, as if you were folding a flag. Lightly coat the finished triangle with butter and place on an ungreased baking sheet. Repeat with the second strip, then continue until all of the phyllo is used.

8 Bake in the top third of the oven for 10 minutes. Brush the triangles with butter again and continue to bake for 10 to 15 minutes longer, or until golden brown. Cool slightly on wire racks and serve warm or at room temperature.

ALTERNATIVE TECHNIQUE: To create Spanakopita rolls, complete the instructions through step 6. Then place 1 rounded measuring teaspoon of the filling in the center of 1 patch. Beginning at the short end, roll the phyllo into a roll to encase the filling. Brush the end of the strip with clarified butter and press to seal the roll. Continue with the instructions in step 7. Instead of folding the strip, roll it up to encase the filling, lightly coating the finished rolls and placing on the baking sheet. Proceed with step 8.

NOTE: If the triangles will be eaten within an hour or so, you can reheat them in a 375-degree-F oven for 10 minutes, or microwave on high for 30 seconds. The triangles can be baked ahead of time and refrigerated in a single layer, covered, until ready to serve. Allow them to reach room temperature before reheating. They can also be frozen in a tightly covered container—take care to stack them carefully. Reheat them, unthawed, in a 375-degree-F oven for about 15 minutes.

Almond Skordalia

Nutty yet light and refreshing, this unusual almond dip is a real treat.

6 ounces (about 6 slices) firm home-style white bread
1 small all-purpose potato (about 3 ounces), peeled and quartered
½ cup coarsely chopped blanched almonds
5 large cloves garlic, minced
3 tablespoons extra-virgin olive oil
2 tablespoons white wine vinegar
1 tablespoon plus 1 teaspoon fresh lemon juice, or more to taste
½ teaspoon sugar
¾ teaspoon salt, or more to taste
Pinch of freshly ground white pepper, or more to taste

1 Assemble *mise en place* trays for this recipe.

2 Trim the crusts from the bread. If not sliced, cut into slices. Lay the slices in a single layer on a baking sheet and let air-dry for 24 hours, turning from time to time.

3 In a small saucepan, cover the potatoes with cool water and bring to a boil over medium heat. Reduce the heat and simmer for about 6 minutes, or until very soft. Remove from the heat, drain, and set aside to cool. Transfer the potatoes to a food processor fitted with the metal blade. Add the almonds and garlic and process until smooth.

4 In a small bowl, combine the oil, vinegar, lemon juice, sugar, salt, and white pepper. Set aside.

5 Fill a large bowl with cool water. One at a time, drop in the dry bread slices. When well soaked, remove and squeeze out most of the water from each slice. The bread should still be moist. With the food processor running, alternately add the bread and the oil mixture to the almond mixture, and process until very smooth. Taste and adjust the seasonings with additional lemon juice, salt, and/or pepper. Transfer to a nonreactive container, cover, and refrigerate for about 4 hours, or until well chilled. If the mixture seems too stiff, beat in a little water. Serve chilled, with pita chips if desired.

White Beans with Garlic

These huge lima beans have a buttery flavor and creamy texture, which make a fabulous amalgam on the appetizer table. For a perfect match, serve with Skordalia.

1 pound dried gigandes (giant white lima beans)
1½ teaspoons salt
½ cup extra-virgin olive oil
¼ teaspoon freshly ground white pepper
1 tablespoon chopped fresh flat-leaf parsley
6 to 8 sprigs fresh flat-leaf parsley

1 Assemble *mise en place* trays for this recipe.

2 Check through the beans and remove any damaged ones or foreign matter. Place in a large bowl and add enough cold water to cover. Discard any beans or skins that float to the surface. Drain in a colander, rinse under cold running water, and return the beans to the bowl. Cover with cold water and soak for 12 hours, or overnight.

3 Drain the beans and transfer to a large heavy saucepan. Add enough cold water to cover by about 1 inch and bring to a boil over high heat. Boil for about 10 minutes, skimming off any foam as it rises to the surface. Add 1 teaspoon salt, reduce the heat, cover, and simmer, stirring occasionally, for 1½ hours, or until the beans are fork-tender. Drain, transfer to a bowl, and cool for about 15 minutes, or until the beans stop steaming but are still very warm.

4 In a small bowl, whisk together the oil, the remaining ½ teaspoon salt, the white pepper, and chopped parsley. Pour over the warm beans and toss gently to coat. Cover and refrigerate for at least 4 hours, or until well chilled and the flavors have blended. Serve at room temperature, garnished with the parsley sprigs.

Fillet of Snapper with Tomato, Onion, and Garlic

This traditional fish preparation is found in homes and restaurants throughout Greece. Its popularity is equaled only by its aromatic flavor and ease of preparation.

¹⁄₃ cup plus 2 tablespoons olive oil
1¹⁄₂ cups chopped onions
1 cup thinly sliced carrots
3 cloves garlic, sliced
1¹⁄₄ cups dry white wine
Two 14¹⁄₂-ounce cans whole tomatoes, drained and chopped
1 cup water
¹⁄₄ cup plus 2 tablespoons chopped fresh flat-leaf parsley
Salt and freshly ground black pepper to taste
Six 6-ounce fillets red snapper, skin on

1 Assemble *mise en place* trays for this recipe.

2 In a large heavy skillet, heat ¹⁄₃ cup of the oil over medium heat. Add the onions, carrots, and garlic and sauté for about 10 minutes, or until very soft but not browned. Stir in the wine and cook, stirring occasionally, for about 15 minutes, or until the wine has evaporated. Stir in the tomatoes, water, ¹⁄₄ cup of the parsley, and salt and pepper to taste, and bring to a boil. Reduce the heat and simmer, uncovered, for about 15 minutes, stirring frequently, until slightly thickened. Set aside to cool slightly.

3 Preheat the oven to 400 degrees F.

4 Rub both sides of the fish with the remaining 2 tablespoons olive oil. Season lightly with salt and pepper and set aside.

5 Spoon about a third of the tomato sauce into a shallow baking dish just large enough to hold the fillets. Arrange the fish, skin side down, on the sauce. Spoon the remaining sauce over the fish and bake for about 12 minutes, or until the fish flakes easily when tested with a fork and the sauce is bubbling.

6 Place the fillets on warm plates, spoon the sauce over, and sprinkle with the remaining 2 tablespoons parsley. Serve immediately, with rice or couscous if desired.

NOTE: You can replace the red snapper with striped bass, black sea bass, or any other firm-fleshed, nonfatty fish fillets.

■ An easy method for chopping canned tomatoes is to cut them up in the can using clean kitchen shears.

CHARLES BOWMAN: *Fillet of Snapper with Tomato, Onion, and Garlic*

Baklava

Known throughout the world as *the* Greek dessert, flaky baklava is incredibly sweet—and incredibly delicious.

2 cups toasted walnuts
2 cups blanched almonds
16 pieces zweibach (or 1 cup dry bread crumbs)
1 tablespoon ground cinnamon
2 tablespoons unsalted butter, softened
One 1-pound package phyllo dough, thawed according to the package directions
1 1/2 cups Clarified Butter, melted
About 18 whole cloves
3 cups sugar
2 1/4 cups water
3/4 cup honey
One 3-inch cinnamon stick
2 tablespoons brandy

■ Special Equipment: Pizza cutter (optional)

1 Assemble *mise en place* trays for this recipe.

2 Place half of the walnuts and almonds in a food processor fitted with the metal blade. Chop fine, using quick pulses and being careful not to pulverize. Transfer to a large bowl. Repeat with the remaining nuts and add to the bowl.

3 Place half of the zweibach in the food processor and process to make fine crumbs. Add to the nuts. Repeat with the remaining zweibach. Add the cinnamon to the nut-crumb mixture and toss to blend.

4 Preheat the oven to 350 degrees F. Butter a 13 x 9-inch glass baking dish with the softened butter.

5 Lay the phyllo sheets on a dry work surface. With a pizza cutter or a long sharp knife, cut the phyllo crosswise in half to make 2 stacks of 12 x 8 1/2-inch sheets. Lay 4 sheets in the pan. (Since the phyllo is not quite long enough to cover the bottom of the pan completely, as you assemble the baklava, alternate the sheets so that every other layer, more or less, reaches the opposite ends of the pan.) Using a pastry brush, coat the sheets of phyllo with clarified butter. Repeat to make 8 layers of phyllo, leaving the final sheet dry.

6 Sprinkle about 1 1/4 cups of the nut mixture over the dry sheet of phyllo. Add 4 more sheets of phyllo, brushing each one with butter but leaving the final sheet dry. Sprinkle with another 1 1/4 cups of the nut mixture. Repeat this procedure two more times, ending with a layer of nuts. Add the remaining sheets of phyllo, brushing each one including the top one with butter.

7 With a long sharp knife, cut the baklava lengthwise into thirds. Then cut these strips on the diagonal into diamond shapes, ending just short of the lengthwise cuts and the sides of the pan. With a short spatula, work around the sides of the pan, tucking the layers of dough in so that the edges are smooth. Stick a clove into the center of each diamond. Bake for about 1 hour, or until golden brown on top. Set on a wire rack to cool completely.

8 In a large saucepan, combine the sugar, water, honey, cinnamon stick, and 3 cloves and bring to a boil over medium heat, stirring with a wooden spoon until the sugar dissolves. Reduce the heat slightly and boil gently for about 10 minutes, until slightly syrupy. Remove from the heat and stir in the brandy. Set aside to cool to lukewarm.

9 Pour the syrup over the cooled baklava. Cover loosely and set aside at room temperature for several hours, or overnight. Finish cutting the baklava just before serving.

CHARLES BOWMAN: *Baklava*

FLAVORS OF THE SUN

Toasted Couscous Risotto

Roast Poussin with Green Olives,
Preserved Lemon, and Garlic

Quick Preserved Lemons

Lemon Curd Napoleon

WINE SUGGESTIONS:

Sauvignon Blanc or Pinot Grigio *(first course)*

Beaujolais or Barbera d'Asti *(second course)*

Late-Harvest Riesling (German or California) *(dessert)*

WHAT YOU CAN PREPARE AHEAD OF TIME

Up to 1 week ahead: Make the Preserved Lemons. Prepare the Chicken Stock (if making your own). Make the Clarified Butter.

Up to 3 days ahead: Make the lemon curd for the Lemon Curd Napoleon.

Up to 2 days ahead: Marinate the chicken for the Roast Poussin.

Early in the day: Prepare the ingredients for the Toasted Couscous Risotto. Roast the garlic for the Roast Poussin, cover, and set aside at room temperature. Bake the phyllo discs, cover, and set aside at room temperature. Clean the raspberries, cover, and refrigerate.

I first met Terrance Brennan in, of all places, the Dominican Republic. He had just finished a stint apprenticing with many of the three-star chefs of France and had taken a break to assist my husband, Alain Sailhac, at the restaurants in Casa de Campo. These jobs, plus his work in many celebrated New York restaurants, were the preparation he needed to achieve his dream: a restaurant of his own. In his travels, the flavors of the Mediterranean had won his heart and so when he was able to, he opened one of the first Mediterranean restaurants in Manhattan. Called Picholine, after the succulent green olive that grows in the South of France, the warm, comfortable bistro has brought a taste of the sun to the city canyons. Terry's menu clearly demonstrates how he has expanded on classical recipes and made them his own. He is truly one of America's great young chefs.

◁ TERRANCE BRENNAN: *Lemon Curd Napoleon*

Toasted Couscous Risotto

This is an absolutely delicious play on classic Italian risotto. And it requires much less stirring time at the stove.

2¹/₂ cups Chicken Stock
¹/₂ cup dry white wine
2 tablespoons olive oil
¹/₂ cup chopped onions
1 tablespoon minced garlic
Pinch of salt, plus more to taste
2 cups toasted Israeli couscous
5 ounces fresh morels, cooked (about 1¹/₂ cups cooked; see Note)
18 medium-sized spears asparagus, trimmed, cut into 1-inch lengths, and blanched
18 ramps or baby leeks, trimmed and blanched
1 cup shelled fresh fava beans or peas, blanched
¹/₂ cup freshly grated Parmesan cheese
3 tablespoons white truffle oil
3 tablespoons unsalted butter, at room temperature
¹/₄ cup chopped fresh flat-leaf parsley
¹/₄ cup snipped fresh chives
Freshly ground white pepper to taste
Parmesan cheese, for shaving

1 Assemble *mise en place* trays for this recipe.

2 In a bowl or large glass measuring cup, combine the stock and wine. Set aside.

3 In a medium-sized saucepan, heat the oil over medium heat. Add the onions, garlic, and a pinch of salt and cook for about 4 minutes, or until just softened. Add the couscous and 2 cups of the stock mixture and cook, stirring occasionally, for about 15 minutes, or until all the liquid has been absorbed. Add the remaining stock mixture and cook for about 4 minutes, beating rapidly with a wooden spoon until the couscous softens and plumps. Stir in the morels, asparagus, ramps, and fava beans and cook for 1 minute.

4 Remove the pan from the heat and stir in the grated cheese, truffle oil, butter, parsley, and chives. Season to taste with salt and white pepper.

5 Spoon into warm shallow soup bowls and garnish with shavings of Parmesan. Serve immediately.

NOTE: Cook the morels by sautéing them in a small amount of olive oil or butter until just tender. If you can't find morels, use any type of small, earthy mushrooms of equal size or use common button mushrooms.

■ Large-grained Israeli couscous does not require the constant stirring rice does when making traditional risotto; stir it only enough to keep it from sticking.

TERRANCE BRENNAN: *Toasted Couscous Risotto*

Roast Poussin with Green Olives, Preserved Lemon, and Garlic

This perfect marriage of flavors is a real crowd pleaser. The saffron provides a rather haunting flavor of exotic places and the preserved lemons add a refreshing zing.

6 poussin, backbones removed
1½ cups olive oil
1 tablespoon chopped garlic
1 tablespoon grated lemon zest
3 pinches of powdered saffron
40 roasted garlic cloves, 10 peeled and 30 left unpeeled
1¼ cups Chicken Stock
2 tablespoons Dijon mustard
1½ cups pitted Picholine olives
Preserved Lemons (recipe follows), well drained
¼ cup chopped fresh cilantro
Salt and freshly ground black pepper to taste

■ Special Equipment: Hand-held immersion blender (optional)

1 Assemble *mise en place* trays for this recipe.

2 Place the poussin in a glass baking dish large enough to hold them comfortably when laid out flat and add ½ cup of the olive oil, the chopped garlic, lemon zest, and saffron. Toss to coat, cover, and refrigerate for 2 days, turning occasionally.

3 Preheat the oven to 500 degrees F.

4 Drain the excess oil from the poussin and place in a roasting pan, skin side up. Bake for about 20 minutes, or until the poussin are just cooked and the skin is crisp.

5 Meanwhile, in a medium-sized saucepan, bring the stock to a boil over medium heat. Remove the pan from the heat, add the peeled garlic cloves and mustard, and blend well with a hand-held immersion blender or a whisk, until the garlic is pureed. Slowly blend in the remaining 1 cup oil. Stir in the olives, Preserved Lemons, and cilantro. Season with salt and pepper to taste.

6 Place a poussin on each warm plate. Spoon the sauce around the poussin and garnish each with 5 unpeeled roasted garlic cloves. Top with some of the preserved lemon zest. (Do not spoon the sauce over the poussin, or the crisp skin will get soggy.) Serve immediately.

NOTE: The poussin, very small young chickens usually weighing about 1 pound, can be replaced with 3 very small broilers, split in half.

■ A hand-held immersion blender quickly and smoothly incorporates hot ingredients into a sauce.

QUICK PRESERVED LEMONS
MAKES ABOUT 2 TABLESPOONS
PREPARATION TIME: ABOUT 5 MINUTES
COOKING TIME: ABOUT 10 MINUTES

This speedy method of preserving lemon zest makes a traditional Middle Eastern flavor accessible to the busy home cook. Once tried, you'll find a million uses for this savory taste.

Zest of 2 large blemish-free lemons, removed with a vegetable peeler or sharp knife and cut into fine julienne
3¼ cups water
2 tablespoons sugar
1 teaspoon salt

1 Assemble *mise en place* trays for this recipe.

2 Put the lemon zest in a small nonreactive saucepan with 1 cup of cold water. Bring to a simmer over high heat and immediately remove from the heat. Drain and repeat. Drain and set aside.

3 Add the water, sugar, and salt to the saucepan and bring to a boil over high heat. Reduce the heat and simmer for about 2 minutes. Add the zest and simmer for about 5 minutes, until softened. Remove the pan from the heat and cool. Use right away or store in the cooking liquid, covered and refrigerated, for up to 2 weeks.

Lemon Curd Napoleon

SERVES 6
PREPARATION TIME: ABOUT 45 MINUTES
COOKING TIME: 4 MINUTES
BAKING TIME: ABOUT 5 MINUTES

This very sophisticated dessert combines two traditional ingredients in a most unusual way. And, as impressive as it is, it's quite easy to put together.

8 large egg yolks
½ cup fresh lemon juice
Grated zest of 2 lemons
¾ cup sugar
8 tablespoons (1 stick) unsalted butter, cubed, at room temperature
6 sheets phyllo dough, thawed according to the package directions
½ cup Clarified Butter, melted
½ cup confectioners' sugar
1 pint raspberries, washed and dried

1 Assemble *mise en place* trays for this recipe.

2 In a medium-sized heat-proof bowl, combine the egg yolks, lemon juice, and zest. Whisk in the sugar and set the bowl over (not in) a pot of simmering water. Do not let the bottom of the bowl touch the water. Cook, whisking constantly, for about 4 minutes, or until thickened.

3 Remove the bowl from the heat and beat in the room-temperature butter, a piece at a time, until completely incorporated.

4 Put the bowl in an ice water bath and stir the curd frequently until cool. Cover and refrigerate until ready to use.

5 Preheat the oven to 400 degrees F. Line 2 baking sheets with parchment paper.

6 Place 1 phyllo sheet on a dry work surface. Using a pastry brush, liberally coat with clarified butter. Top with 2 more sheets, brushing each with butter. Make a second stack with the 3 remaining sheets of phyllo, buttering each one. Using a sharp round 3-inch cookie cutter, cut out 12 circles from each stack. Sprinkle with confectioners' sugar and arrange on the baking sheets. Cover each baking sheet with a sheet of parchment paper and put another baking sheet on top to hold the phyllo discs flat. Bake for about 5 minutes, or until golden. Remove the baking sheets and parchment from the top of the phyllo disks and cool on the baking sheets.

7 Place a small dollop of lemon curd in the center of each plate. Place a phyllo disc on top and dab each with a tablespoon of curd. Arrange 4 raspberries on the curd and top each dessert with another phyllo disc. Repeat to make 4 layers, ending with a phyllo disc. Sprinkle with confectioners' sugar and serve immediately.

NOTE: The raspberries can be replaced with any other berry except strawberries, which are too large for an attractive presentation.

■ When washing raspberries, mist them with a sprayer and turn them upside down on paper towels to dry. If they are handled too much, they tend to disintegrate.

■ The curd can be made with any citrus fruit.

◁ TERRANCE BRENNAN: *Roast Poussin with Green Olives, Preserved Lemon, and Garlic*

GREAT SUNNY FLAVORS

Seared Scallops in Gazpacho-Thyme Sauce

Vegetable Paella

Coffee Granita with Lemon-Scented Ice Milk

BLANCO Y NEGRO

WINE SUGGESTIONS:

Sauvignon Blanc *(first course)*

Sparkling Wine or Beer *(second course)*

WHAT YOU CAN PREPARE AHEAD OF TIME

Up to 1 week ahead: Prepare the Vegetable Stock (if making your own).

Up to 2 days ahead: Prepare the milk mixture for the Lemon-Scented Ice Milk.

Up to 1 day ahead: Make the Gazpacho Thyme Sauce. Make the Coffee Granita and Lemon-Scented Ice Milk.

Early in the day: Julienne, salt, and drain the vegetables for the Vegetable Paella, cover, and refrigerate. Blanch the vegetables for the paella, cover, and refrigerate.

Dominick Cerrone first made his mark at the famed Le Bernardin in New York City. His Spanish roots and childhood memories served him well as a most talented master of fine fish dishes with origins in Spain. However, when he wanted to recreate the tastes of his family table more clearly, he opened Solera, a modern Spanish bistro, in Manhattan. Here, he updated his memories with the techniques and flavors he had learned as a professional chef to bring a worldly menu to sophisticated diners. In the recipes he shared with us at De Gustibus, we were given a sunny taste of the Mediterranean in a new and exciting way.

◁ DOMINICK CERRONE: *Vegetable Paella*

Seared Scallops in Gazpacho-Thyme Sauce

SERVES 6
PREPARATION TIME: ABOUT 1 HOUR
COOKING TIME: ABOUT 7 MINUTES

The ubiquitous gazpacho reaches a totally new dimension when it's served as a sauce for sea scallops. The zesty flavors intermingle with the sweet, firm-fleshed shellfish, giving new meaning to the opening of a fine meal.

SAUCE:

1 red bell pepper, cored, seeded, and chopped
1/2 green bell pepper, cored, seeded, and chopped
1/2 yellow bell pepper, cored, seeded, and chopped
1 large ripe tomato, cored and chopped
1 rib celery, chopped
1/2 hothouse cucumber, chopped
1/4 small onion, chopped
1 clove garlic, chopped
6 fresh basil leaves, chopped
2 cups plus 1 tablespoon tomato juice
2 tablespoons plus 1 teaspoon sherry wine vinegar
1 tablespoon extra-virgin olive oil
Fine sea salt and freshly ground white pepper to taste
Pinch of cayenne pepper, or to taste
1 large sprig fresh thyme

SCALLOPS:

1/2 hothouse cucumber, cut into fine julienne (avoid the seedy center)
1 small zucchini, trimmed and cut into fine julienne (avoid the seedy center)
1 small yellow squash, trimmed and cut into fine julienne (avoid the seedy center)
Fine sea salt to taste
1 red bell pepper, cored, seeded, and finely diced
1/2 green bell pepper, cored, seeded, and finely diced
1/2 yellow bell pepper, cored, seeded, and finely diced
30 sea scallops
Freshly ground white pepper to taste
2 tablespoons extra-virgin olive oil
1 tablespoon fresh thyme leaves
6 small sprigs fresh thyme

1 Assemble *mise en place* trays for this recipe.

2 To make the sauce, in a food processor fitted with the metal blade, combine the chopped bell peppers, tomatoes, celery, cucumbers, onions, garlic, basil, tomato juice, vinegar, and oil. Process until smooth. (For a more refined sauce, strain through a fine sieve.) Transfer to a nonreactive container and season to taste with salt and white pepper and cayenne. Add the thyme sprig and set aside.

3 To prepare the scallops, in a colander, combine the cucumber, zucchini, and yellow squash. Lightly salt and toss well. Set the colander on a plate and drain for about 15

DOMINICK CERRONE: *Seared Scallops in Gazpacho-Thyme Sauce*

minutes. Rinse the vegetables under cold running water, pat dry, and lay on paper towels.

4 In a large saucepan of boiling water, blanch the bell peppers for 10 seconds. Drain, rinse under cold running water, and pat dry. Set aside.

5 Wash the scallops and pat dry with paper towels. Season to taste with salt and white pepper. In a large nonstick skillet, heat the oil over high heat. Add the scallops and sear for about 3 minutes, or until golden on the bottom. Turn and sear for 2 minutes longer, or until the scallops are golden on both sides and firm to the touch. Transfer to a warm baking sheet and cover to keep warm.

6 In the same skillet, sauté the julienned vegetables for 1 minute, or just until they absorb some scallop flavor and soften slightly. Do not overcook.

7 Pour about ¼ cup of the sauce onto the center of each plate and allow to spread to cover the plate. Sprinkle the diced peppers over the sauce. Pile equal portions of julienned vegetables in the center of each plate and surround with an equal number of scallops (or create a balanced design of your choice with the julienned vegetables and scallops). Sprinkle with the fresh thyme leaves and garnish each plate with a thyme sprig. Serve immediately.

NOTE: The julienned vegetables are salted and drained to reduce their moisture content so that they do not release liquid into the sauté pan.

■ Chef Cerrone suggests canned Sacramento-brand tomato juice and either a spicy green Lerida olive oil or a sweet yellow oil from southern Spain.

■ You will have lots of extra sauce, which you can use to garnish other fish dishes or chicken or as a salad or vegetable dressing. The sauce may also be frozen for up to 1 month.

Vegetable Paella

SERVES 6
PREPARATION TIME: ABOUT 1½ HOURS
COOKING TIME: ABOUT 30 MINUTES

This is a dazzling vegetarian dish that can be adapted to any time of the year using fresh seasonal vegetables. When presented at the table, it resembles an edible kaleidoscope.

1 large tomato, peeled, cored, seeded, and chopped
2 tablespoons minced onion
7 cups Vegetable Stock
1½ tablespoons saffron threads
1½ tablespoons Hungarian paprika
1 bay leaf
⅓ cup extra-virgin olive oil
3 cups Arborio rice
½ cup fresh peas
⅓ cup diced roasted red bell pepper
½ to ¾ cup each of at least 6 of the following: blanched sliced carrots, fennel, celery, asparagus, and/or artichoke hearts; blanched corn kernels, sliced broccoli, and/or sliced cauliflower florets; blanched trimmed string beans, sugar snap peas, snow peas, and/or sliced mushrooms; shredded spinach and/or endive

¼ cup chopped fresh herbs [1 tablespoon each parsley and chives combined with any other herb(s) you desire]
Olive oil spray (optional)

■ Special Equipment: Paella pan or other wide shallow two-handled pan (about 14 inches in diameter)

1 Assemble *mise en place* trays for this recipe.

2 In a small bowl, toss the tomatoes and onions to combine.

3 In a medium-sized saucepan, combine the stock, saffron, paprika, bay leaf, and tomato mixture and bring to a boil over medium-high heat. Immediately reduce the heat to a simmer.

4 Heat the paella pan over medium-high heat. Add the oil and when very hot, stir in the rice. Cook, stirring constantly, for about 3 minutes, or until golden brown. Add 6 cups of the simmering stock, reduce the heat until barely simmering, and cook, without stirring, for about 20 minutes, or until the rice is barely *al dente* (see Note); place the vegetables decoratively over the rice as it cooks. Begin with the peas and roasted peppers and add the other vegetables according to the degree of doneness you desire. When the rice is *al dente,* turn off the heat and rest for about 10 minutes.

5 Sprinkle the paella with the herbs and, if desired, spray a bit of olive oil spray over the dish to make it glisten. Serve immediately, bringing the pan to the table.

NOTE: The extra cup of stock should be added if all the liquid has been absorbed before the rice is done. When setting up the decorative vegetable pattern, use one vegetable, such as asparagus, to outline sections.

■ If the paella pan is larger than the stove burner, set it off center and rotate it frequently for even cooking.

Coffee Granita with Lemon-Scented Ice Milk

SERVES 6
INFUSING TIME (MILK MIXTURE ONLY): 12 HOURS
PREPARATION TIME: ABOUT 30 MINUTES
FREEZING TIME: 2 HOURS

Blanco y Negro

Here is a summer dessert that is perfection! Because it is icy-cold, it must be made well in advance. The granita is wonderfully invigorating, rather like eating a refreshing frozen cappuccino.

2/3 cup plus 6 tablespoons granulated sugar
3 cups milk
1 cup heavy cream
Zest of 1 large lemon, removed with a vegetable peeler or sharp knife and cut into strips
One 3-inch cinnamon stick
3 cups very hot espresso (or other strong coffee)
4 large egg whites, at room temperature
Cocoa for dusting (optional)
6 sprigs fresh mint

■ Special Equipment: Hand-held immersion blender

1 Assemble *mise en place* trays for this recipe.

2 In a medium-sized saucepan, combine the 2/3 cup sugar with the milk, cream, lemon zest, and cinnamon stick and bring to a boil over medium heat, stirring to dissolve the sugar. Immediately remove the pan from the heat and pour into a nonreactive container. Cover and refrigerate for at least 12 hours.

3 Dissolve 3 tablespoons of the remaining sugar in the coffee and pour onto a rimmed baking sheet. Place in the freezer and freeze, frequently breaking up the frozen edges with a fork to prevent the mixture from freezing in a solid block. When completely frozen, transfer to a small freezer container and keep frozen.

4 Put a 9 x 13-inch pan in the freezer. Place 6 goblets or coupes in the refrigerator.

5 In a large bowl, using an electric mixer set at medium-high speed, beat the egg whites with the remaining 3 tablespoons sugar until they hold stiff peaks. Refrigerate this meringue.

6 Using a hand-held immersion blender, whip the chilled milk mixture until it holds firm peaks. Fold into the chilled meringue, scrape into the chilled pan, cover, and freeze for 2 hours.

7 When ready to serve, scrape the coffee granita *(Negro)* into the chilled goblets. Place a scoop of ice milk *(Blanco)* on top. Serve immediately, dusted with cocoa if desired, garnishing each with a mint sprig and a cookie.

NOTE: You could also flavor the ice milk with either lemon grass or lemon verbena.

DOMINICK CERRONE: *Coffee Granita
with Lemon-Scented Ice Milk* ▷

A MAGICAL MEDITERRANEAN BUFFET

Baba Ganoush

Sofrito of Baby Lamb with Romesco Sauce

Fattoush

Blueberry Clafoutis

WINE SUGGESTIONS:

Champagne *(first course)*

Merlot or Pinot Noir *(second course—lamb and fattoush)*

Ruby Port *(dessert)*

WHAT YOU CAN PREPARE AHEAD OF TIME

Up to 2 days ahead: Prepare the Baba Ganoush and the Romesco Sauce.

Up to 1 day ahead: Chop the vegetables for the Sofrito of Baby Lamb. Place in a plastic bag and refrigerate. Bake the pita for the Fattoush. Make the dressing for the Fattoush, cover, and refrigerate.

Early in the day: Prepare the Sofrito of Baby Lamb. Reheat for about 15 minutes in a 325-degree-F oven before serving. Prepare the vegetables and herbs for the Fattoush. Place in plastic bags and refrigerate. Make the Blueberry Clafoutis. Reheat for about 10 minutes in a 300-degree-F oven before serving.

Andy D'Amico is a De Gustibus treasure. Over the years, he has taught many classes, always pleasantly surprising us with the versatility of his repertoire. Executive Chef at New York's Sign of the Dove and partner with Joe, Berge, and Henny Santo in a host of other restaurants, Andy presented this buffet as a home cook's dream. I had enjoyed a similar table at The Sign of the Dove at a baby shower given for a dear friend, Dorothy Cann Hamilton, the founder of The French Culinary Institute in New York City. At both the party and the De Gustibus class, all the dishes stood up to the demands of an evening sitting out on the table. They were all prepared in advance and offered an abundance of flavors that married well.

◁ ANDREW D'AMICO: *Baba Ganoush, Sofrito of Lamb with Romesco Sauce, Fattoush, and Blueberry Clafoutis*

Baba Ganoush

Andy's tangy version of the famous Lebanese dip has the added flavor of smoky eggplant. For a stunning visual effect, complete the dish with the traditional pomegranate seed garnish. Serve this with pita bread, crackers, or toasted country-style bread rubbed with garlic.

1 large eggplant, about 1 pound
2 cloves garlic
1/4 to 1/3 cup fresh lemon juice
Salt to taste
2 to 4 tablespoons tahini
2 tablespoons olive oil
Ground cumin to taste
Freshly ground black pepper to taste

GARNISH (OPTIONAL)

3 tablespoons pomegranate seeds, or 1 tablespoon chopped fresh flat-leaf parsley, or 1/8 teaspoon ground sumac, or 1 tablespoon extra-virgin olive oil

1 Assemble *mise en place* trays for this recipe.

2 Prepare a charcoal or gas grill or preheat the broiler.

3 Using a fork, puncture the eggplant in several places. Roast the eggplant on the grill or under the broiler for about 20 minutes, turning occasionally, until the skin is completely charred and the eggplant is soft. Cool until cool enough to handle. Halve and scrape out the pulp, put it in a fine sieve, and hold under gently running cold water to wash away any bitterness. Shake dry and use your hands to squeeze out as much liquid as possible.

4 In a food processor fitted with the metal blade, combine the eggplant pulp, garlic, 1/4 cup lemon juice, and salt to taste. Process until smooth. Add 2 tablespoons tahini and process just to incorporate. Taste and, if necessary, adjust the flavors with additional lemon juice and tahini. With the processor running, add the oil. Season to taste with cumin, salt, and pepper. Transfer to a small serving bowl, cover, and chill for at least 30 minutes, or up to 2 days.

5 Garnish with pomegranate seeds, parsley, sumac, or a drizzle of olive oil if desired, and serve.

NOTE: To retrieve pomegranate seeds neatly, barely cut into the tough skin and then peel it back as you would peel an orange. The seeds will fall out without staining your hands with the intense red juice.

ANDREW D'AMICO: *Baba Ganoush*

Sofrito of Baby Lamb with Romesco Sauce

This succulent dish traces its beginnings to the Spanish countryside. This is served with the meat removed from the bone and kept warm in a beautiful chafing dish. If serving the lamb as an entrée, add roasted potatoes and a crisp green vegetable.

1/4 cup olive oil
One 6-pound leg of lamb
2 bulbs garlic, split in half crosswise
2 cups finely diced onions
1 cup finely diced fennel
2 sprigs fresh thyme
2 sprigs fresh rosemary
2 sprigs fresh cilantro
2 bay leaves
Romesco Sauce (recipe follows)
Coarse salt to taste

1 Assemble *mise en place* trays for this recipe.

2 Preheat the oven to 350 degrees F.

3 In a roasting pan or casserole with a tight-fitting lid, heat the oil over medium heat. Add the lamb and sear, turning frequently, for about 6 minutes, or until brown on all sides.

4 Add the garlic, onions, and fennel and sauté for about 10 minutes, or until the vegetables are golden brown. Add the thyme, rosemary, cilantro, bay leaves, and 3 cups of water. Cover and roast for 45 minutes.

5 Turn the meat and check the water level. If the vegetables look dry, add 1 more cup of water. Continue to roast, turning and adding water, 1/2 cup at a time, when necessary, for an additional 1 hour and 15 minutes.

6 Using a pastry brush, thinly coat the lamb on all sides with Romesco Sauce. Sprinkle with salt. Cover and return to the oven for 1 hour longer.

7 Turn the lamb, brush with Romesco Sauce, and season with coarse salt. Return to the oven, uncovered, and roast for approximately 45 minutes longer, or until the meat easily falls from the bone. Transfer to a large chafing dish and serve with the remaining sauce on the side.

ANDREW D'AMICO: *Sofrito of Lamb with Romesco Sauce*

ROMESCO SAUCE
MAKES ABOUT 1 1/2 CUPS

3 plum tomatoes, halved
2 fresh hot green chiles, such as jalapeño or serrano, halved and seeded
1 red bell pepper, cored, quartered, and seeded
1 small bulb garlic, separated into cloves
1/2 cup sliced unblanched almonds
1 dried New Mexican red chile
1 cup water
3 tablespoons red wine vinegar
2 tablespoons chopped fresh flat-leaf parsley
1 tablespoon sweet paprika
1/2 cup olive oil
Salt and freshly ground black pepper to taste

1 Preheat the oven to 350 degrees F.

2 Place the tomatoes, fresh chiles, bell pepper, garlic, and almonds on a nonstick baking sheet, keeping each ingredient separate, and bake for about 20 minutes, removing the items as they are cooked: The almonds will brown quickly, while the vegetables will probably require the full time for their skins to blister and their flesh to soften. Cool, then peel the peppers and garlic. Finely chop the almonds in a spice grinder or finely grind them with a mortar and pestle.

343

3 In a small saucepan, combine the dried chile and water and bring to a boil over high heat. Reduce the heat and simmer for about 10 minutes, or until the liquid is reduced to ¼ cup. Remove the pan from the heat and cool slightly. Seed and stem the chile and set aside. Reserve the cooking water.

4 In a food processor fitted with the metal blade, combine the green chiles, bell pepper, garlic, dried chile and cooking water, vinegar, parsley, and paprika and process until smooth. With the processor running, slowly add the oil. When well blended, season to taste with salt and pepper. Transfer to a nonreactive bowl and fold in the almonds. Use immediately or cover and refrigerate until ready to use.

■ Any leftover sauce can be used as a base for a soup or as a glaze for grilled meats.

■ You can cook veal shanks, beef shanks, or rack of lamb or rack of veal in this manner. The sauce also serves as a glaze for roast rack of lamb.

Fattoush

SERVES 6
PREPARATION TIME: ABOUT 30 MINUTES
TOASTING TIME: ABOUT 10 MINUTES

This hearty bread salad has its roots in Syria. Related to the Tuscan panzanella, an equally filling side dish, fattoush is an excellent accompaniment to grilled or roasted meats.

6 day-old 6-inch pita breads, cut into ½-inch squares
2 cloves garlic, minced
1 serrano chile, seeded and minced
1 teaspoon salt, plus more to taste
½ cup fresh lemon juice
½ teaspoon ground sumac
¼ cup extra-virgin olive oil
¼ cup virgin olive oil
Freshly ground black pepper to taste
3 large ripe but firm tomatoes, peeled, cored, seeded, and cut into ¼-inch dice
2 scallions, cut into ¼-inch dice
1 small red onion, cut into ¼-inch dice
1 small red bell pepper, cored, seeded, and cut into ¼-inch dice
1 large cucumber, peeled, seeded, and cut into ¼-inch dice
1 large head Romaine lettuce, inner leaves only, coarsely chopped
½ cup chopped fresh flat-leaf parsley
½ cup chopped fresh mint
½ cup chopped fresh cilantro

■ Special Equipment: Mini food processor

1 Assemble *mise en place* trays for this recipe.

2 Preheat the oven to 350 degrees F.

3 Place the pita on a nonstick baking sheet and bake for 10 minutes, or until golden brown. Set aside.

ANDREW D'AMICO: *Fattoush*

344

4 In a mini food processor fitted with the metal blade (or in a mortar and pestle), process (or grind) the garlic, chile, and salt until a paste forms. Transfer to a small bowl and stir in the lemon juice and sumac. Whisk in the oils and season to taste with salt, if necessary, and pepper.

5 In a salad bowl, combine the tomatoes, scallions, onions, bell peppers, cucumbers, lettuce, parsley, mint, and cilantro. Add the dressing and toss to combine. Toss in the toasted pita and serve immediately.

Blueberry Clafoutis

SERVES 6 TO 8
PREPARATION TIME: ABOUT 20 MINUTES
BAKING TIME: ABOUT 40 MINUTES

This easy-to-prepare, pudding-like dessert is always well received, especially if the fruit is ripe and sweet. Although French, clafoutis is not from the Mediterranean area but from the Limousin region, where it is traditionally made with dark, juicy cherries.

$1/2$ cup plus 2 tablespoons confectioners' sugar
2 large egg yolks
1 large egg
8 tablespoons (1 stick) unsalted butter, cut into pieces, softened
1 cup all-purpose flour
1 cup hot boiled milk
2 tablespoons kirschwasser, rum, or Chambord
$2^{1}/2$ cups ripe blueberries, picked over, rinsed, and dried

■ Special Equipment: 9-inch round flan dish or cake pan

1 Assemble *mise en place* trays for this recipe.

2 Preheat the oven to 400 degrees F. Generously butter a 9-inch flan dish or cake pan.

3 In a large bowl, using an electric mixer set on medium speed, beat $1/2$ cup of the sugar and the egg yolks for 2 to 3 minutes, or until thick. Beat in the whole egg and then gradually beat in the butter, a piece at a time. Beat in the flour. Beat in the milk and kirschwasser and mix until smooth.

4 Pour into the prepared pan and distribute the berries evenly over the top. Bake on the lower rack of the oven for about 40 minutes, or until the top is golden and the center is set. Cool on a wire rack for 10 minutes. Sprinkle with the remaining 2 tablespoons sugar and serve warm.

NOTE: Any ripe berry can be used in place of or in combination with the blueberries. If the berries are not naturally sweet, toss with $1/4$ cup of sugar and let stand for 30 minutes before adding to the batter. The clafoutis will be puffed when it comes out of the oven, similar to a soufflé, and although it deflates quickly, it will still taste delicious.

ANDREW D'AMICO: *Blueberry Clafoutis*

TRIBUTE TO THE SOUTH OF FRANCE

Warm Shrimp Salad
with Crisp Marinated Vegetables

St. Pierre Roasted on a Bed of Fennel
with Fresh Tomato Purée and Niçoise Olives

Sautéed Pears with Honey Ice Cream

WINE SUGGESTIONS:

Chardonnay or White Côtes-du-Rhône *(first course)*

Pinot Grigio or Sauvignon Blanc *(second course)*

Tawny Port *(dessert)*

WHAT YOU CAN PREPARE AHEAD OF TIME

Up to 1 week ahead: Make the Honey Ice Cream.

Early in the day: Prepare the vegetables for the Warm Shrimp Salad. Place in plastic bags and refrigerate. Make the tomato puree and prepare the basil and olives for the St. Pierre Roasted on a Bed of Fennel. Cover and refrigerate. Sauté the pears for the dessert (undercook them slightly, cover, and refrigerate). Reheat before serving.

Just a mention of the world-renowned Alain Ducasse brings a smile to my face. Currently, he is the only chef in a hotel to have three Michelin stars—for the extraordinary Louis XV Restaurant in Monte Carlo. I met Alain many years ago in New York while he was the executive chef at the Hotel Terrasse in Juan-les-Pins. He asked to teach at De Gustibus, a request I was reluctant to encourage, as he spoke no English. But, of course, he convinced me and an incredible class resulted. Even though most of us there spoke no French, the passion and love he brought to the classroom transcended all boundaries. We were enthralled.

Alain Ducasse is best known for his ardor for the fresh, near-perfect ingredients found in the South of France and for the simple but simply delicious preparations to which they lend themselves. He always maximizes basic flavor and frequently does little to alter the inherent taste of his ingredients. In the years since we first met and he mesmerized the De Gustibus classroom, I have had the good fortune to dine several times at Louis XV. Each time I am dazzled by his talents. Vive le Chef Ducasse!

◁ ALAIN DUCASSE: *Warm Shrimp Salad with Crisp Marinated Vegetables*

Warm Shrimp Salad with Crisp Marinated Vegetables

SERVES 6
PREPARATION TIME: ABOUT 30 MINUTES
COOKING TIME: ABOUT 3 MINUTES

This dish embodies everything great food should be; it's light, colorful, and filled with flavor. You must have absolutely peak-of-freshness vegetables for it to be perfect.

1/2 pound pencil-thin asparagus, trimmed, stalks finely minced and tips reserved

1/2 pound very ripe tomatoes, peeled, cored, seeded, finely diced, and drained

2/3 pound very young fava beans, shelled and peeled, or baby lima beans, shelled

4 baby artichoke hearts, finely diced (see Note)

1/2 cup plus 1 tablespoon extra-virgin olive oil

Juice of 1/2 lemon

Coarse salt and freshly ground black pepper to taste

2 pounds peeled and deveined medium-sized shrimp (2 1/2 to 3 pounds shrimp in the shell)

1 cup shredded fresh basil

1 Assemble *mise en place* trays for this recipe.

2 In a nonreactive bowl, combine the asparagus, tomatoes, beans, and artichokes. Add 1/2 cup of the oil, the lemon juice, and coarse salt and pepper to taste. Toss and let marinate for about 5 minutes.

3 In a large sauté pan, heat the remaining 1 tablespoon oil over medium-high heat. Add the shrimp, season to taste with coarse salt and pepper, and sauté for about 3 minutes, or until pink and just opaque throughout. Remove from the heat.

4 Place equal portions of the marinated vegetables on each plate. Top with the shrimp and garnish with the shredded basil. Serve immediately.

NOTE: For baby artichoke hearts, buy tiny artichokes and peel away only the tough outer leaves. If the choke is tough, cut it away. Very often, in very small artichokes the choke may be tender enough to eat.

■ If any of the vegetables are not available in their pristine state, replace them with those that are.

St. Pierre Roasted on a Bed of Fennel with Fresh Tomato Purée and Niçoise Olives

SERVES 6
PREPARATION TIME: ABOUT 30 MINUTES
COOKING TIME: ABOUT 20 MINUTES

Here again, the flavor of the dish depends on the quality of the ingredients. Each should be at the height of its goodness—the fish fresh from the sea, the tomatoes picked from the vine, and the basil snipped from its stalk—and the olive oil and olives of the finest quality.

2 pounds very ripe tomatoes, peeled, cored, seeded, and diced

Three 2 1/2- to 3-pound St. Pierre (John Dory) or red snapper, well cleaned, heads removed

Coarse salt and freshly ground black pepper to taste

1/4 pound dried fennel twigs (see Note)

1/2 cup water

1/2 cup extra-virgin olive oil

8 tablespoons (1 stick) unsalted butter, softened

Juice of 1/2 lemon

1/2 cup pitted and quartered Niçoise olives

3 tablespoons minced fresh basil

1 tablespoon slivered fresh basil

1 Assemble *mise en place* trays for this recipe.

2 Preheat the oven to 400 degrees F.

3 In a food processor fitted with the metal blade, process the tomatoes until smooth. Transfer to a fine sieve lined with cheesecloth and allow to drain thoroughly, then transfer to a medium-sized nonstick sauté pan and set aside. (Reserve the juice for another use.)

ALAIN DUCASSE: *St. Pierre Roasted on a Bed of Fennel with Fresh Tomato Purée and Niçoise Olives (red snapper substituted in photograph)* ▷

4 Pat the fish dry and season to taste with coarse salt and pepper. Put the fennel twigs in a baking dish large enough to hold the fish comfortably. Add the water and set the fish on the twigs. Sprinkle with 6 tablespoons of the oil and tightly cover with aluminum foil.

5 Bake for about 15 minutes, or just until the fish flakes when pierced with a fork and the flesh is opaque throughout. Transfer to a warm serving dish and cover loosely to keep warm.

6 Strain the pan juices into a small saucepan and place over medium heat. Whisk in the butter, bit by bit. Whisk in the remaining 2 tablespoons oil. When well blended, whisk in the lemon juice and season to taste with coarse salt and pepper. Remove from the heat and keep warm.

7 Set the tomato purée over medium heat and add the olives and minced basil. Stir and cook for 2 minutes, or until just warm.

8 Lift the fillets from the fish and place 1 on each plate. Spoon a little tomato purée around the fish. Add the slivered basil to the butter sauce, stir gently, and spoon on either side of the fish. Serve immediately.

NOTE: Dried fennel twigs are available at specialty stores. One large bunch of basil should be sufficient for this recipe.

■ You can replace the St. Pierre with any other firm-textured, nonfatty fish, such as striped bass or black sea bass. If whole fish are not available, use 6 fillets about 1 inch thick.

SERVES 6
PREPARATION TIME: ABOUT 20 MINUTES
COOKING TIME: ABOUT 10 MINUTES
FREEZING TIME (ICE CREAM ONLY): ABOUT 7 HOURS

Sautéed Pears with Honey Ice Cream

The honey ice cream brings a full-bodied taste of the Mediterranean to this dessert. Use pears or choose another seasonally ripe fruit (apples or nectarines, for example) that complements the honey flavor.

2 cups milk
1 cup heavy cream
4 large egg yolks
1 cup honey
8 tablespoons (1 stick) unsalted butter
4 Bartlett or other firm pears, peeled, cored, halved, and sliced
1/4 cup granulated sugar

■ **Special Equipment: Ice cream freezer**

1 Assemble *mise en place* trays for this recipe.

2 Pour the milk into a medium-sized saucepan and the cream into a small saucepan. Bring each to a boil over medium heat, remove from the heat, and immediately pour the cream into the milk.

3 In a small bowl, whisk the egg yolks and honey together. Whisk in a bit of the hot milk mixture to temper the eggs and then whisk the eggs into the milk mixture. Return to medium heat and, whisking constantly, bring to a simmer. Cook for 2 minutes, whisking constantly, or until the mixture thickens enough to coat the back of a spoon. Cool to room temperature and then refrigerate until chilled. Or chill in an ice water bath.

4 Strain the mixture through a fine sieve into an ice cream freezer. Freeze according to the manufacturer's directions. When frozen, transfer to a container with a tight-fitting lid. Cover and freeze for at least 6 hours before serving.

5 In a large sauté pan, melt the butter over medium heat. Add the pears and sugar and sauté for about 5 minutes, or until golden. Place an equal portion in each shallow bowl and top with a scoop of ice cream. Serve immediately.

◁ ALAIN DUCASSE: *Sautéed Pears with Honey Ice Cream*

WHAT YOU CAN PREPARE AHEAD OF TIME

Up to 3 days ahead: Prepare the Fish Stock (if making your own). Make the Gateau Rolla.

Early in the day: Prepare the vegetables and citrus juices for the Spanish Fish Soup. Cover and refrigerate. Prepare the Aïoli. Prepare the vegetables for the Spaghetti with Saffroned Onions. Cover and refrigerate.

CALIFORNIA ON THE MEDITERRANEAN

Spanish Fish Soup

CALDO DE PERRO

Spaghetti with Saffroned Onions, Greens, Fennel, Sun-Dried Tomatoes, and Currants

Gateau Rolla

WINE SUGGESTIONS:

Sparkling California Wine, Spanish Cava, or White Sangria *(first course)*

Pinot Grigio *(second course)*

Joyce Goldstein is the grand doyenne of Mediterranean cuisine in America. The menu at her San Francisco restaurant, Square One, has evolved from her love of these robust foods, further refined by the personal touch she brings to everything she has accomplished. Because of her enthusiasm and precision, her classes at De Gustibus are always met with great anticipation. Joyce's articulate manner clearly defines her recipes; the hows and whys of each dish are readily understood by the home cook. Each of two main dishes presented here can easily stand alone. Serve either one with a green salad, a cheese course, and a great bottle of wine and you will have created a wonderful meal.

◁ JOYCE GOLDSTEIN: *Spanish Fish Soup*

Spanish Fish Soup

Caldo de Perro

The classic *caldo de perro* from Cadiz is made with only fish, fish stock, and the juice of bitter oranges. Joyce is a bit more expansive in her interpretation. She has added some shellfish, a little heat in the form of hot pepper flakes, and a marvelous orange-and-almond aïoli garnish.

¼ cup olive oil
4 cups finely diced yellow onions
3 large cloves garlic, minced
1 tablespoon red pepper flakes, or to taste
1 bay leaf
4 cups Fish Stock
1 cup fresh orange juice
¼ cup fresh lime or lemon juice
2 teaspoons grated orange zest
Salt and freshly ground black pepper to taste
60 Manila or other very small clams, well scrubbed
1½ pounds monkfish, cleaned and cut into 2-inch chunks
1 pound sea scallops, trimmed of tough side muscle
Orange-Almond Aïoli (recipe follows)

1 Assemble *mise en place* trays for this recipe.

2 In a large sauté pan, heat the oil over medium heat. Add the onions and sauté for about 10 minutes, or until soft and translucent. Stir in the garlic, red pepper flakes, and bay leaf and sauté for 3 minutes. Add the stock and bring to a simmer. Reduce the heat and simmer for 15 minutes. Stir in the orange and lime juices, zest, and salt and pepper to taste.

3 Carefully drop the clams and fish chunks into the pan. Cover and simmer for about 5 minutes, or until the clams open. Carefully drop in the scallops and simmer for another 2 to 3 minutes, or until just cooked through and opaque.

4 Ladle into warm soup bowls. Place a dollop of the aïoli in the center of each bowl and serve immediately.

■ Flounder or rockfish can be substituted for the monkfish; add to the soup after the clams have cooked for 3 minutes.

■ You can garnish the soup with large croutons if desired.

■ Manilla clams are tiny clams, a little larger than a nickel. Substitute small cherrystones if necessary.

ORANGE-ALMOND AÏOLI
MAKES ABOUT 1½ CUPS

1 cup mayonnaise
¼ cup fresh orange juice
1 teaspoon fresh lemon juice
½ cup toasted sliced almonds, crushed
2 teaspoons puréed garlic
2 teaspoons grated orange zest
¼ teaspoon salt
Pinch of freshly ground black pepper

In a nonreactive bowl, whisk together the mayonnaise and orange and lemon juices. Whisk in the almonds, garlic, orange zest, and salt and pepper. Cover and refrigerate until ready to use.

NOTE: To prepare the crushed almonds, grind in a mortar and pestle or crush them with a rolling pin. To prepare the puréed garlic, process a few cloves in a mini food processor or grind in a mortar and pestle.

Spaghetti with Saffroned Onions, Greens, Fennel, Sun-Dried Tomatoes, and Currants

This unusual pasta dish finds its roots in Sicily, with the Arabic influences of saffroned onions and currants combined with indigenous fennel and sun-dried tomatoes. It is complex in flavor and rich in taste, yet inexpensive and easy to prepare.

1 cup currants
¼ teaspoon crushed saffron threads
2 tablespoons dry white wine
Coarse salt to taste
1 pound spaghetti
¾ cup olive oil
4 onions, sliced ¼ inch thick
2 cups ⅛-inch-thick fennel slices
¾ to 1 cup finely julienned dry-packed sun-dried tomatoes (see Note)
2 tablespoons minced anchovy fillets
1 tablespoon minced garlic
1½ pounds Swiss chard or escarole, trimmed, washed, dried, and cut into a fine chiffonade

1 Assemble *mise en place* trays for this recipe.

2 In a small bowl, combine the currants and hot water to cover. Set aside to plump for at least 10 minutes. In a small cup, combine the saffron and wine. Set aside to soak.

3 Bring a large pot of salted water to a boil over high heat. Add the spaghetti and stir to prevent clumping. Cook for about 12 minutes, or until *al dente*.

4 Meanwhile, in a large sauté pan, heat the oil over medium heat. Add the onions and sauté for about 4 minutes, or until soft. Add the saffron mixture and cook for 1 minute. Stir in the fennel, sun-dried tomatoes, anchovies, and garlic and sauté for 3 minutes.

5 Drain the currants and add to the onion mixture. Stir in the Swiss chard and cook, stirring, for about 2 minutes, or until wilted.

6 Drain the pasta and transfer to a large shallow bowl. Add the sauce, toss to combine, and serve immediately on warm plates.

NOTE: Sun-dried tomatoes vary widely in quality and saltiness. If they are sweet, use the larger amount called for in the recipe; if salty, use the lesser.

Joyce says "no cheese, please" on this pasta. However, she says, you could add some chunks of grilled tuna for an even more flavorful and filling dish.

JOYCE GOLDSTEIN: *Spaghetti with Saffroned Onions, Greens, Fennel, Sun-Dried Tomatoes, and Currants*

Gateau Rolla

MAKES ONE 9-INCH CAKE; SERVES 6
PREPARATION TIME: ABOUT 1 HOUR
BAKING TIME: ABOUT 1 HOUR
CHILLING TIME: ABOUT 13 HOURS

This rich dessert is a real crowd pleaser! And it is an even greater boon to the home cook as it is best made at least one day in advance.

MERINGUE LAYERS:

About 2 tablespoons flavorless vegetable oil
5 large egg whites, at room temperature
Pinch of salt
1 cup granulated sugar
1 teaspoon pure vanilla extract
3/4 cup finely grated almonds

FILLING:

6 ounces sweet chocolate, coarsely chopped (see Note)
2 tablespoons nonalkalized cocoa powder
3 large egg whites
3/4 cup granulated sugar
1 1/2 cups (3 sticks) unsalted butter, at room temperature

1 Assemble *mise en place* trays for this recipe.

2 Preheat the oven to 250 degrees F. Trace a circle 9 inches in diameter onto each of four 10-inch squares of parchment paper. Lightly oil 4 baking sheets with vegetable oil and place a piece of parchment paper onto each sheet, tracing side down. Lightly oil the paper. (See Note.)

3 To make the meringue layers, in a large bowl, using an electric mixer set on high speed, beat the egg whites with the salt until they hold stiff peaks. Gradually beat in 3/4 cup of the sugar and continue to beat until stiff and glossy. Lower the speed and beat in the remaining 1/4 cup sugar and the vanilla. Fold in the almonds just until blended.

4 Spread or pipe the meringue into rounds about 1/4 inch thick on the parchment, staying within the outlines of the circles. Bake for about 1 hour, or until just dry. Carefully lift the meringues and paper off the baking sheets and cool on the paper on wire racks.

5 While the meringues are baking, make the filling: Melt the chocolate with the cocoa in the top half of a double boiler set over barely simmering water, stirring frequently until smooth. Set aside to cool.

6 Put the egg whites in a heatproof bowl and set it over a pan of hot water. Using an electric mixer set on high speed, beat until foamy. Gradually beat in the sugar until soft peaks form. Beat in the butter, a bit at a time, then beat in the chocolate mixture until smooth. Transfer to a clean bowl, cover, and refrigerate for about 1 hour, or until firm enough to spread.

7 Carefully peel the cooled meringue off the parchment paper. (If a meringue cracks or breaks, you can patch it with the filling.)

8 Spread equal portions of the chocolate filling over 3 of the meringue circles, spreading it about 1/4 inch thick. Stack them on a cake plate. Place the remaining meringue on top and carefully frost the top and sides with the remaining chocolate filling.

9 Refrigerate the cake for about 1 hour, or until the frosting has set. Cover and allow to chill for at least 12 hours, or up to 2 days. Bring to room temperature before serving.

NOTE: This recipe calls for sweet chocolate, which is dark sweet chocolate, sweeter than bittersweet or semisweet chocolate. The most widely available brand in the United States is Baker's German Sweet Chocolate.

Only one 10-inch parchment paper square will fit on a baking sheet. You may have to bake these in two batches if your oven is not large enough to hold 4 baking sheets.

JOYCE GOLDSTEIN: *Gateau Rolla* ▷

A NIGHT IN MOROCCO

*Ahi Tuna Tartare with Fennel, Caraway Toast,
and Green Olive Tapenade*

Lamb Tagine with Almonds, Dates, and Toasted Bulgur

Caramelized Pear and Cranberry Upside-Down Cake

WINE SUGGESTIONS:

Champagne or Sparkling Wine *(first course)*

Syrah (French, California, or Australian) *(second course)*

Tawny Port or Muscat de Beaumes-de-Venise *(dessert)*

WHAT YOU CAN PREPARE AHEAD OF TIME

Up to 1 week ahead: Make the Green Olive Tapenade. Cover and refrigerate. Prepare the Chicken Stock (if making your own).

Up to 2 days ahead: Make the Lamb Tagine with Almonds, Dates, and Toasted Bulgur, but omit the almonds and the final parsley addition. Cover and refrigerate. Reheat and garnish just before serving.

Early in the day: Make the Toasted Bulgur. Reheat as directed in the recipe note. Bake the Caramelized Pear and Cranberry Upside-Down Cake. Reheat as directed in the recipe note.

Up to 3 hours ahead: Prepare the Caraway Toasts for broiling.

Up to 1 hour ahead: Prepare the Ahi Tuna Tartare. Cover and refrigerate.

Up to 30 minutes ahead: Make the Fennel Salad.

Matthew Kenney is a New York chef who has been greatly influenced by the cuisines of the Mediterranean countries. He first came to my attention when he was chef at the very trendy Banana Cafe, but he became even more noticeable after he opened the stylish Matthew's Restaurant on Third Avenue in Manhattan. His food is well seasoned and full of flavor, with definite Mediterranean overtones. The menu that follows was a De Gustibus highlight, resulting after Chef Kenney attended an international food conference in Morocco. He returned enchanted with the foods that he had encountered and immediately began introducing them on his menu. His class benefited from his enthusiasms—we all caught the Moroccan magic and Matthew enthralled us with his gentle, earnest approach in the kitchen. The dishes are imaginative, light, and redolent with Moroccan influences.

◁ MATTHEW KENNEY: *Caramelized Pear and Cranberry Upside-Down Cake*

Ahi Tuna Tartare with Fennel, Caraway Toast, and Green Olive Tapenade

For this dish to be perfection, you must use sushi-grade tuna. If it is unavailable, substitute very fresh salmon. For a different take on this aromatic recipe, you could also marinate tuna fillets for about an hour in the tartare ingredients and then grill them.

3/4 **pound very fresh sushi-grade tuna, cut into** 1/8-**inch dice**
1 **tablespoon plus** 1 1/2 **teaspoons grated lemon zest**
1 **tablespoon plus** 1 1/2 **teaspoons olive oil**
1 1/2 **teaspoons light soy sauce**
1/4 **cup plus 1 tablespoon minced fresh chives, flat-leaf parsley, or cilantro**
Tabasco sauce to taste

Salt and freshly ground black pepper to taste
Fennel Salad (recipe follows)
Green Olive Tapenade (recipe follows)
Caraway Toast (recipe follows)
1/4 **cup sliced pitted Picholine olives**
2 **tablespoons minced fresh fennel fronds (fennel tops)**
Cracked black pepper to taste

1 Assemble *mise en place* trays for this recipe.

2 In a medium-sized bowl, combine the tuna, lemon zest, oil, soy sauce, and chives. Toss gently. Add the Tabasco and salt and pepper to taste.

3 Place equal portions of the salad on 6 plates and spoon the tuna mixture on top. Spoon some tapenade around the edge and put a small amount on top of each portion of tuna. Arrange 4 toast quarters next to each salad and garnish the plates with the sliced olives and fennel fronds. Sprinkle with cracked pepper and serve.

■ To prevent sticking when cutting tuna (or other fish), rub the knife with a lightly oiled paper towel.

FENNEL SALAD
SERVES 6

2 **medium-sized bulbs fennel, cut into small dice**
1 **tablespoon plus** 1 1/2 **teaspoons minced shallots**
3/4 **teaspoon freshly ground toasted coriander seeds**
3 **tablespoons fresh lemon juice**
1 **tablespoon plus** 1 1/2 **teaspoons sherry wine vinegar**
1/2 **to** 2/3 **cup walnut oil**
Salt and freshly ground black pepper to taste

1 Put the fennel in a bowl.

2 In another bowl, combine the shallots, coriander, lemon juice, and vinegar. Whisk in the oil and season to taste with salt and pepper. Pour over the fennel and toss to combine. Serve immediately.

NOTE: Fennel quickly discolors, so it should not be cut more than 30 minutes before use. Although lemon juice inhibits discoloration, do not use more than called for in the dressing, as it would make the salad too acidic.

Green Olive Tapenade

MAKES ABOUT ½ CUP

3 ounces Picholine olives, pitted
1½ teaspoons drained small capers
1½ anchovy fillets, patted dry
1½ teaspoons fresh lemon juice
¼ cup plus 2 tablespoons olive oil
About 2 tablespoons water
Salt and freshly ground black pepper to taste (optional)

1 In a blender, purée the olives, capers, and anchovies. Add the lemon juice and blend well. With the machine running, add the oil. Add enough water to make a thin sauce-like mixture. Season to taste with salt and pepper, if necessary.

2 Strain through a fine strainer into a bowl, pressing against the solids with the back of a spoon. Cover and refrigerate until ready to use.

Caraway Toasts

MAKES 6 SLICES

2 tablespoons unsalted butter, at room temperature
1½ teaspoons freshly ground toasted caraway seeds
Pinch of salt
Six ¼-inch-thick slices slightly stale brioche, challah, or other egg-rich bread

1 Preheat the broiler.

2 Combine the butter, caraway, and salt. Spread on 1 side of each slice of brioche.

3 Toast under the broiler, butter side up, until lightly browned. Turn and toast the other side until lightly browned. Cut into quarters and serve warm.

NOTE: The bread can also be toasted on a charcoal or gas grill.

Lamb Tagine with Almonds, Dates, and Toasted Bulgur

SERVES 6
PREPARATION TIME: ABOUT 1 HOUR
COOKING TIME: ABOUT 2 HOURS

A tagine is a slowly simmered stew that is traditionally cooked in a wide earthenware dish with a conical lid (also called a tagine). This particular stew brings Morocco right into your kitchen by relying on the exotic dimension of sweet almonds, dates, and honey. It could also be served with couscous in place of bulgur.

¼ cup olive oil
1½ pounds boneless lamb shoulder, cut into 3/4-inch cubes
1 large onion, halved and sliced
1½ cups sliced carrots
¾ cup minced shallots
3 cloves garlic, minced
One 1-inch piece fresh ginger, peeled and minced
½ teaspoon saffron threads
1 tablespoon freshly ground toasted cumin seeds
1 tablespoon paprika
1 tablespoon ground cinnamon
1 teaspoon ground cardamom
¼ teaspoon ground allspice

About 3 cups Chicken Stock
¾ cup honey
¼ to ½ cup sliced pitted dates
Salt and freshly ground black pepper to taste
Cayenne pepper to taste
¼ cup plus 2 tablespoons chopped fresh flat-leaf parsley
Toasted Bulgur (recipe follows)
1 cup chopped toasted almonds

1 Assemble *mise en place* trays for this recipe.

2 In a large Dutch oven, heat the oil over medium heat. Add the lamb and sear for about 5 minutes, or until well browned on all sides. Transfer to paper towels to drain.

3 Add the onions, carrots, shallots, garlic, and ginger to the Dutch oven and stir to combine. Add the saffron, cumin, paprika, cinnamon, cardamom, and allspice and cook, stirring occasionally, for about 10 minutes, or until the vegetables soften.

MATTHEW KENNEY: *Lamb Tagine with Almonds, Dates, and Toasted Bulgur*

TOASTED BULGUR
SERVES 6

1½ cups coarse-ground bulgur
3 tablespoons olive oil
1 large onion, chopped
¼ teaspoon hot green chile, such as jalapeño or serrano, seeded and chopped, or to taste
2 teaspoons tomato paste
1¾ cups plus 2 tablespoons boiling water
1 tablespoon plus 1½ teaspoons fresh lemon juice
¼ cup chopped fresh flat-leaf parsley
Salt and freshly ground black pepper to taste

1 Preheat the oven to 300 degrees F.

2 Spread the bulgur on a baking sheet and toast in the oven, stirring frequently, for about 7 minutes, or until light brown. Take care not to let bulgur get too dark, or it will taste burned. Set aside.

3 In a large skillet, heat the oil over medium heat. Add the onions and chile and sauté for about 4 minutes, or until the onions are soft and translucent. Stir in the bulgur and tomato paste, add the water, and bring to a boil. Stir gently, reduce the heat, cover, and cook for about 20 minutes, or until all the water has been absorbed and the bulgur is tender. Stir in the lemon juice, parsley, and salt and pepper to taste. Remove from the heat, cover, and let rest for 5 minutes before serving.

NOTE: If you prepare the bulgur early in the day, do so only up to the point of adding the lemon juice and parsley. To reheat, moisten with about ¼ cup Chicken Stock (see page 10) and warm over low heat. Add the lemon juice, parsley, and salt and pepper to taste just before serving. This may also be served at room temperature.

4 Return the lamb to the Dutch oven, stir, and add just enough stock to barely cover the lamb. Reduce the heat, cover, and simmer gently for about 1 hour, or until the lamb is fork-tender and the liquid has reduced to a sauce-like consistency. Do not allow to boil.

5 Stir in the honey and ¼ cup dates. Taste for sweetness and add up to ¼ cup more dates if desired. Season to taste with salt and pepper and cayenne. Stir in ¼ cup of the parsley.

6 Mound the bulgur in the center of 6 plates. Spoon the tagine over the top and garnish with the almonds and the remaining 2 tablespoons parsley. Serve immediately.

NOTE: You can add chopped celery, potatoes, turnips, or other firm vegetables as well as diced prunes to the tagine.

Caramelized Pear and Cranberry Upside-Down Cake

MAKES ONE 9-INCH CAKE; SERVES 6
PREPARATION TIME: ABOUT 20 MINUTES
COOKING TIME: ABOUT 5 MINUTES
BAKING TIME: ABOUT 30 MINUTES

Although this dessert is not Mediterranean in flavor, it is one of Matthew Kenney's trademarks and he wanted to share it with the class—and our readers.

11 tablespoons plus 1 teaspoon unsalted butter
3/4 cup lightly packed light brown sugar
1/3 cup dried cranberries
2 firm but ripe pears, peeled, cored, halved, and sliced 1/8 inch thick
1 2/3 cups all-purpose flour
2 teaspoons baking powder
1/4 teaspoon salt
2/3 cup granulated sugar
2 large eggs
1 teaspoon pure vanilla extract
2 cups milk
Vanilla ice cream or frozen yogurt (optional)

■ Special Equipment: 9-inch round cake pan

1 Assemble *mise en place* trays for this recipe.

2 Preheat the oven to 350 degrees F and put a baking sheet on the center rack. Lightly grease a 9-inch round cake pan.

3 In a medium-sized saucepan, melt 6 tablespoons of the butter over medium heat. Stir in the brown sugar and cook, stirring constantly, for about 5 minutes, or until the sugar dissolves. Immediately pour into the prepared cake pan. Sprinkle the cranberries over the sugar syrup and arrange the pear slices on top in a slightly overlapping circular pattern. Set aside.

4 In a small bowl, whisk together the flour, baking powder, and salt.

5 In a large bowl, using an electric mixer set on medium-high speed, cream the remaining 1/3 cup butter and the granulated sugar for 2 to 3 minutes, or until light and fluffy. Add the eggs 1 at a time, and beat until well combined. Add the vanilla. Add the dry ingredients, alternating them with the milk and beating until well blended. Pour the batter over the pears and spread with a spatula to cover the fruit.

6 Set the cake on the preheated baking sheet and bake for about 30 minutes, or until the edges are golden and a cake tester inserted in the center comes out clean. Cool on a wire rack for 5 minutes.

7 Position a serving plate over the cake pan and gently invert. Tap gently to release, and lift the pan off the cake. Serve warm, with scoops of ice cream or yogurt if desired.

NOTE: The dessert pictured was prepared as individual 6-inch cakes. If you chose to bake individual cakes, divide the pears and batter among the smaller cake pans and decrease the baking time to about 20 minutes, or until the edges are golden and a cake tester inserted in the center comes out clean.

Baking the cake on the hot baking sheet helps to caramelize the sugar. If making the cake in advance, invert it onto an oven-proof plate. Just before serving, reheat it in a 300-degree-F oven for about 10 minutes.

A ROBUST WINTER DINNER

Baked Cod with Bulgur

Braised Lamb Shanks with White Bean Purée

Pistachio-Fig Tart

WINE SUGGESTIONS:

Sauvignon Blanc or Chardonnay *(first course)*

Merlot or Pinot Noir *(second course)*

Tawny Port *(dessert)*

WHAT YOU CAN PREPARE AHEAD OF TIME

Up to 1 week ahead: Prepare the Veal Stock and Chicken Stock (if making your own).

Up to 3 days ahead: Prepare the Braised Lamb Shanks up to point of straining off the liquid. Cover and refrigerate. Reheat as directed in the recipe note. Prepare the White Bean Purée. Cover and refrigerate. Reheat as directed in the recipe note.

Up to 1 day ahead: Make the Pistachio-Fig Tart.

Early in the day: Prepare the vegetables for the Baked Cod with Bulgur, cover, and refrigerate.

Whenever Tom Valenti teaches at De Gustibus, we know we are in for a special evening. Not only is his food always scrumptious and easy to prepare, his sense of humor keeps the kitchen rocking. Plus, he manages to make everything look almost effortless—a wonderful combination of qualities in a chef.

I first met Tom when he was working at New York's Gotham Bar and Grill and arrived at De Gustibus as assistant to Chef Alfred Portale. Chef Valenti later moved on to much acclaim at the warm and friendly Alison on Dominick. In the spring of 1994, he became chef and co-owner at Cascabel, where he delights diners with his unique blend of French and Italian cooking. The recipes he shares with us here are some of our all-time favorites and represent but a few of Tom's signature dishes.

◁ TOM VALENTI: *Braised Lamb Shanks with White Bean Purée*

Baked Cod with Bulgur

Cod is not often on the De Gustibus menu, but after tasting Tom's version, we decided it should be a regular item. Although he served it as a first course, I think it makes a terrific, easy-to-put-together entrée.

15 Sicilian or other large green olives, pitted and sliced
9 shallots, thinly sliced
3 tomatoes, cored, seeded, and chopped
3 cloves garlic, sliced
1 lemon, peeled and sectioned
1 teaspoon minced fresh tarragon
1 teaspoon minced fresh oregano
3/4 cup dry white wine
1/2 cup water
Salt and freshly ground black pepper to taste
Six 6-ounce pieces skinless cod fillet
1 1/2 cups bulgur
2 1/2 cups plus 2 tablespoons boiling salted water
3/4 cup extra-virgin olive oil

1 Assemble *mise en place* trays for this recipe.

2 Preheat the oven to 450 degrees F. Lightly oil a baking dish large enough to hold the fish easily.

3 In a medium-sized bowl, combine the olives, shallots, tomatoes, garlic, lemon, tarragon, oregano, wine, water, and salt and pepper to taste. Pour into the baking dish and lay the fish on top. Cover tightly with aluminum foil. Reduce the oven temperature to 400 degrees F and bake for about 15 minutes, or until the fish is firm to the touch. Set aside uncovered to cool slightly.

4 Meanwhile, put the bulgur in a heat-proof bowl. Add the boiling water, cover tightly with plastic wrap, and set aside for about 15 minutes, or until all the water has been absorbed.

5 Carefully pour the cooking liquid from the baking pan into a blender and process until smooth. With the motor running, slowly add the oil, blending until the mixture is emulsified and smooth.

6 Spoon an equal portion of bulgur onto each plate. Place a fish fillet on top, arrange the vegetables on top of the fish and the bulgur, and drizzle with the sauce. Serve immediately.

TOM VALENTI: *Baked Cod with Bulgur*

Braised Lamb Shanks with White Bean Purée

SERVES 6
PREPARATION TIME: ABOUT 30 MINUTES
SOAKING TIME (BEANS ONLY): 8 HOURS
COOKING TIME: ABOUT 2 HOURS AND 40 MINUTES

This is Chef Tom Valenti's best-known signature dish and I guarantee it deserves its starring role on his menu. It is a terrific do-ahead winter meal!

6 lamb shanks
Salt and freshly ground black pepper to taste
1/2 cup olive oil
8 ribs celery, sliced
2 large carrots, sliced
1 large onion, diced
5 cloves garlic, minced
2 cups red wine
2 cups Veal Stock (see page 10)
Two 32-ounce cans Italian plum tomatoes, drained and crushed
6 anchovy fillets
20 black or green peppercorns
2 bay leaves
White Bean Purée (recipe follows)

1 Assemble *mise en place* trays for this recipe.

2 Preheat the oven to 325 degrees F.

3 Season the shanks with salt and pepper to taste. In a large sauté pan, heat the olive oil over medium heat. Add the shanks and sear for about 6 minutes, or until browned on all sides. Transfer to a large flame-proof casserole or roasting pan.

4 In the same pan, sauté the celery, carrots, onions, and garlic over medium heat for 30 seconds, taking care not to burn any particles that have stuck to the bottom of the pan. Add 1 cup of the wine and stir to deglaze the pan. Scrape the mixture over the shanks.

5 Add the veal stock, the remaining 1 cup wine, the tomatoes, anchovies, peppercorns and bay leaves to the casserole. The shanks should be almost covered with liquid; if necessary, add some water. Stir to combine. Bring to a boil over medium-high heat, remove from the heat, and cover tightly.

6 Bake for 2 1/2 hours, or until the meat is almost falling off the bone. Using tongs or a slotted spoon, remove the shanks and set aside, covered with aluminum foil to keep warm. Strain the cooking liquid through a fine sieve into a medium-sized saucepan and simmer for about 5 minutes over medium heat, or until reduced and thickened slightly.

7 Place an equal portion of bean purée on each plate. Place a shank alongside and spoon some sauce over the top. Pass the remaining sauce on the side.

NOTE: You can prepare the shanks ahead of time, up to the point of straining off the liquid. Reheat them in a 350-degree-F oven for about 20 minutes and complete the recipe as instructed.

WHITE BEAN PURÉE
SERVES 6

1 pound dried Great Northern beans
4 cloves garlic, 3 crushed and 1 minced
4 sprigs fresh thyme
2 bay leaves
3 cups Chicken Stock (see page 10), or more if needed
1/2 cup white wine
Salt and freshly ground black pepper to taste
1/2 cup olive oil
1 to 2 tablespoons unsalted butter, at room temperature (optional)

1 Rinse the beans in cold water, discarding any damaged or broken ones. Place in a large bowl, add cold water to cover, and soak for 8 hours, changing the water 3 or 4 times. Drain.

2 In a large saucepan, combine the beans, crushed garlic, thyme, bay leaves, stock, and wine and bring to a simmer over medium heat. Cook for about 1 1/2 hours, or until the beans are tender, adding additional stock or water if the beans get too dry. Season to taste with salt and pepper.

3 In a food processor fitted with the metal blade, purée the beans. With the motor running, slowly add the olive oil and minced garlic and process until smooth. (This may have to be done in batches.) If the purée seems too thick, fold in the butter. Serve hot.

NOTE: You can prepare the beans ahead of time. Reheat over low heat, adding extra stock or water if necessary.

Pistachio-Fig Tart

Tom told us that, as a boy, he adored Fig Newtons. When he learned to cook, one of his goals was to make a "grown-up" version of his childhood favorite. This is his delicious tribute to the famous cookie, devised with Paula Smith, the original pastry chef at Alison on Dominick.

FILLING:

1¼ pounds dried figs, stems removed
1½ cups granulated sugar
3 tablespoons ground cinnamon
1 tablespoon ground cloves
½ teaspoon ground mace
Pinch of salt
1 teaspoon freshly ground black pepper
1½ cups water
1 cup white wine

PASTRY:

1½ cups plus 3 tablespoons all-purpose flour
1 cup granulated sugar
1 cup finely ground pistachios
2 teaspoons baking powder
Grated zest of 1 lemon
1 cup (2 sticks) plus 2 tablespoons unsalted butter, at room temperature
3 large eggs
1 large egg yolk
1 teaspoon pure vanilla extract
2 tablespoons milk

■ Special Equipment: 10-inch tart pan with removable bottom; pastry bag fitted with No. 5 plain tip

1 Assemble *mise en place* trays for this recipe.

2 To make the filling, in a large nonreactive saucepan, combine the figs, sugar, cinnamon, cloves, mace, salt, pepper, water, and wine and bring to a boil over medium-high heat. Reduce the heat and simmer for about 30 minutes, or until the figs are tender and the liquid has reduced to a thick syrup. Set aside to cool to room temperature.

3 In a food processor fitted with the metal blade, purée the figs with their liquid. Transfer to a bowl and set aside.

4 Preheat the oven to 350 degrees F. Lightly oil a 10-inch tart pan with a removable bottom.

5 To make the pastry, in a large bowl, combine the flour, sugar, pistachios, baking powder, and lemon zest. Add the butter and, using an electric mixer set on low speed, mix until blended. Add 2 of the eggs, the egg yolk, and vanilla and beat on medium speed until combined.

6 Spread half the dough in the bottom of the prepared tart pan. Top with the fig mixture, leaving a 1-inch border all around.

7 Place the remaining dough in a pastry bag fitted with a No. 5 plain tip. Pipe a lattice design on top of the tart, allowing the ends to fall over the edges of the pan. Fold the ends under themselves and pat into place so they adhere to the bottom crust.

8 In a small bowl, whisk together the milk and the remaining egg. Using a pastry brush, coat the lattice with the egg wash. Bake for about 30 minutes, or until the pastry is golden brown. Cool on a wire rack for about 10 minutes, cut into wedges, and serve warm.

◁ TOM VALENTI: *Pistachio-Fig Tart*

A WORLD OF FOOD

Hot and Sweet Red Pepper Dip with Walnuts and Pomegranate
MUHAMMARA

Flaked Parsley Salad with Black Olives

Couscous with Greens

Sweet and Sour Pumpkin or Butternut Squash

Mussels "Saganaki"

Walnut Roll

WINE SUGGESTIONS:

Dry Spanish Wine or Dry Rosé *(red pepper dip)*

Gavi or Pinot Grigio *(parsley salald, couscous, and squash)*

Sauvignon Blanc *(mussels)*

Tawny Port *(dessert)*

WHAT YOU CAN PREPARE AHEAD OF TIME

Up to 1 week ahead: Make and freeze the Walnut Roll. Thaw in the refrigerator before serving. Make the Hot and Sweet Red Pepper Dip.

Up to 2 days ahead: Prepare the Sweet and Sour Pumpkin or Butternut Squash.

Early in the day: Prepare the parsley for the Flaked Parsley Salad. Wrap in damp paper towels and refrigerate. Steam the greens for the Couscous with Greens. Cover and refrigerate. Prepare the Mussels "Saganaki" up to the addition of the feta. Before serving, soak the feta and proceed as directed in the recipe through step 5.

Paula Wolfert was one of the original teachers at De Gustibus more than fifteen years ago. She was, in fact, one of the first cooks to bring the foods of the Mediterranean to the classroom—it was she who introduced us to the then-unfamiliar preserved lemons, which now are almost commonplace. Paula brought so much passion, romance, and history to the stove that we were all entranced. She has returned many times to tell us tales of her culinary adventures as she roams the Mediterranean countries looking for traditional recipes to bring back to the home cook.

◁ PAULA WOLFERT: *Couscous with Greens, Mussels "Saganaki," and Sweet and Sour Pumpkin*

Hot and Sweet Red Pepper Dip with Walnuts and Pomegranate

MAKES ABOUT 3 CUPS
PREPARATION TIME: ABOUT 15 MINUTES
CHILLING TIME: AT LEAST 8 HOURS

Muhammara

This is a very tasty dip that, if covered and refrigerated, will last for at least a week. Serve with crisp bread, crackers, or pita triangles.

6 to 8 red bell peppers (about 2¹/2 pounds), roasted, peeled, and seeds and membranes removed

1¹/2 cups coarsely ground walnuts (about 6 ounces)

¹/2 cup crumbled unsalted crackers

2 tablespoons pomegranate molasses

1 tablespoon fresh lemon juice

¹/2 teaspoon ground cumin, plus a pinch

¹/2 teaspoon granulated sugar

³/4 teaspoon salt

3 tablespoons olive oil

2 small hot chiles, such as Fresno or hot Hungarian, roasted, peeled, and seeds and membranes removed, or to taste

2 tablespoons toasted pine nuts

PAULA WOLFERT: *Hot and Sweet Red Pepper Dip with Walnuts and Pomegranate* and *Flaked Parsley Salad with Black Olives*

1 Assemble *mise en place* trays for this recipe (see page 7).

2 Spread the bell peppers, smooth side up, on paper towels and drain for about 10 minutes.

3 In a food processor fitted with the metal blade, combine the walnuts, crackers, pomegranate molasses, lemon juice, ¹/2 teaspoon of the cumin, the sugar, and salt and process until smooth. Add the bell peppers and process until puréed and creamy. With the motor running, add 2 table-spoons of the oil in a thin stream. Add the chiles. If the dip seems too thick, thin it with 1 to 2 tablespoons water. Transfer to a nonreactive container, cover, and refrigerate for at least 8 hours.

4 Place the dip in a serving dish and sprinkle with the pine nuts and the pinch of cumin. Drizzle with the remaining 1 tablespoon oil.

Flaked Parsley Salad with Black Olives

SERVES 6
PREPARATION TIME: ABOUT 25 MINUTES

This unusual recipe uses everyday curly parsley and is delicious with fish. Do not mix this ahead of time.

¹/4 pound (about 2 large bunches) very fresh curly parsley, washed and thoroughly dried

24 Kalamata or Niçoise olives, rinsed, drained, pitted, and slivered

3 tablespoons minced shallots

¹/2 teaspoon Worcestershire sauce

3 tablespoons olive oil

1 tablespoon cider vinegar or rice wine vinegar

Salt and freshly ground black pepper to taste

3 tablespoons freshly grated Pecorino-Romano cheese

1 Assemble *mise en place* trays for this recipe.

2 Remove the parsley leaves from the stems, discarding the stems, and tear each leaf into tiny bits. You should have about 4 loosely packed cups of parsley flakes.

3 In a large bowl, combine the parsley, olives, shallots, Worcestershire, oil, vinegar, and salt and pepper to taste and toss gently. Transfer to a serving bowl and sprinkle with the cheese. Serve immediately.

NOTE: To insure the parsley is completely dry use a salad spinner.

Couscous with Greens

This is a delicious, nutritious entrée for vegetarians and those looking for healthy alternatives in their diets.

½ pound (about 4 bunches) fresh flat-leaf parsley, thick stems discarded, and chopped
¼ pound (about 2 bunches) fresh dill, chopped
¼ pound fennel fronds (fennel tops), chopped
¼ pound (about 2 bunches) scallions, chopped
¼ pound leeks, chopped
½ cup chopped carrot greens or celery leaves (optional)
½ cup olive oil
1 cup chopped onions
3 tablespoons tomato paste
2 tablespoons crushed garlic, plus 6 whole garlic cloves, peeled
2 teaspoons sweet paprika
2 teaspoons ground coriander or tabil
1 teaspoon ground caraway seeds
2 teaspoons salt, or more to taste
1½ to 2 teaspoons red pepper flakes, preferably Aleppo, Turkish, or Near East
2 cups hot water
1 pound (about 2½ cups) medium-grain couscous
1 red bell pepper, cored, seeded, and cut into 6 pieces
1 hot green chile, seeded and minced

■ Special Equipment: Couscous cooker (couscousière), or a large steamer or a large colander that fits inside a large saucepan

1 Assemble *mise en place* trays for this recipe.

2 In the perforated top of a *couscousière* (or a steamer basket or large colander), combine the parsley, dill, fennel, scallions, leeks, and carrot greens or celery leaves, if using, and set over boiling water. Cover and steam for 30 minutes. Remove from the heat, uncover, and let stand until cool enough to handle. Squeeze out the excess moisture and set aside.

3 In a large sauté pan, heat the oil over medium heat. Add the onions and sauté for 3 minutes, or until tender. Stir in the tomato paste and cook, stirring constantly, for about 2 minutes, or until the paste glistens. Stir in the crushed garlic, paprika, coriander, caraway, salt, and red pepper flakes. Reduce the heat and sauté for about 3 minutes, or until the garlic softens. Add 1 cup of the water, cover, and cook for 15 minutes.

4 Remove from the heat, add the couscous, and stir until well combined. Add the steamed vegetables and herbs and stir to combine. Fold in the bell pepper, chile, and garlic cloves.

5 Fill the bottom of the *couscousière* with water and bring to a boil over high heat. Fasten on the perforated top and put the couscous mixture in the top. (Or put it into the steamer basket or large colander and set over boiling water.) Cover and steam for 30 minutes.

6 Transfer the couscous to a warm serving dish and break up any lumps with a fork. Remove and reserve the garlic cloves and bell pepper. Stir the remaining cup of hot water into the couscous, taste, and adjust the seasoning. Cover with aluminum foil and let stand for 10 minutes. Remove the foil and garnish the couscous with the reserved bell pepper and garlic.

PAULA WOLFERT: *Couscous with Greens*

Sweet and Sour Pumpkin or Butternut Squash

This is an interesting way of preparing squash. It serves as either a condiment or a side dish.

One 2 1/2-pound pumpkin or butternut squash
About 2 tablespoons coarse salt
1/4 cup olive oil
1 1/3 cups (about 1/2 pound) thinly sliced onions
1 teaspoon granulated sugar
1/4 cup plus 3 tablespoons white wine vinegar
1/3 cup water
3/4 teaspoon salt
1/2 teaspoon freshly ground black pepper
1/4 cup torn fresh mint leaves

1 Assemble *mise en place* trays for this recipe.

2 Peel the pumpkin or squash, removing a little flesh with the peel. If using pumpkin, cut the flesh into 1/4-inch-thick slices approximately 2 1/2 inches by 3 1/4 inches. If using butternut squash, start at the neck end and cut into 1/4-inch-thick rounds. When you reach the bulb end, cut lengthwise in half, remove the seeds and pulp, and slice the flesh into 1-inch squares about 1/4 inch thick. Sprinkle the pumpkin or squash lightly with coarse salt. Using paper towels, blot off the excess moisture, but do not dry completely.

3 In a large nonreactive skillet, heat the oil over medium-high heat. Add the pumpkin or squash, without crowding, and cook for about 5 minutes, turning once or twice, or until golden brown on both sides. Remove with tongs and drain on paper towels, then cover and set aside.

4 Reduce the heat to medium and add the onions and sugar to the skillet. Cook for about 5 minutes, or until the onions are soft and golden brown and just beginning to caramelize. Raise the heat, add the vinegar and water, and bring to a simmer. Cook for about 4 minutes, or until the liquid has reduced by half. Remove from the heat and set aside to mellow for 3 to 4 hours.

5 Layer the pumpkin or squash on a large serving dish, sprinkling the layers with the salt and pepper. Pour the onion mixture over the slices. Garnish with half the torn mint leaves, cover, and refrigerate for about 1 hour, or until chilled.

6 Serve chilled, garnished with the remaining mint leaves.

NOTE: For the sweetest flesh, purchase pumpkin or squash with dull skin that feels heavy for its size. It is essential to use a mild wine vinegar for this recipe. Try the Sasso brand or French Corcellet white wine vinegar for best results. Avoid vinegar with more than 6 percent acidity.

◁ PAULA WOLFERT:
Sweet and Sour Pumpkin

PAULA WOLFERT:
Mussels "Saganaki" ▷

Mussels "Saganaki"

A saganaki is a shallow pan with two handles, but any deep sauté pan will work just about as well for this combination of shellfish and feta cheese. The flavors may surprise your taste buds, but I'm sure you will find it quite delicious.

3 pounds mussels
1 tablespoon coarse salt, plus more to taste
1/2 cup water
1 to 2 tablespoons fresh lemon juice, or more to taste
1/4 teaspoon freshly ground black pepper, plus more to taste
1 tablespoon olive oil

2 teaspoons minced seeded long hot green chile, or more to taste
1/3 cup plus 2 tablespoons chopped fresh flat-leaf parsley
1/2 cup peeled, seeded, and chopped fresh tomatoes or drained, seeded, and chopped canned tomatoes
1/2 teaspoon mashed garlic
5 large fresh spearmint or other mint leaves, torn into shreds
1/4 teaspoon crumbled dried oregano, preferably Greek
1 teaspoon dry mustard
Pinch of red pepper flakes
3 ounces imported feta cheese, preferably Bulgarian

1 Assemble *mise en place* trays for this recipe.

2 Scrub the mussels and pull off the beards. Rinse in several changes of water and put in a bowl of cool water. Add the sea salt and let stand for at least 30 minutes to purge the mussels of sand. Drain.

3 Place the mussels in a saganaki or large deep sauté pan. Add the water, cover, and cook over high heat for about 2 minutes, or just until the mussels open; do not overcook. Using tongs or a slotted spoon, transfer the mussels to a bowl to cool. Strain the cooking liquid through several layers of damp cheesecloth into a bowl and set aside.

4 Remove the mussels from their shells and cut off any remaining beards. Strain any liquid collected in the bowl and add to the reserved mussel broth. Sprinkle the mussels with lemon juice and pepper to taste.

5 In a medium-sized nonreactive skillet, heat the olive oil over medium-low heat. Add 2 teaspoons minced chile and 1/3 cup of the parsley and cook for 1 minute, stirring. Add the reserved mussel cooking liquid, the tomatoes, garlic,

mint, oregano, mustard, red pepper flakes, and the remaining 1/4 teaspoon pepper. Raise the heat to high and bring to a boil. Reduce the heat and simmer for 5 minutes, stirring often, or until the sauce has reduced to about 1 1/4 cups. If desired, add more minced green chile to taste. Return to the boil for just a second. Transfer to a bowl and allow to cool for about 10 minutes, until tepid. Add the mussels to the sauce, cover, and refrigerate.

6 Twenty minutes before serving, soak the feta in cold water for 15 minutes. Drain and cut into 1/2-inch cubes.

7 In a large skillet, heat the mussels and sauce over medium-low heat just until heated through. Do not allow the sauce to boil. Add the feta cheese and cook, stirring, for 2 minutes. Taste and adjust the seasoning. Serve immediately, sprinkled with the remaining 2 tablespoons chopped parsley.

■ If you buy cultivated, farm-raised mussels, there is no need to soak them. Ask the fish merchant where the mussels come from; soaking diminishes their flavor.

Walnut Roll

MAKES ONE 17-INCH ROLL; SERVES 6 TO 8
PREPARATION TIME: ABOUT 30 MINUTES
BAKING TIME: ABOUT 15 MINUTES
CHILLING TIME: AT LEAST 2 HOURS

This dessert is rich enough to end any meal in grand style.

CAKE:

2 tablespoons unsalted butter, at room temperature
5 large eggs, separated
1/2 cup granulated sugar
Pinch of salt
1 1/4 cups finely ground walnuts (about 5 ounces)
1/2 teaspoon baking powder

FILLING:

1 1/2 cups ground walnuts (about 6 ounces)
1/2 cup hot milk
8 tablespoons unsalted butter, at room temperature
1/3 cup granulated sugar
2 tablespoons Cognac
1 cup heavy cream, whipped to soft peaks
About 1/2 cup confectioners' sugar

■ Special Equipment: 11 x 17-inch jelly roll pan

1 Assemble *mise en place* trays for this recipe.

2 Preheat the oven to 375 degrees F. Using 1 tablespoon of the butter, grease an 11 x 17-inch jelly-roll pan. Line the pan with wax or parchment paper, leaving a 2-inch overhang at each end, and press down on the butter. Using the remaining 1 tablespoon butter, grease the paper.

3 To make the cake, in a large bowl, using an electric mixer set on medium-high speed, beat the egg yolks until foamy. Beat in the sugar and salt until pale and thick. Using a large wire whisk, fold in the nuts and baking powder.

4 In another large bowl, using the mixer set on medium-high speed, beat the egg whites until they hold stiff peaks. Using a spatula, fold the egg whites into the yolk mixture. Spread evenly in the prepared pan.

5 Bake for 15 minutes, or until a cake tester inserted in the center comes out clean. Cool slightly on a rack, cover with a damp kitchen cloth, and refrigerate for 30 minutes.

PAULA WOLFERT: *Walnut Roll*

6 To prepare the filling, put the walnuts in a bowl and pour the milk over them. Allow to cool.

7 In a large bowl, using an electric mixer set on medium-high speed, cream the butter. Gradually add the sugar and beat until light and fluffy. Beat in the nut mixture and the Cognac. Using a spatula, fold in the whipped cream.

8 Sprinkle the cake with confectioners' sugar. Lay a 20-inch-long sheet of wax paper over the cake. Grip the ends of the jelly-roll pan, holding the wax paper firmly in place, and quickly invert the cake and pan onto a work surface. Remove the pan and peel the paper from the cake. Using a spatula, spread the filling over the cake. Using the second sheet of wax paper to help guide it, roll up the cake like a jelly roll. Cover with foil and refrigerate for at least 1½ hours, or until the filling is set. Just before serving, dust the top of the cake with confectioners' sugar.

NOTE: Use a nut grinder to grind the nuts fine for the cake and the grating blade of a food processor to grind them less fine for the filling.

Index